The Acquisition of Sociolinguistic Competence in a Study Abroad Context

SECOND LANGUAGE ACQUISITION
Series Editor: Professor David Singleton, *Trinity College, Dublin, Ireland*

This series brings together titles dealing with a variety of aspects of language acquisition and processing in situations where a language or languages other than the native language is involved. Second language is thus interpreted in its broadest possible sense. The volumes included in the series all offer in their different ways, on the one hand, exposition and discussion of empirical findings and, on the other, some degree of theoretical reflection. In this latter connection, no particular theoretical stance is privileged in the series; nor is any relevant perspective – sociolinguistic, psycholinguistic, neurolinguistic, and so on – deemed out of place. The intended readership of the series includes final-year undergraduates working on second language acquisition projects, postgraduate students involved in second language acquisition research, and researchers and teachers in general whose interests include a second language acquisition component.

Full details of all the books in this series and of all our other publications can be found on http://www.multilingual-matters.com, or by writing to Multilingual Matters, St Nicholas House, 31–34 High Street, Bristol BS1 2AW, UK.

SECOND LANGUAGE ACQUISITION
Series Editor: David Singleton

The Acquisition of Sociolinguistic Competence in a Study Abroad Context

Vera Regan, Martin Howard and Isabelle Lemée

MULTILINGUAL MATTERS
Bristol • Buffalo • Toronto

Et lui répondit que la beauté du cosmos est donnée non seulement par l'unité dans la variété, mais aussi par la variété dans l'unité.
Umberto Eco, *Le Nom de la Rose* (p. 19).

Library of Congress Cataloging in Publication Data
A catalog record for this book is available from the Library of Congress.
Regan, Vera.
The Acquisition of Sociolinguistic Competence in a Study Abroad Context/
Vera Regan, Martin Howard, Isabelle Lemée.
Second Language Acquisition
Includes bibliographical references and index.
1. Second language acquisition. 2. Sociolinguistics. 3. Language and languages--Variation. 4. Foreign study. 5. French language--Study and teaching--Foreign speakers. 6. French language--Acquisition.
I. Howard, Martin II. Lemée, Isabelle - III. Title.
P118.2.R425 2009
401'.93–dc22 2009009446

British Library Cataloguing in Publication Data
A catalogue entry for this book is available from the British Library.

ISBN-13: 978-1-84769-157-6 (hbk)
ISBN-13: 978-1-84769-156-9 (pbk)

Multilingual Matters
UK: St Nicholas House, 31–34 High Street, Bristol BS1 2AW, UK.
USA: UTP, 2250 Military Road, Tonawanda, NY 14150, USA.
Canada: UTP, 5201 Dufferin Street, North York, Ontario M3H 5T8, Canada.

Copyright © 2009 Vera Regan, Martin Howard and Isabelle Lemée.

All rights reserved. No part of this work may be reproduced in any form or by any means without permission in writing from the publisher.

The policy of Multilingual Matters/Channel View Publications is to use papers that are natural, renewable and recyclable products, made from wood grown in sustainable forests. In the manufacturing process of our books, and to further support our policy, preference is given to printers that have FSC and PEFC Chain of Custody certification.TheFSCand/orPEFClogoswillappearonthosebooks where full certificationhasbeengrantedtotheprinterconcerned.

Typeset by Techset Composition Ltd., Salisbury, UK.

Contents

Acknowledgements ix

1 Second Language Acquisition and Linguistic Variation 1
   Introduction: Aims and Scope of this Book 1
   Contextual Approaches to Second Language Acquisition
      Research and Sociolinguistics 4
   Context of Acquisition 6
   The Role of Input in Second Language Acquisition 8
   Study Abroad as a Context for Acquiring a
      Second Language 11
   The Variationist Paradigm and Second Language
      Acquisition 13
   Variation and Sociolinguistic Norms in French 14
   The Acquisition of Native Speaker Variation Speech
      Patterns: A New Research Thread 16

2 Linguistic Outcomes and Study Abroad 19
   Introduction 19
   Study Abroad as Context 19
   L2 Acquisition in a Study Abroad Context 20
   L2 Development During Study Abroad 21
   Study Abroad and the Acquisition of Sociolinguistic
      Competence 24
   Study Abroad and the Acquisition of Sociopragmatic
      Competence 27
   The Effect of Study Abroad on the L2 Learner's Lexical
      Acquisition 28
   The Effect of Study Abroad on Structural Aspects of the
      Learner's Grammar 30
   The Effect of Study Abroad on L2 Fluency 34
   Summary 37

3 Extralinguistic Factors Affecting L2 Development
   During Study Abroad 39
      Proficiency Level 39
      Other Extralinguistic Factors Affecting the Linguistic
         Outcome of Study Abroad 41
      Concluding Remarks Concerning the Effect of
         Extralinguistic Factors on the Learner's Linguistic
         Development During Study Abroad.................. 45
      Synthesis 49

4 The Research Investigation: An Overview................ 51
      Introduction 51
      Aims and Objectives 51
      The Learner-Informants 53
      Data Collection...................................... 57
      Data Analysis Within the Variationist Paradigm 59

5 The Acquisition of *ne* deletion by Irish-English
   speakers of French L2 during the Year Abroad........... 62
      Negation in French 62
      Variable Use of *ne* in Spoken French................ 63
      Ne Deletion in Non-native Speaker French: Advanced
         vs Early and Intermediate Learners 65
      Ne Deletion and the Classroom Learner.............. 67
      Ne Deletion in the Native Speech Community by
         L2 Speakers...................................... 67
      Ne Deletion and French Immersion Learners in Canada........ 68
      Ne Deletion and Irish Year Abroad Learners................. 68
      Research Questions in Relation to *Ne* Deletion
         by Irish L2 Speakers in a Study Abroad Context 69
      Results.. 71

6 The Variable Use of *Nous/On* during the Year Abroad............ 79
      The Variable Use of *Nous/On* in Metropolitan French 82
      The Variable Use of *Nous/On* in Canadian French 84
      The Variable Use of *Nous/On* in Canadian Immersion
         L2 Speakers' Speech.............................. 86
      Acquisition of Variable *Nous/On* in L2 Speakers and
         the Year Abroad 87
      Acquisition of the Variable Use of *Nous/On* by Irish
         Learners of French L2 89
      Results.. 89
      Conclusion 93

7 The Acquisition of /l/ Deletion in French by Irish
   Study Abroad Speakers.................................... 96
   /l/ Deletion in Metropolitan French L1.................... 96
   /l/ Deletion in Canadian French L1........................ 97
   /l/ Deletion in L2 Speech: The Case of French
      Immersion Speakers in Canada, L2 Canadian
      and American Year Abroad Speakers..................... 97
   Acquisition of Variable /l/ Deletion by Irish L2
      Speakers of French.................................... 98
   Results... 98
   Conclusion 102

8 The Variable Use of Future Temporal Reference during
   the Year Abroad 105
   Future Tense in French 105
   The Variable Use of Future Temporal Reference
      in Metropolitan French............................... 107
   The Variable Use of Future Temporal Reference
      in Canadian French................................... 108
   Canadian Immersion and L2 Speakers and
      the Future Tense..................................... 109
   Acquisition of the Future Temporal Reference
      by Irish L2 Speakers Back from a Year Abroad......... 111
   Results.. 112
   Conclusion 115

9 The Role of Gender in the Acquisition of Sociolinguistic
   Competence in an L2 During the Year Abroad............... 117
   Women and Language 117
   Quantitative Findings on Language and Gender............ 118
   The Second or 'Later' Wave of Labovian Research
      on Women's Use of Language........................... 120
   Gender and L2 Acquisition 122
   Variationist Perspectives on Gender and Second
      Language Acquisition................................. 125
   The Acquisition of Sociolinguistic Variation Patterns:
      Gender and the Year Abroad........................... 128
   Gender as a Factor in Relation to Four Linguistic
      Variables in French L2: /l/ Deletion, *Nous/On*
      Alternation, *Ne* Retention and the Expression of
      the Future 129
   Conclusion 131

10 Spending a Year Abroad: Do We Acquire Sociolinguistic
    Competence? 133
    Introduction: Findings from our Research.................. 133
    Research Questions 133
    What have we Learnt about Sociolinguistic
        Competence and Study Abroad?......................... 134
    Implications of the Research 137
    Theoretical Implications: Research Issues 138
    Group and Individual Variation in
        Relation to L2 Speakers............................... 139
    The Acquisition of Sociolinguistic Competence:
        Process and Product 141
    Practical Implications: Programmatic and Policy Issues 142
    Future Research 142

References... 144

Index.. 167

Acknowledgements

We have been very fortunate in the support of numerous people and institutions in the production of this book, and financial support for the research on which this book is based, and we would like to thank:

- University College Dublin, for granting Vera Regan a President's Award to research this project.
- University College Cork, for granting Martin Howard, a Research Grant from the College of Arts, Celtic Studies and Social Sciences.
- The Irish Research Council for the Humanities and Social Sciences for several research fellowships to Vera Regan and Martin Howard for funding which greatly assisted research for the book.
- The Government of Canada for Canadian Studies research funding for both Vera Regan and Martin Howard.
- The Quebec Government, for funding, through the awarding of the Prix du Québec, to both Vera Regan and Martin Howard.
- The Sociolinguistics Laboratory at the University of Ottawa for Visiting Professorships to Vera Regan, the Sociolinguistics Laboratory and the Graduate School of Education at the University of Pennsylvania equally for Visiting Professorships.
- The United States Fulbright Commission for two Research Fellowships for Vera Regan, which permitted research combining sociolinguistic and second language acquisition expertise.
- The numerous colleagues and students whose support was enormously important to all three authors and whose contributions through discussions and feedback to conference papers greatly assisted the development of the volume; these include Jean-Marc Dewaele, Raymond Mougeon, Shana Poplack and Tere Pica. Also to Doug Adamson and Caitriona Ni Chasaide, who read several extracts.

We also wish to warmly thank the anonymous L2 speakers who generously gave of their time to share their experiences of study abroad through participation in our data collection.

Our special gratitude goes to David Singleton, the SLA series editor, for his unfailing encouragement and support during the process of writing the book, as well as Multilingual Matters, and the anonymous reviewer for valuable suggestions to the manuscript. Of course, any remaining shortcomings are our own.

Chapter 1
Second Language Acquisition and Linguistic Variation

Introduction: Aims and Scope of this Book

One might well ask the reason for another book on learning languages, especially one which does not exclusively focus on learning English. In our 21st century global village, are we not all traversing the globe, either physically or virtually, with English as our passport? Perhaps those of us whose first language is not English should be investing all our resources in learning English and forgetting any other languages we may happen to have. The new technologies and the role they play in our lives have surely made clear that only English matters any more. However, contrary to predictions from a few generations ago, it appears that the story is not so clear cut. In fact, language still matters, and language diversity is far more enduring than some might have thought a few decades ago. In our globalised world, greater contact with other societies and other people highlights issues of language learning and language competence.

It might have seemed that with the internet leading to global homogeneity, English, being the 'international' language, would increasingly be the only important one. However, this is turning out to be a far too simplistic view of how things are developing. The internet is global, but the content that it carries is local; if you access the internet, you receive advertisements that are adapted to local conditions and interests. The news that you receive is tailored to your locality. So that people in southeast France, for example, find advertisements on the internet tailored to their specific needs and interests, and will only be effective if the language used is appropriate. In fact, recent developments in the internet are to enable language other than English. Language diversity on the internet is only one example. In international trade, it is now clear that one must be sensitive to local conditions, needs and cultures, and this also implies local languages. This is why language competence in many languages remains important today, contrary to the dire predictions some years ago. And in the same way that communication involves specific knowledge of individual local cultures, it also involves knowledge of the detail of languages, not just a generalised 'inter-nation' knowledge of the structure and shape of those languages, but how they are embedded in use for the communities who use them. This implies knowledge of the detailed texture of the language, the sociolinguistic detail and variation which is part of every language in social use and is indeed an integral part of linguistic competence. Competence at this level of language is what permits people to communicate fully with others in a manner which respects fully their humanity as social beings, over and above what is needed for more immediate aims such as trade. This is a book about the acquisition of sociolinguistic variation in other languages, how and where it happens.

Since the beginning of research in Second Language Acquisition (SLA), we have learnt a lot about language learning, but there are aspects that have received less attention until recently. One of these is the acquisition of sociolinguistic competence. This describes the dimension of SLA which colours the way the second language (L2) speaker relates to the community or communities they are living in and may wish to be a part of in some way: how they want 'to be' in the particular group or community, what in fact is their linguistic identity within this group and how they construct this identity through language. Needless to say the effect of this dynamic is two-way: the community is affected as much by the presence of the L2 speaker as (s)he is by the community. For a long time in SLA research, this area of SLA was considered a sort of frill around the 'real' issue of learning grammar, something like icing on the cake; if indeed it was considered at all in a heavily linguistic-orientated approach which pertained for much of the beginning of SLA research. However, we are now beginning to understand that this aspect of language acquisition and its related areas is as crucial in enabling learners to communicate with other people as is grammar.

Another somewhat unexamined notion about language learning has been the assumption that the best way to learn a language was to go to the country where the language is spoken. Until recently, however, there has not been a lot of data to prove this. We are now beginning to understand more about this particular way of learning second languages such that it is increasingly clear that the context or surroundings in which people learn second languages is very important. The 'year abroad' for university students – a stay in the community of the L2 we wish to acquire – is one such context. In fact, these two dimensions of language learning are interlinked. The aim of this book is to demonstrate the link between the acquisition of sociolinguistic competence, on the one hand, and learning language by immersing oneself in another society, on the other. We aim to show that the year abroad is one context, perhaps one of the best contexts available to certain categories of second language learners, for acquiring sociolinguistic competence.

These issues have policy as well as theoretical implications. In a globalised, multicultural, multilingual world, communities are constantly shifting and coalescing, and individuals move in and out of communities and are members of multiple communities simultaneously. The vast majority of the world's population today is multilingual; the monolingual speaker is in a minority (Cook, 2002: 1, 2003: 4). L2 (or L3, L4) speakers adapt to the constant shifts in communities and identity, finding a space of their own in the speech community or communities they happen to be part of at the time. Knowledge of grammatical and structural elements of the L2 is only part of the skills and competencies which are necessary for this process of adaptation. Sociolinguistic and sociocultural competences are equally important. These competences condition the L2 speaker's view of themselves in the L2 speech community, their view of their own community as well as the way the L2 community perceives them, and this consequently affects the place they occupy in, and progress through, that community or communities. People rarely remain in one fixed community or have a fixed identity for the span of their lifetime but undergo multiple changes of identity as they move in and out of different, sometimes overlapping, communities depending on what is happening to them at any particular moment. Sociolinguistic approaches to SLA or multilingualism in particular have been recently focused on these issues in SLA (Bayley & Regan, 2004; Bayley & Schecter, 2003; Bucholtz, 1999; Pavlenko & Blackledge, 2004; Rampton, 1995).

We wish to take a close look at how the L2 speaker acquires and uses language in a way which permits them to negotiate their identity and place in different communities. We particularly wish to provide detailed, empirical, close-up language data of negotiation and use by individuals. We look closely at the language practices of speakers in different situations and examine one particular situation of language learning; the one where the learner goes abroad and tries to learn by being in the country or community of the target language. We base our findings on research which we have carried out over a number of years, using multiple studies of L2 speakers and their study abroad experiences and the very rich databases resulting from this work. The studies we have carried out are both longitudinal and cross-sectional. It can seem recently that language itself is currently sometimes neglected in the area of sociolinguistics and so also in sociolinguistic studies of SLA, and we would like to redress this balance by providing a body of fine-grained studies of the acquisition of sociolinguistic competence in one context: the Year Abroad. Only by the placing of such linguistic detail centrally in the analysis can we gain the fullest picture of SLA and use. Recent work, as we said, quite rightly focuses on the ethnographic aspects of L2 acquisition in a line of research within the variationist tradition,[1] beginning with Eckert (1990) and continuing with Bayley (1996), Meyerhoff (2006) and others, in relation to issues such as language socialisation or communities of practice. This work addresses the earlier lack of emphasis on the L2 speaker as member of community and communities. However, the language which the speaker uses constitutes in itself invaluable data in the exploration of the full picture of the speaker and for this reason we feel it should be placed central to inquiries in second language acquisition and use. To explore these issues as indicated earlier, we take as a case-study the instance of year abroad in SLA, where previously instructed and (frequently) advanced learners[2] spend an extended period in the country of the target language. We examine in detail how the year abroad experience affects the acquisition of sociolinguistic competence.

The Year Abroad itself has become the subject of increasing investigation in SLA research. Recent work in the area generally covers a range of issues, some dealing with language issues, others with more social and cultural aspects, for example Freed (1998), Collentine and Freed (2004), Dufon and Churchill (2006). Thanks to this research, we are gradually beginning to have a better understanding of the year abroad experience. This is crucial not only for what it can tell us about the SLA process, but also for policy and programmatic considerations. Simply, considerable financial and other resources are being devoted worldwide to year/study abroad programmes on the basis of fairly generalised notions of their putative benefits. There still remains a shortage of very detailed investigations of the actual language use of those acquiring a language in this particular context – although such studies are increasing.[3] This book aims to contribute to the growing literature on Study Abroad, by investigating the development of sociolinguistic competence by L2 learners in this particular context.

Contextual Approaches to Second Language Acquisition Research and Sociolinguistics

Among the central question asked by SLA researchers are the following:

- Who learns a second language?
- What does it mean to acquire a second language?
- What does the learner learn?

- How does the learner learn?
- Where does learning happen?
- Why are language learners different?

In fact the experience of learning a second language in a study abroad context can explain a considerable amount in relation to each of these questions. So viewing the acquisition process through the prism of the case of Year Abroad is an invaluable method of gaining a more complete picture of SLA. Theoretical positions in research on these major issues in SLA range broadly from nativist approaches, through interactionist ones, to sociocultural ones. Each of these approaches describes different aspects of SLA and they broadly complement each other. SLA research needs to find answers to the questions while taking account of both product and process in acquisition.

Until recently, through the 1960s, 1970s and 1980s, SLA research generally tended to confine itself to mainly psychological approaches. Long (1997: 320), however, has suggested that 'a broader, context-sensitive, participant-sensitive, generally sociolinguistic orientation might prove beneficial for SLA research'. In fact, for some time now, there has been a sharp rise in sociolinguistic and contextual approaches to SLA research, with many different perspectives from different areas of sociolinguistics. One particular approach within sociolinguistics – the variationist perspective – has been particularly influential in exploring the social aspects of second language acquisition. Variation studies have thrown light on many areas of acquisition and, through quantitative as well as qualitative studies of learner language, have furthered our understanding of second language acquisition by frequently highlighting aspects not taken into account or perhaps noticed by research from other paradigms. General accounts of SLA from a variationist perspective can be found in Gass *et al.* (1989), Preston (1989), Adamson (1988, 2005), Bayley and Preston (1996), Regan (1998a, 1998b) and Young (1999).

In the past 20 years or so, the two fields of SLA and sociolinguistics have increasingly tended to inform each other with mutually beneficial results. Researchers in SLA with a sociocultural interest increasingly use methods, concepts and constructs drawn from sociolinguistics to explore and elucidate aspects of acquisition. Approaches, both qualitative and quantitative, emanating from sociolinguistics have come from many subfields (Bayley & Regan, 2004). As we have noted, SLA at its inception tended to be predominantly psychological in approach and indeed currently has a strong cognitivist focus.[4] An understanding of the process of acquisition requires an explanation also of the sociocultural context of this process. Since the late 1970s, there has been a small but consistent interest in the sociocultural aspects of SLA which has developed in parallel with, and in a complementary way, to purely language-internal approaches.

The increasing interest in sociolinguistic approaches to SLA has resulted in several general accounts of the area. Young (1999) points to the importance of social context in L2 acquisition in such domains as pragmatics, classroom second and foreign language learning, literacy and multilingualism. He describes questions explored by sociolinguistic research in SLA in the area of language variation and face-to-face communication: how patterns of conversation differ from one culture to another, why L2 speakers speak differently in different situations and with different people, causes of miscommunication, and whether bilingual speakers transfer patterns from their first language (L1) to their L2. He reviews what he considers the four main areas of SLA and use: interlanguage variation, cross-cultural communication, conversational phenomena and social identity. Social context plays a major role in all of these domains.

Context of Acquisition

Even before the application of sociolinguistics to SLA, researchers were aware that learning another language entails more than just learning linguistic structures. We have been aware of this since Hymes (1971) pointed out the inadequacy of the notion of linguistic competence to account for second language acquisition in any broad sense. His concept of 'communicative competence' is described by Saville-Troike (2006: 100) as 'what a speaker needs to know to communicate appropriately within a particular language community'. Other researchers since then have contributed to the definition of communicative competence, for instance, Swain (1985), Savignon (1997) and Bachman (1990). In this volume we take communicative competence to mean a general notion of the use of appropriate language in the relevant context and sociolinguistic competence as an essential component of communicative competence. These terms will be further teased out in the course of the work.

Current research on many fronts goes beyond the original concept of interlanguage – or learner language – as the progressive acquisition of target language grammar. Exciting new developments have taken place, for instance, in the area of pragmatics since initial work by Kasper and Dahl (1991), Blum-Kulka (1982) and Kasper and Schmidt (1996). More recently, studies by Kasper and Rose (1999), Bardovi-Harlig (1999) and Kasper (2000) investigate the relationship between morphosyntactic and pragmatic competence. There is some debate as to whether pragmatic competence remains low if grammatical level is low or rather if there is little connection between the two competences, although in fact there does seem to be evidence of correlation between grammatical and pragmatic proficiency. In addition, current research in pragmatics indicates that context of acquisition may be crucial in the acquisition of pragmatic competence, which seems to develop through stages, like the acquisition of grammatical competence. Young (1996) emphasises 'the modularity of linguistic competence'. Acquisition involves the ability to use the necessary strategies to be able to communicate in another language and also involves knowledge of the social and cultural aspects of that language. It equally involves knowledge of what it means to have a role and an identity in a group or community.

Recently, as we have already noted, the notion of community has been expanding to encompass the constantly shifting nature of groups and communities as they form and reform. The majority of the world's multilingual population tend to be members of more than one language community and may interact to a greater or lesser extent with one or other community at any particular moment. Currently, for instance, the issue of language socialisation in SLA is receiving increasing attention in the literature (Bayley & Schecter, 2003; Byron, 2006; Eckert, 2000; Firth & Wagner, 1997; Grusec & Hastings, 2007; Rast, 2006; Watson-Gegeo & Nielsen, 2003). In the context of language socialisation, Watson-Gegeo and Nielsen point out, neither a purely cognitivist nor a purely socioculturist view is, in itself sufficient to fully explain language learning.

> [T]heory in L1 acquisition seems ahead of SLA theory in recognizing, on the basis of both experimental and qualitative research, that cognition itself is constructed and shaped in the context of experience and through social interaction. (Watson-Gegeo & Nielsen, 2003: 156)

The arbitrary nature of the dichotomy which the field had previously taken for granted between the two approaches, cognitivist and sociocultural, had indeed already been commented on. Recently, the study of language socialisation, from previously dealing only with children, has broadened to include older children, adolescents and adults and 'attends closely to patterns of meaning suggested by the use of different linguistic codes in speech and literacy performances, as well as ideologies concerning the symbolic importance of different languages' (Bayley & Schecter, 2003: 1). Language socialisation is seen as an ongoing process where those acquiring other languages are not seen as passive but acting with and through the community in which they are operating. Language choice is central to this process. From the perspective we adopt here, cognition is born out of social interaction, and constructing new knowledge is both a cognitive and a social process.

The Role of Input in Second Language Acquisition

This construction of knowledge through both cognitive and social channels is closely linked with the linguistic input to which the speaker has access. Input is one of the most crucial topics in SLA research; input and its effect on acquisition have been looked at in many ways. Context is closely linked to the kind of input the learner has available to him/her. The way in which L2 speakers interact with the many speech communities they are in contact with conditions their access to input. Input is crucial for both L1 and L2 acquisition. However, its role is more problematic in L2. The perception of this role varies considerably depending on the approach chosen. There exists an important body of literature on the issue of input (Gass, 1997; Pica & Doughty, 1985; Long, 1996, among others). For example, behaviourist approaches see input as the crucial element to which learners react and which they imitate. Krashen (1985) considers that 'comprehensible input' is all that is needed for acquisition. Universal Grammar (UG) approaches see input only as a trigger for language-internal mechanisms to take over. Connectionist approaches hold that the quantity and quality of input determine acquisition. Interactionist approaches view input as facilitating – but not causing – acquisition.[5]

Input is generally seen as fundamental to the acquisition process. If the L2 speaker does not have any access or even sufficient access to input, then acquisition is unlikely to take place. Many sociocultural approaches see input as actually determining what features of language are learnt, as we saw earlier. A large body of important work deals in detail with the interplay of input, interaction and intake (Long, 1983, 2000; Pica, 1983, 1987, 1988, 1994; Pica *et al.*, 1986). These researchers all found that learners' interaction with interlocutors was as important as the input. This research demonstrated how learner and interlocutor modify their speech progressively until comprehension is achieved. Further studies on the 'negotiation of meaning' – for example, Pica *et al.* (1989, 1991) and Gass and Varonis (1994) – showed that in negotiating meaning, speakers rephrased, repeated and highlighted words in a systematic way. Modifications like this provided repeated access to L2 forms as they encoded function. Study abroad provides a useful mixture of naturalistic as well as classroom learning. During study abroad, the interaction with native speakers potentially provides opportunities for getting feedback so the speakers are actually aware of it, on condition of their 'noticing'. Feedback is not effective if the learner is not aware of it. Research by Long (2000), Pica *et al.* (1989) and others shows that interaction-modification by negotiation is critical to the acquisition process – for comprehensibility leads to comprehension. A lack of shared meaning is an important stimulation to negotiation which leads to understanding and to acquisition.

Speakers need also to focus on form, however. In a study abroad context, not only does the learner have the input from the naturalistic situation but also in the formal setting, they have the possibility to focus on form. However, focus on form is best used for linguistic items that are not salient or frequent in the input. For those which are frequent and salient, learning in a naturalistic setting may be helpful. For this reason, we chose to study phenomena which were very frequent in the input the learner receives with contact with native speakers during study abroad.

Input and context

Both input and interaction are important in the acquisition process; and access to input is closely linked with context of acquisition. Context has been an important element in sociolinguistic inquiry into SLA, though not always defined nor operationalised.[6] Hymes (1967) proposed a componential model of context for the analysis of native speech. This included a number of categories such as setting, participants, end, act sequence, instrumentality, norms of interaction and interpretation and genre (S-P-E-A-K-I-N-G). This model has tended to underlie work on variation in L2 speech, though often implicitly. Young (1999) develops the nuance of Hymes' notion of context in relation to interlanguage variation. Young elaborates two different approaches to context, one essentially static, involving a focal event – language – and a field of action within which that event is embedded. The other approach is dynamic. The first view describes the setting of language use, as well as participants' cultural background, L1, L2 proficiency, gender, social status and other social categories independently of language use. The other view – which is now more frequently taken – sees context as emerging and dynamic and negotiated by the participants through interaction. This latter view is producing exciting research as outlined above and is influential in much of the work currently being carried out on the area of sociolinguistics and SLA. Saville-Troike (2006), in a discussion of context of acquisition, describes what she calls 'circumstances of learning'. This is a useful notion for studying the role of context in acquisition. It involves, for example, such factors as the learner's prior educational experiences, which can be culture-specific and affect acquisition. Traditionally in SLA research an important factor in situational circumstances is whether learning is formal or instructed, on the one hand, or informal or naturalistic on the other. In the community, the learner interacts with native speakers of the L2. The type of input that the classroom provides is very different from that available to those learners living in the native speech community. In the latter environment, the L2 speaker may wish to participate in the life of the community. This has been referred to as the 'integrative' motivation for language learning. Competence here involves the wider skills referred to earlier, that is, knowledge of the community's culture. Foreign language learners in the classroom, on the other hand, learn within the context of their own culture and have limited opportunity for interacting with native speaker interlocutors. A learner of an 'auxiliary' language is even more narrowly focused. The goal here is often referred to as 'language for specific purposes', for example, for scientific or technological ends. Saville-Troike comments on context of acquisition:

> Within the definition of communicative competence, the content of 'what a speaker needs to know', as well as judgements of relative success in attaining that knowledge, depend on the social context within which he or she learns and is using the language. (Saville-Troike, 2006: 101)

SLA researchers have long wondered why some L2 speakers seem to integrate better into the society they are living in and why some seem to become more proficient and more native-like. These studies range from Schumann's (1975, 1978) speculations on Alberto and his lack of 'acculturation' in his famous study, to Meisel (1983), who applied a similar model to his investigation of guest workers in Germany. Schumann's acculturation model takes account of the distance the learner perceives between him/herself and the culture of the target-language. Whether the speaker 'acculturates' is crucial to how they learn and how much they learn. Interaction with native speakers provides the input which is crucial for acquisition to take place. Schumann's study of Alberto is an example which demonstrates that acculturation can be a major causal variable. In this case, Alberto, a Spanish-speaking learner of English, did not acculturate and was thus more or less cut off from the input which was so crucial to his linguistic development. He failed to move along the habitual path and at the usual rate of L2 speakers of English in relation to acquisition of negation. Schumann interpreted the reason for his limited success in the acquisition of negation in English as due to limited acculturation. Meisel (1983) re-invoked the effect of lack of acculturation and the issue of explaining lack of progress along the expected developmental path in some L2 speakers. He studied guest workers in Germany and found among other things that those who acculturated more had better grammatical competence. These speakers socialised more with German L1 speakers.

Second language acquisition, like child language acquisition, is characterised by developmental sequences and processes. All learners go through the same series of steps. Everyone learns word order rules, for instance; this is due to psycholinguistic constraints. Linguistic constraints also operate on language development as it proceeds in a predictable direction. However, psychosocial factors also affect development and these may be particularly important in the development of other features of language. Grammatical morphology, for instance, is sensitive to social factors in acquisition and we find that the acquisition of features such as inflections is considerably affected by psychosocial features. These two strands are picked up in Corder (1981) who distinguishes between, what he terms, 'the vertical and the horizontal continuum'. This construct has been adopted later by others.[7] Corder proposed that variability in L2 speech could be accounted for by these two continua; the vertical one, along a dimension of increasing or decreasing complexity, and the horizontal one, where the speaker shifted from one variety or lect to another. For both dimensions, access to input is crucial. A desire to integrate into a speech community may be one of the motivations for the impetus for 'sounding like a native speaker'. It is perfectly possible, for instance, to communicate one's message without mastering the structures relating to plural forms, but in relation to the speech community, knowledge of grammatical morphemes can have an important integrative function. In this way, Turkish guest workers putting a third person singular ending on a verb in German, or Polish workers in Ireland using target-like morphology in Irish-English may be taking, consciously or unconsciously, a particular position *vis-à-vis* their perception of themselves and the host community. Studies such as Schumann's and Meisel's have affirmed that input and context as well as a desire to relate to the target culture, all have a role to play here.[8]

Study Abroad as a Context for Acquiring a Second Language

One particular context of acquisition is what is known as study abroad or year abroad. Study abroad covers such different situations as spending a year in France for European or American students or spending time in a different linguistic region within the same country, such as Anglophone Canadian speakers learning French in Home Stay situations in Quebec. Collentine and Freed (2004), in a volume focusing on learning context and SLA, provide a welcome comprehensive account of the notion of context as it relates to study abroad. Collentine and Freed (2004: 168) report that the research presented provides no evidence that 'one context of learning is uniformly superior to another for all students, at all levels of language learning, and for all language skills'. They find that the foreign language classroom favours control of morphosyntax and that native-like phonological control appears equally successful in 'at home' learners. There are, on the other hand, gains in lexical breadth and narrative ability. However, there is less discussion of research on the acquisition of sociolinguistic competence. For the most complete picture of language in context and for the best understanding of the role of context as a causal variable, a close examination of the acquisition of sociolinguistic competence is crucial.

We will consider this particular context of acquisition (study/year abroad) in detail in Chapters 2 and 3, and will provide detailed empirical evidence relating to the acquisition of sociolinguistic competence. We will examine the effect of the year abroad context as a causal variable on L2 acquisition. The results of our research for 15 years of sociolinguistic studies of this area reveal new findings in relation both to the general issue of sociolinguistic competence in SLA and specifically in relation to the particular case of study abroad. This evidence confirms previous findings from other perspectives, in some cases, contradicts it in others and adds new information in yet other instances. We aim to provide a better understanding of the role of setting or circumstances of learning in the first instance, and the wider one of context in L2 acquisition ultimately. We investigate how sociolinguistic competence is acquired, taking into account the multiple factors which affect it: psycholinguistic, linguistic and social. These factors include linguistic environment, input, proficiency level, gender, social class, length of stay in the L2 speech community, contact with native speakers, long term effects of study abroad.

Sociolinguistic research in SLA aims to address the major questions posed earlier in this chapter from the particular viewpoint of the social context in which the L2 is learnt. It tries to describe, explain and predict outcomes by describing minutely the process, looking at the effect of multiple factors on this process both in terms of what the learner learns and in what setting. In this book we will address the following issues and questions:

- What the learner learns involves not just structures in the language, but also the social and cultural knowledge involved in the language and the more detailed sociolinguistic knowledge implied by these.
- How does the L2 speaker behave in social situations in the other community?
- How must he or she behave linguistically to be able to function in such a group?

- What is it in the language and in the linguistic context, which affects the L2 speaker's relationship with the host community and that of the community with the L2 speaker?
- What are the linguistic patterns used by the L2 speaker?
- What difference does setting for learning make to integration into the speech community if such is desired?
- Does it make a difference whether the language is learnt in a classroom in the speaker's native speech community or must they spend time in the L2 speech community?

All of these questions relate to what it means to be competent in the use of another language and to create an identity through language in another community.

The Variationist Paradigm and Second Language Acquisition

One specific paradigm within sociolinguistics is the variationist paradigm. Broadly speaking, this is the study of the social significance of language variation. There are now several accounts of what sociolinguistic research contributes to SLA research (Adamson, 1988, 2005; Preston, 1996b), so we will not linger on the theoretical issues involved. We content ourselves with a few remarks on the contribution of variationist sociolinguistics to SLA. For a long period the research agenda has been set by researchers with a UG perspective, very much as linguistics itself in the 20th century was driven by a search for the invariant.

Preston (1996a, 1996b) supports the relevance of sociolinguistics to SLA. He considered that sociolinguistics is 'concerned with variation in language – the product, process, acquisition and cognitive location of ... variation' (Preston, 1996a: 230). He says also that 'it concerns itself with sociological and social-psychological aspects of language. These aspects are crucial in the account of variation in the structural units of language' (Preston, 1996b: 3).

A strong contribution of Labovian approaches to SLA is that of a dynamic model of language. Given that interlanguage is both highly variable and also changes over time, the Labovian approach held much interest for SLA researchers when they began to apply the models and constructs of sociolinguistics to L2 data. When Tarone (1979, 1985), began using Labovian approaches to SLA, it was Labov's interest in the incorporation of variable models in the construction of theories of language acquisition which strongly influenced her early work on SLA.

Another aspect of variation research which is of considerable interest to SLA researchers is the issue of form-function relations (Young, 1996). The process of SLA could be seen as a progressive and evolving relationship between form and function, as the L2 speaker progressively makes one-to-one matches between the two. Variationist sociolinguistic analysis is multivariate and takes account of the multiplicity of factors which influence language choice. Variability in L2 language is subject to multiple influencing factors (both language internal and social context factors) and an approach which provides as full an account as possible of these multiple and frequently interacting factors is a very useful one for such data. UG approaches explain an enormous amount about SLA and the principles and parameter approach to acquisition successfully accounts for the existence and structures of utterances. But a UG approach is interested in the simple fact of something being present in the language – for example, in French the fact that one can delete the complementizer *que* or not. However, for a UG approach it is enough to know the fact. The fact that the complementiser is more likely to occur after certain structures or before others is of no interest. But these are precisely the facts which interest sociolinguists. Sociolinguists wish to know not only about the fact of the occurrence of a phenomenon but also they wish to predict when it occurs, and how often. They wish to add probabilistic information to the model used. Their approach is a probabilistic and not a deterministic one. In SLA, variationists want to understand the variability in L2 speech to determine what makes it systematic even though highly variable. SLA is centrally concerned with language change within the individual, and so sociolinguistic understanding of the mechanism of language change over time is of great interest; where the individual may variably use two or more forms at a single point in time until one form wins out. So, in fact, a dynamic model of language which adequately accounts for language change is ideal for capturing the psycholinguistic reality of language change within the individual. In this way, sociolinguistics can help us to grasp the cognitive procedures involved in acquisition theory, which is not an interest of UG research. Many scientific disciplines quite separate from linguistics are currently focusing on the variable and taking a noncategorical approach. Variation linguistic theory sees things not as either/or, but more or less, as quantitative.

Variation and Sociolinguistic Norms in French

For those working within the variationist paradigm, variation is an intrinsic part of languages and is apparent at every level of language. We proceed on the premise that an understanding of language is incomplete without an account of variability. Native speaker variation patterns and related issues such as vernacular norms are important ones in relation to spoken language in general. Part of acquiring a language is a knowledge of register, formality and informality. Some languages are more concerned with the notion of norm, especially prescriptive norms, than others. In these cases, a learner is less likely to breach communication by violating the 'rules' pertaining to such norms. The issue of linguistic norms in general is especially pertinent when French is the language being acquired, as French is a language particularly concerned with these issues.

French has had a long history of prescriptive norms since the period of Port Royal. For this reason, the choice of French as the L2 to be studied is significant in that it could be said that French is one of the most 'normative' languages in Europe. Since the 17th century, French has had a history of relentless normalising and homogenisation, for political and social reasons.[9] The Académie Française is a very real presence in academic, intellectual and even everyday life for French speakers and they are acutely aware from an early age of prestige norms from intense prescriptive pressure. French L1 speakers, while they are variable users of variants which form an intrinsic part of daily speech, such as the informal deletion of *ne* (part of the negative structure), use of *on* (as opposed to *nous* which is the more prestigious variant), and the deletion of /l/, frequent in rapid spoken French, are nevertheless acutely aware of the status of these variants as nonprestige (these three variants are in fact very mildly stigmatised). It is therefore of interest to explore the extent to which the issue of the norm in French is salient for L2 speakers of French today. The acquisition of vernacular norms in French by L2 speakers is consequently a relatively sensitive and important issue which does not necessarily take place easily or smoothly and is affected by multiple linguistic and social factors. This is an area where the success of a learner in acquiring sociolinguistic competence is palpably felt and so almost easy to measure, as well as an area in which the learner is likely to be highly motivated to learn in order to become part of the speech community.

In this volume we take as examples of the acquisition of sociolinguistic community norms areas of variability in contemporary spoken French such as the variables mentioned above which have a high frequency in oral language: *ne* deletion, *nous/on* alternation, /l/ deletion as well as the variable use of future temporal reference. We analyse how they are acquired and used by Irish-English speakers. We explore the effect of spending a year in a francophone country (France or Belgium) on the use of these variables on L2 speakers. We compare their use by the L2 speakers before the period of time abroad and afterwards,[10] as well as tracking the evolving use of the variants. We also consider research done in Canada and make a general comparison of the results of year abroad, with the effects of the immersion classroom in Canada on the one hand, and with regard to similar variables on the other. The interest of this comparison is ultimately to address the role of context as a causal variable in the acquisition of native speaker variation patterns. Ultimately the research should help us to better understand the role of context and the related issue of the role of input in SLA.

The Acquisition of Native Speaker Variation Speech Patterns: A New Research Thread

Much variation work has examined the acquisition of grammatical features that are generally regarded as obligatory in the target language, characterised, as we have seen as the vertical continuum. Recently, however, there has grown another related research thread which sees knowledge of variation as part of speaker competence. The implication of this position is that second language learners also sometimes wish, depending on their desire to establish a particular identity *vis-à-vis* the community in which they are living and interacting, to acquire native-speaker (NS) patterns of variation. What we have referred to as the horizontal continuum is referred to by Mougeon *et al.* (2004) as 'Type 2' variation. The 'vertical continuum' refers to an increase in proficiency, and the 'horizontal continuum' to the use of noncategorical native-speaker patterns of variation (Bayley & Regan, 2004). Adamson and Regan (1991) provide an example of the vertical continuum in relation to Schumann's continuum of negative constructions for Spanish speakers learning English negative constructions. This continuum consists of four stages:

- Stage 1   no + verb   'She no understand'
- Stage 2   don't_verb   'She don't understand'
- Stage 3   AUX+ not   'She can't play'
- Stage 4   DO+ not   'She doesn't understand'

The *horizontal continuum* on the other hand is rather a continuum of social dialects in the speech community. The L2 speaker who receives in the input both standard and nonstandard forms may use structures with pronoun reduplication, for example: 'My father, he's a doctor' and also use variably 'My father is a doctor' (Adamson & Regan, 1991). The L2 speaker of French can variably say 'Je suis allée au cinéma avec Pierre hier soir' or 'On est allé au cinéma avec Pierre hier soir', alternating between the more prestige form 'je' and the less formal 'on'.

The research agenda of this new research thread involves investigating L2 variation patterns, asking whether they are similar to native speaker variation patterns, the relationship between this usage and the creation of an 'L2 identity' and also trying to chart the evolution of the acquisition of variation patterns in the L2 speaker's speech. Related issues include the effect of context on this process, the role of input in the acquisition of NS patterns of variation, whether the behaviour of the L2 speaker is the same in a case of a stable sociolinguistic variable as in the case of a variable that is undergoing change. We will address these issues by investigating closely the speech of Year Abroad L2 speakers.

A number of studies have addressed some of these questions. For example, Adamson and Regan (1991) examined the acquisition of NS patterns of use of the (ing) variable, for example, *working* vs *workin'*, by Vietnamese and Cambodian immigrant speakers of English as an L2 and found that the variation patterns of the L2 speakers approximated the native speaker patterns. The L2 speakers tried in particular to approximate native speaker gender patterns. Bayley (1996) investigated the acquisition of target-like patterns of consonant cluster reduction (CCR) by Chinese learners of English. He found that more proficient learners, with more native speaker contacts, approached target language patterns of CCR with mono-morphemes. Recently, Major (2004) looked at variation in native-like phonological forms by investigating gender and stylistic differences in the English of native speakers and of native speakers of Japanese and Spanish. He found that there are significant differences based on gender and style. Like Adamson and Regan (1991), Major's study shows the importance of gender as an influencing factor.[11]

In the presentation of the variables we will look at, we have compared the results of our quantitative multivariate studies of speech of Irish L2 Year Abroad speakers with both naturalistic learners and traditional classroom Canadian learners. For example, Sankoff *et al.* (1997) studied the use of discourse markers by non-native speakers of French in Montreal and concluded that appropriate use of these markers is an indication of the speaker's integration into the francophone community. Nagy *et al.* (2003) studied subject-doubling in the French of anglophone Montrealers. They found that contact with francophone speakers positively affected rates of subject doubling. Mougeon *et al.* (2001) studied the acquisition of sociolinguistic competence by students enrolled in French immersion programmes. (We understand by 'immersion' the definitions and descriptions provided in Fortune & Tedick, 2008: 9.) They investigated a number of variables, of varying degrees of formality. They found that immersion speakers make 'nil to marginal use of vernacular variants' (Fortune & Tedick, 2003: 25). The authors did find though that immersion students made somewhat greater use of mildly marked variants than of vernacular variants. Equally in relation to classroom learners, Dewaele and Regan (2001), who studied the use of familiar lexemes in the speech of classroom learners of Continental French found little use of 'slang' terms which would be common in the speech of equivalent young people in the native speech community.

It is in the context of this new research thread that our book situates itself in its investigation of the year abroad as a causal variable in second language acquisition. The use of the variationist paradigm provides empirical data on the process by which L2 learners, through the input they access in the year abroad context, acquire sociolinguistic competence (as evidenced by their proficiency in community speech norms in French) and succeed in creating new identities.

Notes

1. A variationist approach involves an analysis of systematic differences in speech which are correlated with contexts of use. This approach will be discussed at greater length in Chapter 4.
2. For a detailed definition of the 'advanced learner', see Chapter 4 of this volume and Bartning (1997a).
3. See Chapters 2 and 3 for a comprehensive account.
4. For more detail, see Pica (2003) and Doughty and Long (2003).
5. For a comprehensive account of interactionist approaches, see Pica (1987, 1994, 1998, 2003).
6. For further discussion, see Young (1999).
7. For instance, among those in the sociolinguistic tradition in second language research, Adamson and Regan (1991), and Rehner *et al.* (2003).
8. A more specifically focused discussion of context in relation to the studies presented in this book will be given in Chapters 2 and 3.
9. Malherbe (1555–1628) was the precursor of formal explicit research conducted in France from the 19th century. His literary theory was the 'un bon artisan du vers doit exprimer des thèmes éternels dans une forme rigoureuse et pure' (A good worker should write on everending topics in the most rigourous and pure form).
10. We will report on a longitudinal study carried out on one of the variants, *ne* deletion, which demonstrates the long term effects of the year abroad.
11. The role of gender will be discussed at more length in Chapter 9.

Chapter 2
Linguistic Outcomes and Study Abroad

Introduction

With a view to illuminating the specific effects of study abroad on second language acquisition (SLA), as opposed to other learning contexts, this chapter aims to provide an overview of the major findings emanating from study abroad research relating to SLA. We firstly review early study abroad research which provided a more general picture of L2 development during study abroad, as opposed to later research which allows a more detailed insight into the learner's development across the various components of his/her linguistic repertoire in the L2. The chapter is the first in a set of two, whereby the following chapter offers a complementary discussion of the range of extralinguistic factors which impinge on that development.

Study Abroad as Context

We understand 'context' here in the traditional sense regarding the dichotomy between naturalistic acquisition in the target language (TL) environment, on the one hand, and foreign language instruction outside this community, on the other. The learner whose access to the L2 is mainly through instruction outside the TL community has typically been considered to be engaged in *Foreign Language Learning*, as opposed to *Second Language Acquisition*, which denotes the naturalistic acquisition which the L2 learner undergoes in the TL community.[1] As noted by Freed (1995b, 1998), such a distinction in terms is somewhat regrettable by potentially implying that language learning is a fundamentally different process in each case. Furthermore, it must not be forgotten that the alternation between the instructed and naturalistic learning environments is the norm for L2 learners. Today, many international exchange programmes make it possible for the instructed L2 learner to partake in 'study abroad', whereby this learner spends a period of residence of varying duration in the TL community.[2] Whilst the participants often follow a course of instruction whilst abroad, study abroad programmes are principally a means of allowing the instructed learner to acquire 'pseudo-naturalistic' status, by engaging in more informal acquisition in the TL community, through naturalistic contact with the L2 in everyday social situations. Following study abroad, the learner is characterised by more balanced access to both formal and informal input than the instructed learner outside the TL community and the naturalistic learner within that community. The study abroad learner therefore presents a particular combination of learner variables which potentially distinguishes his/her acquisitional development from that of the 'standard' naturalistic or instructed learner. SLA in a Study Abroad context therefore provides us with an important insight into the role of context in SLA, by illuminating 'the relationship between exposure, intake and use' (Regan, 1998b: 64).

L2 Acquisition in a Study Abroad Context

Given the balance in formal and informal input which characterises the study abroad learner's exposure to the L2, there is a general consensus that a period of time spent in the TL community by the instructed learner is beneficial to the acquisition process. However, whilst such a folklinguistic consensus may exist, there has been relatively little empirical evidence to suggest that it is actually true, due to a traditional dearth of studies in this area. For example, Freed (1993) suggests that there has been a number of projects investigating this general area from within a framework other than that which focuses on the language skills of the learner. For example, some projects investigate the role of study abroad in the nonlanguage learner in relation to such issues as personal, academic and social development. Those studies dealing specifically with the specialist language learner, that is, the learner who goes abroad for language learning purposes, have also tended to focus on similar pragmatic issues such as the learner's attitudinal changes in terms of career plans, interests, opinions, and so on. For example, Coleman (2001) investigates the recruitment of study abroad graduates in the job market.

Even in the case of those studies which have specifically investigated the learner's linguistic development during study abroad, Freed (1993) notes that early research provides a limited insight into the conclusions that can be drawn about the linguistic benefits of study abroad. This is because early research tended to be based on general language tests which measure increased proficiency in a very objective way.[3] For example, a number of studies, such as Carroll (1967), Dyson (1988), and Magnan

(1986), is based on various 'discrete point' tests, which do not describe the changes that occur in real language use. Such tests simply offer a global score as indicative of linguistic development, without analysing progress on specific aspects of the learner's linguistic repertoire. For example, they note general increased proficiency on reading and listening tests, without detailing the developmental changes which take place, to allow the learner to demonstrate improved reading and listening skills. Freed (1998) suggests that another difficulty with 'discrete point' tests is their ceiling effects: whilst they may reveal development in the less-advanced learner, development in the more advanced stages may be less noticeable, because of difficulties in discriminating progress at these stages.

A final difficulty concerns the fact that early research has also tended to investigate specific language skills, such as the learner's reading and aural skills. As such, it is difficult to attain a global picture of how the various benefits in each domain qualitatively lead to an all-round more proficient learner. Thus, Coleman (1995a: 22) underscores the need to identify whether certain aspects of the learner's proficiency benefit more than others: 'language proficiency, after all, is not a single entity but a multidimensional construct, and progress in the different aspects – vocabulary, grammar, pronunciation, and so on – may be expected to take place at different rates'.

Having outlined some of the insufficiencies which have traditionally characterised early research on the study abroad learner, the following section will detail results of that research before considering more recent studies, which document the linguistic benefits of study abroad on specific aspects of the learner's linguistic repertoire, namely in the areas of fluency; sociolinguistic and pragmatic competence; lexical acquisition; and grammatical development.[4]

L2 Development During Study Abroad

The linguistic benefits of study abroad have traditionally been investigated in terms of development on the learner's general language skills in reading, writing, listening and speaking. For example, Coleman's (1995b, 1996, 1998) large-scale cross-sectional investigation of European study abroad learners points to the important development made by study abroad learners, as evidenced by their significantly higher post-residence abroad score on the C-Test. Meara (1994) provides an investigation of European learners of English in the UK based on an analysis of introspective questionnaires. He finds that the majority of his learners felt that their oral-aural competence had improved during residence abroad, but less than half felt their reading and writing skills showed equal improvement.

The more important benefits of study abroad for the learner's oral-aural skills as opposed to their written and reading skills are reiterated in a number of other studies. For example, Dyson (1988) reports on a longitudinal investigation of the effect of a year abroad on British learners of French, German and Spanish. Findings from the learners' self-reports mirrored their test results: their listening and speaking skills greatly increased, while their reading skills showed some progress, but relatively no progress was shown in their writing skills. A large-scale study of British study abroad learners by Willis *et al.* (1977) similarly provides evidence of such self-held beliefs by drawing on pre- and post-test results to detail the increased development that occurs on their learners' speaking and aural skills. Batardière (1993) also finds that a group of Irish students self-report that their oral skills had improved in French, but their written skills had not. Whilst such studies are concerned with writing and reading skills in languages that use the Roman alphabet, Huebner points out that little study abroad research has been done on languages that use other systems. He makes the important point that '[S]tudents studying languages with familiar or easily accessible orthographies may be in a better position to take advantage of environmental print for vocabulary development, for example, during their sojourns abroad, than students of languages with less accessible orthographies' (Huebner, 1998: 9). An exception, however, is the study presented by Huebner (1995), which shows that *ab initio* learners of Japanese in Japan perform better on a reading text compared to their counterparts on a language course in the United States.[5] Whilst such increased proficiency is not found to be statistically significant, it is nonetheless reflected in the learners' more positive attitude towards their introduction to the Japanese writing system which can be seen as fulfilling their requirement to become literate in an environment where they were otherwise illiterate. In a further study of the acquisition of reading skills in L2 Japanese, Dewey (2004) finds that study abroad learners report feeling more confident at reading than their immersion learner counterparts in the United States. Whilst important, this, however, is the only difference that emerges between the learners: results concerning a free-recall test as well as vocabulary knowledge did not reveal significant differences.

Lapkin *et al.* (1995) investigate the linguistic gains made by a group of Canadian Anglophone learners participating in a three-month submersion programme in a French-speaking province. As a means of counteracting the methodological problems associated with language tests, as described above, the study reports on self-assessment ratings provided by the learners.[6] The results suggest that the learners made important gains on both their aural and oral skills.

Various studies by Brecht, Davidson and Ginsberg (Brecht & Davidson, 1992; Brecht & Ginsberg, 1991; Brecht & Robinson, 1995; Brecht *et al.*, 1993, 1995), investigating the acquisition of Russian by American learners during study abroad, also point to the linguistic gains of study abroad, particularly in relation to language aptitude, as well as increased speaking skills in Russian. This is particularly true when a comparison is made with learners who do not participate in such programmes. For example, the researchers find that only a small percentage of learners who do not go abroad reach an advanced level, which is considered to be the minimal level of functional ability. In contrast, for learners who spend a semester in Russia, the percentage stands at 40%. The authors also find some interesting correlations between findings, which underscore the complex effects of study abroad. For example, the higher the score on grammar tests before going abroad, the higher the gain in the learners' speaking, listening, and reading skills. Such findings lead the authors to suggest that a solid foundation in grammar and reading skills is important for development in other areas of language proficiency.

The studies reviewed specifically point to an important effect for study abroad on the learner's oral and aural skills. In contrast, the effect is less evident in the case of the learner's reading and writing skills. However, the general sense that study abroad has a generally beneficial effect on the learner's language development is equally borne out in studies which attempt to provide a more introspective insight into the learner's perspective on his/her development during study abroad through the use of learner diary entries. For example, based on her survey of American study abroad learners in Russia, Pellegrino (1998) reports that learners are overwhelmingly satisfied with their progress over one semester. However, leaving aside this study which provides an alternative perspective on L2 acquisition during study abroad from the learner's perspective, being based on general language tests, the other studies reviewed simply offer a more general insight into the benefits of study abroad. They say little about the specificity of development on particular aspects of the learner's linguistic repertoire which gives rise to improvements on real language use. However, a number of more recent studies has investigated the effects of study abroad on specific aspects of the learner's linguistic repertoire such as fluency, sociolinguistic and pragmatic competence, and lexical acquisition. As such, current research specifically responds to the need to understand how the study abroad learner uses his/her linguistic knowledge in real communication. In contrast to such aspects, the learner's grammar has been relatively less focused upon, perhaps reflecting the general belief that study abroad is less important for development on a structural level, than in other areas, such as fluency, sociolinguistic competence and lexical acquisition.

The following sections will detail the general findings of those studies which have investigated the different constituents of the learner's global linguistic repertoire in the L2, with a view to considering the differential effect of study abroad on the various components which constitute that repertoire. We will begin by considering development of the learner's sociolinguistic and sociopragmatic competence in the L2, before considering the effects of study abroad on the L2 learner's fluency, and grammatical and lexical development.

Study Abroad and the Acquisition of Sociolinguistic Competence

Perhaps due to the greater access and exposure to sociolinguistic markers available in the TL community than in the foreign language classroom, as well as increased opportunities for their use, the L2 learner's sociolinguistic and sociopragmatic competences are an interesting domain for studies investigating the role of target language contact on the L2 learner's linguistic development during study abroad. For example, in her review of studies examining the effects of study abroad on sociolinguistic competence, Regan (1998b) notes that increased contact with the native speaker is an important causal factor in the development of sociolinguistic competence, whereby the study abroad learner tries to approximate native speech norms on use of different sociolinguistic markers. Typically, variation rules constrain the native speaker's use of sociolinguistic markers, whereby (non)use of the markers is highly dependent on a range of contextual factors. Thus, the problem for the L2 learner is to learn how such factors constrain (non-)use of such markers.

Japanese lends itself particularly well to the study of the variable use of politeness forms, which is the focus of studies by Marriot (1993, 1995), Marriot and Enomoto (1995) and Siegal (1995, 1996). Marriot investigates the variable use of honorifics in the highly complex system of Japanese by Australian learners of Japanese before and after a stay in Japan. Results of the study suggest that, whilst the learners become more sensitive to such variation, they nonetheless fail to use honorifics according to native speaker norms.

A similar study investigating the acquisition of variable sociolinguistic markers in Japanese is provided by Hashimoto (1994). He finds that sensitivity to such variation is the main characteristic of development during a stay in Japan by a single Australian learner of Japanese. However, the manifestation of such variable features in the learner's speech did not occur until after the learner had returned to Australia.

Japanese aside, studies of other L2s are few. Indeed, findings concerning the role of differential language contact on the acquisition of sociolinguistic variation are more often implicitly stated, and therefore must be inferred. Exceptions concern the important work on the acquisition of French by Dewaele (1992, 2004), Rehner and Mougeon (1999), Nadasdi et al. (2003) and Mougeon et al. (2002).

In a series of studies on the acquisition of a range of sociolinguistic variables by Canadian anglophone immersion learners of French, Mougeon, Rehner and Nadasdi investigate, amongst other issues, the effects of the learners' differential level of exposure to the target language outside the immersion classroom. Their results suggest an important effect for this factor in terms of the favourable effect of the learners' interaction with native speakers on the use of informal variants. For example, Rehner and Mougeon (1999) specifically investigate the variable deletion of the negative particle '*ne*'. Amongst other findings, they find that the rate of deletion is a function of level of exposure to the target language outside the classroom. However, they also find that the factor of amount of time spent in a French-speaking environment is ambiguous, affecting learners in different ways. Nonetheless, the factor of amount of time spent with a French-speaking family was found to correlate with an increased level of deletion. Dewaele (1992) similarly investigates the acquisition of French by Flemish speakers in relation to their acquisition of variable '*ne*' deletion. He equally finds an effect for out-of-classroom input in terms of informal target language exposure through television and holidays. In later work, Dewaele (2004) also reports on the important impact on the learner's sociolinguistic choices of more wide-ranging sociopersonal factors which characterise him/her.

In a similar study concerning the acquisition of the native speaker's alternation between the subject pronouns '*on*' and '*nous*', Rehner et al. (2003) equally find an important effect for extracurricular French language exposure: 'as such exposure increases, either as a result of greater French media consumption or of extended stays with Francophone families or in Francophone environments, the students' use of on also increases', where '*on*' constitutes the informal variant (Rehner et al., 2003: 147). Other Canadian studies which provide a similar insight into the important role of naturalistic contact with the L2 outside the target language classroom include Blondeau and Nagy's (1998) study of subject doubling; Nadasdi *et al.*'s (2001) and Nagy *et al.*'s (1996) studies of the deletion of /l/ such as in '/i/ sort'; Sankoff *et al.*'s (1997) study of the use of discourse markers such as *'bon'* and *'ben'*; and Mougeon and Rehner's (2001) study of the use of restrictive adverbs such as *'seulement'* and *'juste'*.

Within a more traditional study abroad framework, Howard (2005a) also focuses on the role of context in the acquisition of sociolinguistic variation, in this case in relation to variable liaison realisation in L2 French. Similar to one of the major findings in relation to the variables to be presented here, his results indicate a very clear effect for naturalistic contact during study abroad on the instructed learner's acquisition of this variable, such that without such naturalistic contact, the instructed learner makes minimal use of this variable in his/her speech. The study is of particular interest because of the specific characteristics of liaison, whereby, in failing to realise this sociophonological variable, the learners are in effect producing the informal variant, in contrast to the formal variant which is only realised at higher rates in the speech of the study abroad learners.

A final noteworthy study, this time in the case of L2 English, is that of Olson Flanagan and Inal (1996) which, although not within the study abroad framework, investigates the effect of differing levels of exposure on use of the English relative pronouns 'that', 'wh-' and '0' by two groups of learners with different source languages. One group had spent longer than two years in the United States, while the other had spent less than two years. A comparison is made with a group of native speakers. The prescriptive rule favours 'wh-', whereas native speaker preferences tend towards '0', and to a lesser extent 'that'. Results suggest that naturalistic exposure is in the direction of TL norms, as indicated by the fact that non-native speakers of English 'begin to accommodate to NS preferences in relative pronoun use the longer they are in an English-speaking environment' (Olson Flanagan & Inal, 1996: 220). The less time spent in the TL community, the more learners tend toward the prescriptive form 'wh-'.

On the basis of the studies reviewed, study abroad appears to have important benefits for the L2 learner's sociolinguistic competence, as demonstrated by the increased usage of sociolinguistic markers. However, study abroad has more limited effects in bringing about appropriate use of such markers in line with target language norms, as noted, for example, by Marriot (1995). That is to say, the learner tends to overuse the markers in inappropriate contexts. Those studies reviewed above are specifically concerned with the development of the L2 learner's sociolinguistic competence during study abroad in terms of the learner's acquisition of variable sociolinguistic markers. In contrast, other studies have been concerned with the related issue of the learner's sociopragmatic development in terms of the learner's 'knowledge of the appropriate contextual use of the particular languages' linguistic resources' for the realisation of particular speech acts, such as making offers and requests, expressing acceptance and refusal, and providing advice, amongst many others (Barron, 2003: 10). Such studies include Barron's investigation of the acquisition of sociopragmatic norms in L2 German, Matsumara's (2003) work on the sociopragmatic development of Japanese learners of English, and Siegal's (1995) case-study of two female learners of Japanese in Japan.

Study Abroad and the Acquisition of Sociopragmatic Competence

Barron (2003) presents a longitudinal study of Irish learners spending a year abroad at a German university, with specific reference to the development of their sociopragmatic competence. Data elicitation was based on a number of instruments including questionnaires, role-plays and interviews, and (free) discourse completion tasks in relation to the speech acts of requests, offers and refusals of offers. Findings from the study point to the important benefits of study abroad for the development of the learners' sociopragmatic competence: whereas at the start of the study, the learners relied considerably on transfer of their L1 formulations to realise these L2 speech acts, not only did the learners use more native-like formulations at the end of the study, but they also demonstrated greater sociopragmatic awareness in terms of their knowledge of how to use such formulations in context. However, the author emphasises the limitations of such development insofar as there nonetheless remained a considerable gap between native-speaker norms and the learners' sociopragmatic usage 'in cases where movements towards the L2 norm was recorded, "towards" was indeed the appropriate word since it was rarely that the L2 norm was actually reached' (Barron, 2003: 238). Such limitations were seen to relate to the learners' perceptions of transferability from their L1 as well as their perceptions of the appropriateness of use of certain formulations in context. For example, transfer of routines from the learners' L1 was not completely eliminated, whilst overuse of L2 formulations continued in contexts where native speakers would not use such forms.

In a similar investigation of the effects of study abroad on the development of the L2 learners' sociopragmatic competence, Matsumara (2001, 2003) presents longitudinal findings for Japanese learners of English spending an eight-month sojourn at a Canadian university. The study focuses on the speech act of providing advice. Similar to Barron's findings, results of this study point to the important development of the learner's sociopragmatic competence during study abroad: on the one hand, the author notes an increase in the learners' awareness of the appropriateness of various advice-giving formulations. On the other hand, the author similarly notes an increase in the degree of approximation existing between native speaker behaviour and that of the learners.

Siegal (1995) offers an insight into the everyday experiences of two female learners from New Zealand, as they attempt to achieve the appropriate politeness effect with limited linguistic means in typical communicative situations in Japan. Siegal finds differences between the learners in terms of their use of politeness markers which may be related to differences in the individual's identity. That is to say, the individual may identify differently with the TL community, and, as such, that individual's use of language to express his/her identity may differ from other learners. In particular, Siegal describes, in the case of one of her informants, how she creates her own identity by rejecting the linguistic and interactional features characteristic of the female gender in Japanese society.

Further studies concerned with the appropriateness of the learner's linguistic and nonlinguistic behaviour in context have been carried out from within an interactionist perspective. For example, Mauranen (1994) investigates the problem of inadequate knowledge of Finnish students in relation to their participation in various interactive situations abroad, in this case in Britain. Such inadequacy arises out of the culture-specific nature of certain encounters, which are quite different from those taking place in the learner's home environment. Ylönen (1994) offers similar evidence in the case of Finnish learners of German.

In summary, the conclusions to be drawn concerning the development of the learner's sociopragmatic competence during study abroad are somewhat similar to those previously made concerning the learner's sociolinguistic competence: whilst the studies reviewed point to the benefits of study abroad in terms of more increased usage of native-like sociopragmatic formulations, as well as greater sociopragmatic awareness of their appropriateness in context, the studies equally note a number of limitations such that a considerable gap remains between learner and native speaker norms.

The Effect of Study Abroad on the L2 Learner's Lexical Acquisition

The benefits of study abroad have more recently been documented in the area of lexical acquisition by Milton and Meara (1995), Ife *et al.* (2000), Howard (2002b), DeKeyser (1991), Collentine (2004) and Dewaele and

Regan (2001). Milton and Meara's study is based on a large-scale investigation of European learners spending at least six months at a British institution. Based on an analysis of introspective questionnaires completed by the informants, the authors report that the learners acquired vocabulary 'five times faster than for those who took classes at home ... and to be gaining vocabulary at a rate of over 2500 words per year'. DeKeyser (1991) also offers similar evidence of the important lexical gains to be made during study abroad by his American learners in a hispanophone country. Similarly, in their study of British learners of Spanish in Spain, Ife et al. (2000) also report on the important lexical acquisition experienced by their learner informants, as demonstrated by an increased vocabulary range. Furthermore, they also find that the learners demonstrated a more native-like organisation of their lexicon. In contrast to such positive findings in the case of L2 Spanish, Collentine (2004) generally fails to find significant lexical differences in his study of classroom learners of Spanish in the United States and learners spending a semester in Spain. His study is based on a comparison of the lexical frequencies of a range of grammatical word types. With the exception of adjectives, both groups of learners demonstrated similar lexical scores. However, lexical differences were evident in terms of the increased occurrence of semantically dense lexemes in the study abroad learners' speech, giving rise to an enhanced quality of informationally rich discourse.

In a study that is more narrow in its approach to lexical acquisition during study abroad, insofar as it specifically focuses on the acquisition of lexical verbs, Howard (2002b) draws on a number of lexical scores, such as the learners' use of sophisticated verbs, to illuminate the more expansive lexical verb repertoire demonstrated by study abroad learners, as compared to classroom learners. Furthermore, the study abroad learners, in this case, Irish learners of French, are more adept at using inflectional morphology with such an increased lexical verb range.

In contrast, the study by Dewaele and Regan (2001) does not report the same lexical benefits of study abroad as the previous studies. However, this may reflect the type of lexical acquisition which the authors focused upon: they specifically investigate the acquisition of colloquial language by advanced Flemish-speaking and Anglophone learners of French. While the learners demonstrate gains in their use of colloquial language, such gains are not extensive. Thus, the effect for study abroad is more limited in the case of the acquisition of colloquial language.

On a general level, the review presented so far has pointed to the general benefits of study abroad for the learner's sociolinguistic and lexical development. The following section will consider whether study abroad is equally beneficial for development on structural aspects of the learner's grammar, in relation to such aspects as structural error and interlanguage grammaticalisation.[7]

The Effect of Study Abroad on Structural Aspects of the Learner's Grammar

In a series of studies, Paul Lennon investigates the acquisition of English by a group of German learners participating in a study abroad programme in England.[8] Lennon (1989) presents a longitudinal study of the learners' grammatical development. Based on introspective methods which tap the learners' strategic approach to the L2 acquisition task, results indicate a decrease during the course of the study in the extent to which the learners focus on formal accuracy during interactive communication. Nonetheless, the results suggest that the learner is conscious of his/her own linguistic shortcomings. For example, Lennon notes that the learners actively seek feedback on the linguistic forms with which they experiment. As such, Lennon finds that his subjects were very much in control of their learning environment, with the intention of promoting their acquisition of formal aspects of the L2. The question for study abroad research is whether the communicative interaction such learners engage in is helpful for interlanguage grammatical development. In the case of the learners studied by Lennon over a period of six months, his findings point to an increase in syntactic complexity along with a decrease in error in their spoken production. A limited number of other studies investigate the question posed.

Collentine (2004) presents a longitudinal study of American learners of Spanish in a study abroad context and in an instructed learning context in the United States. Based on a comparison of the learners' scores on their use of various grammatical features in spoken discourse, Collentine finds that the classroom context promoted accuracy on use of a range of discrete grammatical features to a greater extent than the study abroad context, with one exception, namely the marking of tense. However, when grammatical development was considered in terms of the learners' 'narrative ability' a more important effect emerged for study abroad, whereby the study abroad learners were more adept at producing narrative discourse. That gain emerged in terms of their enhanced score concerning the use of a number of features characterising narrative discourse such as past tense verbs, third person morphology, past and present participles and public verbs such as verbs of communication.

The findings presented by Collentine contrast with those presented by Herschensohn (2003) in her longitudinal comparison of two learners of

French, one in a classroom environment in the United States, and the other spending a semester in France. Based on analysis of their spoken interlanguage, Herschensohn finds that, whilst both learners demonstrated substantial development over the course of the study on their use of inflectional morphology, the study abroad learner attained a superior level of accuracy, approaching near-categorical levels after six months. Herschensohn (2003: 39) concludes by stating that 'mastery of morphosyntax may be fostered by an instructed environment as well as a naturalistic setting'.

Möhle and Raupach (1983) report on a cross-linguistic project investigating German learners of French participating in a study abroad programme in France and French learners in Germany. They find limited grammatical gains in the case of their learners of French. As such, they suggest that the learner's grammar does not change in a noticeable way. In contrast, however, they find that their learners of German made considerable progress in terms of a reduction in formal error. The authors suggest, that this may have to do with the nature of German grammar: they note that progress was notably in the area of inflectional morphology, an integral part of German grammar. As such, the results point to an effect for the TL under investigation.

In a preliminary study, Cox and Freed (1988) make a comparison between American learners who spend a year in France and those who do not. They find that the study abroad learners have greater control over different morpho-syntactic forms, including aspects of morphology, relative clauses, and use of the subjunctive. However, the authors do add that the procedures for carrying out the study were not rigorous.

Kihlstedt (1994), in her analysis of the effects of a stay in France on the acquisition of past time morphology by two Swedish learners, has differing findings: for one learner, stay abroad increased past-time marking, whereas for the other learner, no differences in past time marking between the time before going to France and after are noticed.

Based on a project involving Irish learners of French, Howard (2001, 2005b, c) provides a study of their acquisition of temporality in an instructed environment and also in a study abroad context. Findings suggest a more important effect for study abroad insofar as the study abroad learners attain a higher level of accuracy in their expression of past time relations. Such increased accuracy is particularly apparent in the use of the 'imparfait' to mark various imperfective values, which pose considerably less difficulty to the study abroad learners than to the instructed learners. Finally, a lexical analysis of the learners' use of past time morphology indicates that the study abroad learners extend such morphology to a larger range of lexical verbs. However, a number of similar lexical restrictions also characterises the learners' use of the past time forms, irrespective of whether they had studied abroad or not. For example, across the learners, the results suggest that the 'passé composé' is extended to a wider range of lexical verbs than the 'imparfait', such that the 'imparfait' is more lexically restricted than the 'passé composé'. Furthermore, use of the past time forms in general is restricted to the most frequently occurring verbs in target language French.

Whilst Howard's work points to a number of differences and similarities between the instructed and study abroad learners, other studies point to more limited benefits of study abroad for the learner's grammatical development. For example, Freed *et al.* (2003) investigate the written productions of a group of learners who have studied abroad and those who have not. In their reactions to these written productions, native speaker judges remarked no differences. Moreover, a formal investigation of the learners' written productions from the point of view of grammatical accuracy and syntactic complexity revealed no differences between the two groups. Such findings further corroborate the general finding in much earlier study abroad research which claims that development is much less evident in relation to the study abroad learner's written skills, as compared to his/her oral skills.

Limited progress in the area of grammatical accuracy is also noted by Walsh (1994) in a study which investigates Irish learners of German. She suggests that lack of preparedness, in the sense of limited linguistic awareness on the part of the learners, may be a factor in their failure, given that progress is noted in fluency, lexis and communicative strategies. Similarly, in his study of American study abroad learners in a hispanophone country, DeKeyser (1991) fails to find evidence of significant grammatical development in relation to their use of the copula *ser/estar*. This is in spite of gains made in other areas of the learners' acquisitional development, such as in relation to the lexicon.

Finally, Huebner (1995) finds that the use of zero anaphora in Japanese shows no differences between study abroad and classroom learners. He investigates two groups of learners of Japanese, one in Japan, the other in America, both following courses of instruction at beginners' level. Results of this study suggest that, whilst study abroad learners may not be more advanced than classroom learners at home, neither are the latter learners more advanced than those who go abroad. Such findings certainly point to the limitations of classroom instruction outside the TL community relative to study abroad.

On the basis of the studies reviewed here, the general evidence regarding the benefits of study abroad as opposed to foreign language instruction for the learner's grammar is rather limited. This appears to be true for the learner in the early stages of acquisition, as demonstrated by Huebner's study, as well as for the learner at a more advanced level, as demonstrated by the other studies. A noticeable trend, however, concerns the fact that, with the exception of DeKeyser's and Huebner's studies, the evidence is not all negative in those studies which focus on a particular aspect of the learner's grammar, such as Collentine, Howard, Kihlstedt and Cox and Freed. In contrast, the evidence is less positive in those studies, which investigate the learner's grammar as a general entity, as described by Herschensohn (1998), Möhle and Raupach (1993), Freed et al. (2003) and Walsh (1994). An important question, therefore, concerns whether development may occur on specific aspects of the learner's grammar, rather than across the learner's grammar as a general entity.

A further important question, as Freed (1995b) points out, concerns the qualitative differences between the study abroad learner and the nonstudy abroad learner in terms of the developmental patterns characterising his/her acquisition of specific aspects of the TL grammar. Ryan and Lafford (1992) investigate such differences in their longitudinal study of the acquisition of 'ser' and 'estar' in Spanish. They make a comparison between their findings for a group of study abroad learners and those reported by VanPatten's (1987) study of the classroom acquisition of the same forms. They find similar acquisition patterns, although not identical, as those proposed by VanPatten, suggesting that differences in input conditions are responsible for the acquisitional differences arising.

Guntermann (1995) also considers the question of differential acquisition patterns demonstrated by the study abroad learner, by comparing her results with those of Ryan and Lafford (1992). Her study, following on Guntermann (1992a, b), investigates the order of acquisition of 'ser' and 'estar', and 'por' and 'para' in Spanish by American Peace Corps volunteers. Results provide similar support for the acquisition patterns proposed in the previously mentioned studies.[9]

A final study of such a question is provided by Howard (2001) in the case of his study of the acquisition of temporality by Irish study abroad and instructed learners of French. Based on a variationist analysis of a range of linguistic factors predicted to constrain the system of variation behind the learner's use of past time markers, results of the study suggest that the factors investigated each have a similar influence on the variation characterising the learners' use of past time markers, irrespective of their learning environment.

Thus, results of the studies by Guntermann, Howard, and Ryan and Lafford generally provide evidence of the similarities between grammatical development in a study abroad context and in the foreign language classroom, in terms of the underlying patterns of development demonstrated by learners in both contexts of acquisition.

The Effect of Study Abroad on L2 Fluency

Freed (1995a) investigates the common belief that the learner who goes abroad speaks more fluently on his/her return. Her study is based on a comparison between American instructed learners of French who do not go abroad and a study abroad group. Native speaker judges evaluated the speech of both groups, with a view to identifying linguistic differences between both groups. Results of the study point to a range of issues behind the perception of improved 'fluency' in the study abroad group. In particular, the study abroad learners were perceived to speak significantly more, to have an increased speech rate and longer streams of continuous speech than the learners who had not been abroad. All in all, the study abroad learners are more at ease when speaking in the L2. Whilst Freed's study presents evidence of the fluency gains to be made during study abroad, a follow-up study by Freed *et al.* (2004a, b) presents a more complex picture of the role of learning context on the development of fluency. In a study that presents a three-way comparison of study abroad, classroom and immersion learners, Freed *et al.* find that it is in an immersion context in the United States that their American learners of French make the most fluency gains. In contrast, whilst the study abroad learners demonstrate fluency gains compared to the classroom learners, those gains are not as significant as in the case of the immersion learners.

In a similar study in the case of L2 Spanish, Segalowitz and Freed (2004) offer similar evidence of the beneficial effects of study abroad in the development of fluency. Their study is based on a longitudinal comparison between university learners in the United States and instructed learners who spent a semester living in Spain. Whilst both groups demonstrated increased development during the course of the study, it was the study abroad group which made the most gains, as seen in more improved oral performance in terms of their score on an Oral Proficiency Interview (OPI) as well as longest speaking turn, and improved oral fluency as captured by three measures, namely speech rate, length of speech run without pauses and longest fluent run. The authors also attempt to provide an insight into the potential cognitive development that might underlie the changes in fluency demonstrated by the learners. From this point-of-view, results show that the learners in both the study abroad and instructed learning context made similar gains in 'fluency-relevant cognitive processing abilities' (Segalowitz & Freed, 2004: 194), as captured by changes in lexical access and attention control. However, a relationship was also noted between the gains made by the learners in terms of their OPI rating and their initial lexical access processing speed at the start of the study. The authors conclude: 'oral gains may depend, to some extent, on cognitive readiness to benefit from the learning opportunities available; fast, efficient abilities to connect words to meanings facilitated learning to speak more proficiently' (Segalowitz & Freed, 2004: 194).

Towell *et al.* (1996) report similar fluency gains for a group of advanced British learners of French participating in a study abroad programme in France. For example, they suggest that mean length of run was the most important of the temporal variables contributing to increased fluency, which gave rise to a more native-like effect in the learners. Working within an information processing perspective, the authors suggest that the increased fluency noted reflects the proceduralisation of various formal aspects of the learner's L2 use which have previously been less controlled. That is to say, the learners automatise their formal knowledge of how the L2 'works' in order to achieve greater fluency in real-time processing of such knowledge. However, the authors also find that the learner tends to hit a fluency plateau, which leads to differences in their fluency compared to the native speaker. (See Towell & Dewaele, 2005 for a follow-up study.)

Laudet (1993) reaches similar conclusions based on her study of Irish learners of French in France: various native-like characteristics, such as drawls and repetitions allow greater time for language processing. Other studies offering similar positive support for the beneficial role of study abroad in relation to fluency include Walsh (1994), who investigates fluency gains in Irish learners of German. Raupach (1984, 1987), in his investigation of German learners of French in France, notes similar gains in global fluency, such as increased rate of speech, more appropriate fillers and better use of compensatory strategies. In contrast to such findings, however, Lennon (1990a, 1990b), in his longitudinal study of German learners of English in England, notes a general increase in dysfluency markers which he sees as constituting 'real negative trade-off effects' (Lennon, 1990a: 312) to grammatical improvement as evidenced chiefly through increased syntactic complexity. He does nonetheless report overall fluency gain for the learners, but this could only be captured in relation to three out of 12 fluency measures.

While not situated within a study abroad framework, Trofimovich and Baker (2006) also offer pivotal insights into fluency development. Their study is based on a comparison of 30 Korean adult learners of English in the United States whose period of residence in the target language community ranged from short (three months) and medium (three years) to extended (10 years). The authors were interested in how length of stay, as well as age of arrival in the United States would impact on a number of features characterising the learners' fluency profile. The findings indicate that, while the learners' amount of contact influenced stress timing, it was their age of arrival that impacted more greatly on the production of other suprasegmentals, namely speech rate, pause frequency and pause duration.

Working within the related area of communicative strategies, Lafford (1995) suggests that the study abroad learner is better capable at dealing with varied communicative situations, in spite of the fact that the classroom learner demonstrates a broader range of communicative strategies than the study abroad learner. Her study is based on a cross-sectional comparison of American study abroad learners of Spanish in Spain and Mexico, and instructed learners who remained in the United States. Results suggest that the study abroad learner is better at coping with the various pragmatic difficulties that everyday communicative situations can throw at them, such as beginning, maintaining and concluding communication. Such increased communicative ability is also found to be related to increased fluency, as manifested by increased rate of speech and more repair by the study abroad learners. In a follow-up longitudinal study of American classroom and study abroad learners of Spanish, Lafford (2004) similarly finds that following their sojourn abroad, the study abroad learners use fewer communication strategies than their classroom counterparts. The author suggests that a possible reason for this difference relates to the increased fluency which the study abroad learners demonstrate, such that there are fewer communication insufficiencies in their speech, which, in turn, gives rise to fewer occasions when communicative strategies need to be deployed.[10] An alternative explanation relates to the greater focus on form which the classroom learners demonstrate, such that they may be more prone to consciously modify their speech through the use of communication strategies.[11]

However, DeKeyser (1986, 1991) finds that a semester spent in Spain by American learners did not entail a radical change in communication processes, despite a general increase in vocabulary and fluency. He concludes that significant differences do not exist between the classroom and the TL community as domains of acquisition. Rather, differences between learners in both domains emerge in terms of how the native speaker views the learner as a language user, which may be related to the tendency for the study abroad learner to make more frequent use of certain communication strategies which are used less frequently by classroom learners.

Communication strategies aside, a final issue which equally underlies the study abroad learner's fluency gains concerns his/her pronounciation skills. Such an issue has not been the focus of investigation in the study abroad literature, with the exception of Díaz-Campos (2004), who presents a comparative analysis of the acquisition of a number of phonemes in L2 Spanish by American classroom and study abroad learners. His results fail to show a more significant effect for study abroad compared to classroom instruction, such that on those phonemes where pronounciation gains were made, the gains were similar across the learner groups.

Summary

At this point, the effects of study abroad have been considered from the more traditional perspective of the L2 learner's general language skills, as well as in relation to development on more specific aspects of the learner's real language use. In the former case, study abroad appears to have a generally positive effect on the learner's oral and aural skills. However, the effect is less positive in the case of the learner's reading and writing skills, where development has been less evident.

In relation to the specific constituents of the learner's linguistic repertoire in the L2, the studies reviewed have noted important fluency and lexical gains in the case of the study abroad learner, as well as increased sociolinguistic and pragmatic competence. However, the benefits of study abroad are less clear in the area of the learner's grammatical competence, where conflicting findings across the various studies make it difficult to draw definitive conclusions concerning the relative benefits of study abroad. As Freed (1995b: 27) writes with regard to structural accuracy, 'there are some findings, at least for advanced learners, that significant changes do not take place within the study abroad context'.

Having outlined the general areas of linguistic development manifested by the study abroad learner, it remains for us to consider the interaction between the development outlined and the various extralinguistic factors which define the learner's experience whilst abroad. Some of these factors have already been hinted at. For example, Huebner's (1995) study provides evidence that a study abroad experience is valuable in the early stages of acquisition, thus calling into question the common belief that it is only worthwhile for the more proficient learner.[12] Proficiency level is but one factor which affects the learner's development during study abroad. The next chapter will look at some of the extralinguistic factors which affect the linguistic outcome of a period of residence abroad by firstly considering proficiency level.

Notes

1. As noted by Gass (1990) and VanPatten (1990), however, the naturalistic learner in the target-language community may also receive classroom instruction within this environment.
2. For discussion of the range of programmes available within a European and North American context respectively, see Coleman (1998) and Huebner (1998). As these authors note, such programmes can also be accessed by nonlanguage students who are specialising in other areas of study, but who nonetheless have the opportunity to engage in L2 learning while abroad. Whilst the number of students partaking in such international exchange programmes has dramatically increased, it should also be borne in mind that learners also organise personal visits to the target language community, and such visits equally constitute study or residence abroad.
3. For further discussion, see Coleman (1995b).
4. For a general overview of research on the study abroad learner, see Coleman (1995a, 1996, 1997, 1998), Freed (1995b, 1998), Howard (2005c) and Parker and Rouxeville (1995).
5. See also Kline (1998) who provides an outline of the learner's everyday social experience of literacy in a study abroad context. Using an ethnographic approach, she reports on a range of conflicts which characterise that experience, whereby the learner is often confronted with a certain tension between their reading experiences and those of the native speaker in terms, for example, of the attitudes which the native speaker holds of the learner's reading material, as well as their own reading material. Such tension is also found to arise in relation to the learners' expectations of the reading experience and their actual experiences in the study abroad context.
6. However, in their conclusions, the authors state that 'the correlational data would not encourage us to dispense with language testing in favour of self-assessment scales' (Lapkin *et al.*, 1995: 93).
7. For discussion, see Howard (2001, 2005c), Regan (1998b).
8. See Lennon (1990a, 1990b, 1991, 1996).
9. Guntermann, however, also notes that a period of instruction before study abroad provides a more beneficial combination for development on a structural level.
10. The increased fluency gains demonstrated by the study abroad learners in Lafford's longitudinal study is documented by Segalowitz and Freed (2004) who provide an analysis of the same learner-informants from the perspective of fluency.
11. That increased focus on form by the classroom learner as opposed to the study abroad learner is documented by Collentine (2004) who presents a complementary study of the same learner-informants investigated by Lafford.
12. For example, Huebner (1995) finds that his study abroad learners in Japan make considerable gains on a test of reading relative to the instructed learners in the United States.

Chapter 3
Extralinguistic Factors Affecting L2 Development During Study Abroad

Whereas the preceding chapter was concerned with the linguistic outcomes of L2 development during study abroad, this chapter aims to provide some complementary insights by considering how some extralinguistic factors may impact on that development. Such factors are wide-ranging, and include issues to do with the type and intensity of the communicative interaction which the learner engages in while abroad, more sociopersonal characteristics such as the learner's motivation and gender, as well as more global issues such as residence type, length of stay abroad and *raison d'être* while abroad. We will begin, however, by considering the relationship between L2 development in a study abroad context and the learner's starting proficiency level.

Proficiency Level

Whilst Huebner (1995), as discussed in the previous chapter, finds that study abroad is beneficial at beginner level, Regan (1998b) cautions that a lot depends on the aspect under investigation. She suggests that more advanced learners may be better capable of attending to more subtle aspects of the L2, whereas learners in the less-advanced stages, due to their limited linguistic resources, have a lot more to cope with, linguistically. From this point of view, one notes the whole range of pragmatic advantages that more advanced learners have. For example, Freed (1990) suggests that they are more likely to seek out contact with native speakers, whereas less advanced learners may shy away from such situations, because of the greater communicative difficulties they entail. That is to say, less proficient learners may be less well equipped, linguistically, to cope with communicative interaction than more advanced learners whose linguistic resources are better developed. Freed concludes that little is known about how high level learners differ from lower level learners in the type of interactive situations they seek out. In her study of American learners participating in a six-week study abroad programme in France, Freed finds that the learners' scores on a grammatical test depended, to a large extent, on their level before taking part in the programme. Gains were evident for less-proficient learners, but for more advanced learners gains were less striking to the point of showing no progress at all. Freed suggests that the opposite tendency occurs, however, when account is taken of the type of language interaction the learner engages in. That is to say, for learners at the lower levels who engage in noninteractive contact, their grammatical test scores showed little change. Freed finds the trend reversed for more advanced learners. As such, she concludes that the learner's relative proficiency level is an important variable which impinges on the level of linguistic progress made during study abroad.

In contrast to Freed's conclusion concerning the important effect of proficiency level on the learner's L2 development during study abroad, Matsumura's (2003) study of the acquisition of sociopragmatic competence by Japanese learners of English during a year abroad in Canada offers opposing findings: '[G]iven the near-zero effects of proficiency, it can be said that Japanese students with a high level of proficiency did not necessarily develop their pragmatic competence in the target speech community and that those with a low level of proficiency might have developed their pragmatic competence' (Matsumura, 2003: 485). However, in line with Freed, the author does note a similar relationship between the learner's level of proficiency and the extent to which they seek out opportunities for more increased exposure to the target language, thus pointing to an indirect relationship holding between the learner's proficiency level and his/her sociopragmatic development. The author expresses such an indirect, as opposed to a direct relationship in the following terms: '[I]n sum, interpretation of the direct and indirect effects of proficiency and exposure on pragmatic competence suggests that: (a) amount of exposure has greater potential to account for development of pragmatic competence than levels of proficiency; (b) amount of exposure is determined in part by levels of proficiency' (Matsumura, 2003: 485).

Other studies draw more definitive conclusions concerning the role of proficiency level on L2 development during study abroad. Brecht and Robinson (1995), Dyson (1988), Lapkin *et al.* (1995) and Milton and Meara (1995) similarly find that lower proficiency learners make the most gains compared to higher proficiency learners, who tend to reach a developmental plateau. Such findings are in spite of differences in languages, age and duration of programme.

In general, it seems that the benefits to higher proficiency learners are more limited than to lower proficiency learners. There is a variety of reasons which might explain such evidence, one of which is the type of communicative interaction the learner engages in, as was noted in Freed's (1990) study. The following section will review some of the other extralinguistic factors affecting the role of study abroad. Such factors have received only limited focus. The presentation will therefore principally concern the issues of level of communicative interaction, learner motivation and gender.

Other Extralinguistic Factors Affecting the Linguistic Outcome of Study Abroad

Results of studies such as Freed (1990), as presented above, point to the need to consider various external factors which influence the level of linguistic development which the learner undergoes during study abroad. In the case of Freed's study, the factor investigated related to the type of interactive communication the learner engages in whilst abroad. Various other studies also note an effect for this factor in terms of the level of contact with the TL whilst abroad.[1] For example, in her longitudinal study of American study abroad learners in Russia, Pellegrino (1998) investigates the learners' expectations of the type of contact which best facilitates their acquisition during study abroad. Both prior to and following study abroad, the learners self-report on the importance that they attach to informal contact with the target language. The greater importance attached to informal contact by study abroad learners, as opposed to formal contact in the form of classroom instruction, is also borne out by Brecht and Robinson (1995) and Miller and Ginsberg (1995) on American learners of Russian.

Still dealing with the issue of language contact during study abroad, other studies have approached the issue of the range of contact opportunities available to the learner, and their relative merits in facilitating opportunities for L2 development. For example, Dewaele (1992), Marriot (1995) and Siegal (1995) each point to the role of differences in level of contact with native speakers as an indicator of development. Such differences may also interact with the level of contact with speakers of the learner's source language. Dewaele's study investigates the acquisition of the sociolinguistic marker '*ne*' by his Flemish-speaking learners of French. He finds that the level of contact that the learners made with native speakers whilst on holiday in France is an important factor in their level of use of this marker. He also finds an effect for more passive interaction through reading, listening to the radio and watching TV. Marriot's (1995) study and that of Siegal (1995) offer similar findings concerning the effect of level of contact with native speakers on their informants' acquisition of politeness markers in Japanese. Such conclusions are reflected in the student questionnaire findings presented by Willis *et al.* (1977) who report on a positive relationship between increased speaking skills and the learners' self-reported use of the L2. This finding is also seen to hold true across the learners' four language skills in the questionnaire study carried out by Meara (1994). In contrast, however, in their large-scale analysis of student questionnaires, Opper *et al.* (1990) find no relationship between increased proficiency and either interactive or passive contact with native speakers. Segalowitz and Freed (2004) similarly fail to find an effect for out-of-class language contact insofar as this factor was not found to account for the more increased fluency gains demonstrated by their American learners of Spanish spending a semester in Spain in comparison with their instructed learner counterparts in the United States. However, the authors do note that their study abroad learners' oral performance levels at the outset of their longitudinal study may impact on the type of communicative activity that they engage in while abroad. For example, those learners producing more hesitation-free speech before going abroad were found to engage in more extracurricular reading.

Differences in the type of interactive activity engaged in by learners are also borne out in Kaplan's (1989) study. Although she does not investigate a particular linguistic variable, she notes that, in their introspective questionnaires, her American learners indicated that they had made more progress in comprehension activities than in production during a six-week residence abroad programme in France. Kaplan notes that such a belief reflects the learners' ample access to comprehension activities during study abroad, such as through the media, but their limited access to genuine opportunities for production, as self-reported by the learners.

On this score, Spada (1985, 1986) indicates that different types of linguistic skills may be influenced by different types of interaction. For example, she finds a negative relationship between out-of-class interaction and development on reading tests. She suggests that low interactive learners make more progress on more passive skills, such as reading, whereas high interactive learners engage less in such activities, and thus, have better oral skills. A general problem, however, involved in dealing with factors such as contact with native speakers, type of interaction and level of motivation, is that information is often provided through self-reporting which, for its success, demands a high level of reliability on the part of the learner.

The quality of native-speaker interaction enjoyed by the learner whilst abroad is also an issue considered by Wilkinson (1998a, 1998b, 2002). Using ethnographic data, she details the sense of frustration experienced by many learners at the limitations to their social integration in the target language community, which is often at odds with the learner's expectations prior to their study abroad experience. Even in the case of learners who are living with host families, Wilkinson reports that genuine opportunities for communicative interaction are often minimal. Similarly, in their comparison of American learners of French in an immersion situation in the United States and in a study abroad context, Freed *et al.* (2004b) find that those learners in the immersion context report greater use of French outside the classroom than in the case of the study abroad learners who actually report using English to a greater extent. This is in spite of the greater range and variety of contact opportunities that the study abroad context potentially offers. Freed *et al.*'s finding, however, contrasts sharply with that of Dewey (2004: 320) who reports a 'greater degree of interaction in Japanese in the SA than the IM context', where SA relates to the study abroad context, and IM to an immersion context in the United States. In view of such differences between the findings of both studies, Dewey (2004: 320) notes that 'the difference in patterns of language contact between these studies highlights the need to be cautious over making any broad claims concerning language use during SA and IM'.

However, a difficulty with drawing conclusions concerning the effect of type and level of interactive contact, is the failure by the various studies to 'tease out' how motivation might be a more relevant factor, given that students who seek out active interactive situations may be more highly motivated than learners who do not. The issue of motivation can be seen in St Martin's (1980) study of learners of English in North America. She finds differences in her learners' TOEFL[2] scores, depending on whether the learners were living with host families or not. Kaplan (1989), previously mentioned, also notes differences in activities engaged in depending on the learner's type of housing during the programme. Such differences reiterate Coleman's (1995a) claim that exposure to a wide range of members of the host country is an important factor, when considering the overall gains made. Kaplan also notes the role of motivation, in that the individual learner's choice to live with a family may indicate a high level of motivation, as in St Martin's study. However, Freed (1990) mentions that learners who choose to go abroad are perhaps, in general terms, at the upper end in a scale of motivation. She finds no relationship between motivation and the pursuit of out-of-class contact for the learners in her study, as previously presented.

Another study which attempts to identify the effect of level of interactive contact and of learner motivation on the learner's linguistic development is that of Yager (1998). He investigates American learners of Spanish engaged in summer study in Mexico. Assessment of the learners' development was based on native speakers' reactions to the learners' productions. Yager finds that increased proficiency in Spanish is demonstrated by those learners who report greater interactive contact, especially at beginner level. As regards the effect of learner motivation, Yager's findings suggest that more integrative and less instrumental motivation correspond with the advanced learners' greater development. Such a conclusion reflects to a certain extent Coleman's (1996) finding that learners demonstrate more integrative motivation following study abroad, although the difference between pre-study abroad and post-study abroad is nonetheless seen to be marginal.

Apart from motivation, a range of affective factors can equally be considered to impinge on the learner's social integration, such as issues to do with culture shock and personality. This has been noted by Pellegrino (1998) insofar as American learners in Russia report not putting a lot of effort into seeking out opportunities for speaking with native speakers outside of the classroom due to difficulties in relation to cultural adaptation. This is a problem which is seen to benefit from pre-study abroad preparation in the form of enhanced intercultural awareness, as discussed by Barro and Grimm (1993), Jordan and Barro (1995) and Barro et al. (1998). Milton and Meara (1995) similarly note the often limited contact that study abroad learners have with the native speaker, insofar as a strong tendency emerges in their self-reports for study abroad learners to socialise with their fellow expatriots, and to a certain extent with other learners of other L1 backgrounds. In their study of lexical acquisition during study abroad, they find no correlation with their learners' reported level of contact with native speakers.

Another possible extralinguistic factor which has, as of yet, gone without thorough investigation is that of the learner's gender. However, Brecht and Davidson (1992) consider the factor in their investigation of study abroad learners in Russia. Their results suggest that women gain less than men in listening and speaking skills. Moreover, men are more likely to attain an advanced level, whereas women tend not to go beyond the upper intermediate level.[3] However, this trend may have more to do with cultural difficulties for women in the country under investigation, namely Russia, which negatively affect their learning opportunities. Such a perspective on the acquisition process is also offered by Polanyi (1995), who finds that sexist behaviour against American female learners in Russia is a common theme in their introspective journal entries. The learners comment that such behaviour negatively affects their language learning insofar as it impinged on the type of opportunities for interaction which they engaged in, and, as such, restricts the type of contact opportunities that they can access. Similar findings are reported by Twombly (1995) in the case of American learners in Costa Rica, as well as by Carlson *et al.* (1990) in a study of American learners in France and Germany.

Concluding Remarks Concerning the Effect of Extralinguistic Factors on the Learner's Linguistic Development During Study Abroad

The review presented has considered a number of extralinguistic factors which have been found to constrain the level of linguistic development experienced by the learner whilst abroad. The factors have principally concerned the type of interaction in which the learner engages, the level of contact with the TL, the learner's proficiency level, learner motivation and gender. Whilst such factors are not definitive, they are nonetheless the factors which have been relatively more often investigated.

However, Coleman (1995a) notes a number of others which have generally not been investigated, such as length of stay abroad, the learner's *raison d'être* whilst abroad, the learner's domicile whilst abroad, as well as a range of affective factors known to influence L2 development. For example, little is known whether the learner's proficiency level tends to reach a developmental plateau after a certain period of time whilst abroad, after which development is relatively limited. The results presented in the case of the studies which have been reviewed in this chapter are based on a mixture of study abroad programmes which vary in duration from six weeks to one year. Carroll's (1967) study suggests that the gains in listening skills during a year abroad are twice those produced by a summer course in the TL community. He states that similar results manifest themselves on other skills. Teichler and Steube (1991) also find that gains in proficiency were dependent on the duration of the study abroad period. They also note that gains in receptive skills tend to reach a developmental block after just four months, and productive skills after seven months. In contrast, however, Barron's (2003) investigation of the acquisition of sociopragmatic skills by Irish learners of German offers an important insight into the gradual development characterising L2 acquisition during study abroad. In the case of these learners who were spending a year in Germany, she finds that some aspects of the learners' development occurred quite rapidly, whilst others took more time, and were only apparent at the end of the period of residence abroad such that development in the direction of native speaker norms continued during the complete duration of the study.

The question of the learner's *raison d'être* during residence abroad has generally not been investigated. For example, little is known about whether a work placement might be more beneficial than a course of classroom instruction during residence abroad. However, Willis *et al.* (1977) find higher proficiency levels in the case of students on work placements, a fact which Coleman (1997) suggests may reflect a range of sociobiographic characteristics such as their higher motivation and more positive attitudes. Meara (1994) and Opper *et al.* (1990) similarly note that learners themselves often hold exchange programmes in lower esteem than work placements, considering the latter to be more beneficial. Such issues are particularly important for planning for study abroad programmes.[4] From this point of view, studies by Brecht and Robinson (1995), Miller and Ginsberg (1995) and Pellegrino (1998) offer interesting findings. Using diary entries made by American study abroad learners in Russia, these studies provide a conflicting insight into the learners' view of the role of classroom instruction during study abroad and how they use that instruction as a basis for their learning. Pellegrino finds that learners report that they see naturalistic interaction as constituting a more beneficial forum for learning than classroom instruction. Miller and Ginsberg (1995) further report that, whilst learners are in certain ways critical of classroom practices, learners try to recreate those same acquisitional opportunities in their interaction outside the classroom. Whilst Brecht and Robinson (1995) also report similar findings, they equally observe a positive relationship between classroom instruction and the learners' self-reported language use outside of the classroom. In contrast, Milton and Meara (1995) report a negative effect for classroom instruction in the case of their study of lexical acquisition in a study abroad context: they find that instructed learners demonstrate more limited lexical gains than learners not receiving classroom instruction.

The issue of classroom instruction aside, another question concerning the learner's *raison d'être* relates to the learner's residence whilst abroad. On this score, Rivers (1998) offers interesting findings in his study which compares the linguistic gains made by learners who reside with host families and learners who live in student accommodation. As Rivers (1998: 492) states 'the Second Language Acquisition community has long held the homestay environment as the *sine qua non* of language study abroad', whereby the homestay environment is considered to offer a more constant level of L2 contact than dormitory placements. However, Rivers' results offer counterevidence to such an intuitive belief. Using the 1979–1996 American Council of Teachers of Russian Students Data Base, he compares the gains made in speaking, listening and reading by learners in homestay and student accommodation. His findings indicate that the homestay learners were less likely to gain on their speaking and listening skills than on their reading skills. Rivers explains such counterevidence by considering the problems faced by the homestay learner in relation to his/her access to and management of the linguistic input available in that domain. Results provided by Wilkinson (1998a, 1998b, 2002) concerning American learners residing during the summer with families in France, corroborate Rivers' findings: the comments made by the learner-participants overwhelmingly point to the limitations for genuine interaction within the host family environment.

In contrast, however, St Martin (1980) fails to find evidence of such a negative correlation between a homestay environment and L2 development during study abroad: she notes that her homestay learners demonstrated higher TOEFL scores compared to non-homestay learners. Such a finding can be explained with reference to Kaplan's (1989) survey of the type of interactive activities engaged in by study abroad learners: '[F]or most students, however, [...] living with a family seemed to provide regular opportunities to use French, whereas living in the résidence offered no compensating advantages' (Kaplan, 1989: 292).

Finally, with regard to affective factors and study abroad, Coleman (1997, 1998) reports on the findings of those few existing studies which have considered how study abroad may impact on their role. For example, based on his 1996 study, he concludes that, in the case of anxiety, study abroad entails a marked decrease in the level of anxiety experienced by learners in general, but especially in the case of female learners. Willis *et al.* (1977) report a similar finding whereby increased proficiency during study abroad occurs in tandem with a decrease in anxiety during study abroad. Such a result is reflected in Opper *et al.*'s (1990) finding that learners experience a decrease in the 'degree of restraint' they feel in using the L2 over the duration of a study abroad programme, feeling minimally restrained at its end. In the case of attitudes, Coleman (1997, 1998) and Willis *et al.* (1977) report that study abroad is often not successful in transforming learners' negative attitudes towards native speakers, such that upon their return, learners were often seen to hold the native speaker in lower esteem than prior to going abroad. This is all the more true in the case of male learners when compared with female learners. In the case of language aptitude, Brecht *et al.* (1993), and Brecht and Davidson (1992) employ the MLAT to demonstrate an important correlation with their learners' reading and listening skills in Russian, but not with speaking skills. A final sociobiographic factor is that of personality, which Coleman (1996: 9) speculates to be possibly 'the most important factor influencing outcomes', notwithstanding the fact that few studies have provided adequate investigations of it, with the exception of Willis *et al.* (1977) who report that greater gains are demonstrated by more extrovert learners.

Final questions concern the long-term effects of study abroad, which can be summarised in terms of how long the linguistic gains acquired during study abroad remain. In other words, on returning to the nontarget language community, where exposure conditions are different to the foreign language classroom, does the learner show a decrease in proficiency over time? It must be acknowledged that the acquisition opportunities in the learner's home country are very different from those to which (s)he is accustomed during residence abroad, perhaps the most important difference being the lack of opportunity to come into everyday contact with the language, and all that such opportunities bring, such as a social desire to acculturate. Raffaldini (1987) investigates the concept of language attrition in a group of American learners of French during the year following a period of residence abroad. On returning to the States, their contact with the TL was through instruction. Despite instruction, the learners' lexical, morphological and structural errors increased, while their communicative competence decreased: a drop in accuracy, appropriateness and general communicative proficiency was noted.

In a study of the long-term retention of the linguistic skills developed during study abroad, but this time in relation to the learner's sociolinguistic skills, Regan (2005) offers interesting insights into the question of whether the learner's sociolinguistic skills can be maintained in a classroom environment. Given the specificity of the social environment that defines the foreign language classroom, in contrast to the naturalistic context, it might be expected that the learner's sociolinguistic skills would decline, due to lack of opportunity to put them into practice in the same way as would be possible in the native speaker social context. However, such a hypothesis is rejected in Regan's study, where the author finds that one year following their return to the classroom context, the L2 speakers had generally consolidated their sociolinguistic competence to maintain the skills developed whilst abroad. We will expand the investigation of long term effects specifically in relation to the acquisition of sociolinguistic variation patterns later (see Chapter 5 of this volume).

Howard (2009) presents a study of L2 development post-study abroad. This is based on an analysis of development on use of aspectuo-temporal morphology in L2 French for the expression of past time. The findings indicate that the issue of development following study abroad is by no means a simple one, but rather the learner's acquisition is best captured in terms of a range of differences and similarities in their use of inflectional morphology during study abroad and a year later. The results are best summarised by the finding that 'overall accuracy in the expression at time III is seen to revert back to its original level at time I, [...] although the functional characteristics of the learner's use of each form have continued to evolve at each stage of the study'. In terms of the patterns underlying use of the past time forms concerned in relation to a number of linguistic and lexical factors seen to constrain their usage, such patterns are generally seen to remain unchanged at each stage of the study. For example, the author concludes that 'lexical restrictions characterising the IMP (= imparfait) remain unchanged between time II and time III, as do the lexical quotients of each form throughout the study'.

A final study to consider the question of the level of progress made by the learner returning from a year abroad is that of Coleman (1995a). Based on the C-test which offers a global proficiency rating, he finds that university learners generally do not make much progress on returning, even in spite of instruction. Such a finding, however, must be taken in the context of the learner's general proficiency level. For example, for less advanced learners, study abroad may provide them with a good communicative basis. On their return to their home country, such communicative skills may be supplemented by a focus on formal aspects of the language, thus improving their grammatical competence. In the case of the more advanced learner, however, (s)he may have acquired a level of proficiency which allows functional communication in the target language. As such, classroom instruction may in some ways have less to offer this learner. An equally valid explanation of the failure to find evidence of further development may relate to the nature of the C-test which may not capture the type of gains made by the learner upon his/her return.

Synthesis

Taken together, this chapter along with the preceding one have presented a general review of previous research on the study abroad learner. In particular, we have been concerned with identifying whether study abroad gives rise to a differential outcome compared with foreign language instruction, in terms of the learner's linguistic development. On a more general level, early studies have identified the benefits of study abroad in relation to the L2 learner's general language skills. From this perspective, the benefits of study abroad have principally been identified in relation to the learner's listening and speaking skills. The learner's reading and writing skills, however, are relatively less affected.

However, more recent studies have investigated development on particular aspects of the learner's linguistic repertoire. From this point of view, increased development has been noted in terms of the learner's fluency gains, more extensive lexical acquisition and increased sociolinguistic and pragmatic awareness. While the evidence reviewed suggests that study abroad has a more beneficial effect in such areas, the question of grammatical gains is, however, open to question, due to the mixed findings of the studies reviewed.

Notes

1. Freed *et al.* (2004a) present the 'Language Contact Profile' which could usefully be used in future studies as a means of counteracting discrepancies in the type of questionnaires that individual studies are often seen to rely upon.
2. Test of English as a foreign language.
3. In this case, the terms advanced and upper intermediate refer to scores attained on a test of proficiency.
4. See Inkster (1993) for a discussion of the role of planning, in the wider sense of the term, in study abroad programmes, both from the learner's perspective, as well as on an institutional level. See also Gillespie *et al.* (1996) for a discussion of the issue of student preparation and assistance, prior to, during and following study abroad; Huebner (1998) for discussion of the evaluation of study abroad programmes from within an educational policy framework; and the special issue of *Frontiers. The Study Abroad Journal* (Fall, 2003) on Assessment in Study Abroad.

Chapter 4
The Research Investigation: An Overview

Introduction

Having presented in the previous chapters an overview of the issues in second language acquisition (SLA) research which are investigated in the research to be presented here, this chapter will present some of the more practical issues related to the project. This chapter will firstly present the general aims and objectives of the research undertaken in relation to the research questions behind our investigation of the acquisition of sociolinguistic competence in a study abroad context. Secondly, we will describe data collection procedures in relation to the learners who participated in our various studies, as well as the data elicitation methods used. Finally, we shall provide an outline of the data extraction and coding procedures behind the studies.

Aims and Objectives

The overall aim of this research is to detail the development of the L2 speaker's sociolinguistic competence in a study abroad context in relation to his/her variable use of a number of sociolinguistic markers in target language French. Specific research questions which stem from this global aim include:

- To what extent is sociolinguistic variation a feature of the instructed learner's language before study abroad?
- To what extent does study abroad facilitate the acquisition of sociolinguistic variation in the case of the instructed learner?
- In variationist terms, what are the characteristics of the underlying system of factors constraining the learner's use of sociolinguistic variables in the L2?
- What are the differences which arise between the native speaker and the L2 speaker in relation both to rates of variant usage, as well as in relation to constraint ordering in the case of L1 and L2 speakers?

- What extralinguistic factors affect the learner's sociolinguistic development in a study abroad context?
- In relation to the acquisition of such variables in a study abroad context, is development similar across learners?
- If differences arise between learners in relation to their level of sociolinguistic development in a study abroad context, what factors give rise to such inter-learner variation?
- Finally are the effects of the sociolinguistic competence acquired during study abroad lasting or simply temporary?

With a view to considering such questions, the findings to be presented here in relation to a range of sociolinguistic variables in target language French stem from a number of quantitative studies carried out by the three authors. The following section will provide the background detail to these projects, firstly in relation to the learner-informants, and thereafter in relation to the data elicitation techniques.

The research project

The studies on which our findings are based were first initiated in the early 1990s, (Regan, 1995, 1996), and have been the subject of intensive ongoing research throughout the last decade with the global aim of documenting the acquisition of sociolinguistic competence in L2 French by Irish classroom and study abroad learners. Our several studies are based on a number of databases of spoken L2 French, collected individually by each of the three authors. In terms of their size, both in relation to the number of learner participants, as well as the amount of data collected from each informant, the databases constitute the most significant collection of spoken French by Irish L2 learners, including data from both university and second level students. The overall corpus includes data from 72 informants, 20 of whom are year abroad students. In Ireland, there are few other existing interlanguage corpora, be they in French or any other L2. This is equally true of spoken and written interlanguage. Exceptions principally concern the oral French corpus established by Seán Devitt based on interviews with naturalistic Irish child informants during a stay in France,[1] the Trinity College Modern Languages Project[2] and Batardière (2003) based on university learners of French.

Having provided some general background information to the research project, we now present the subjects of the studies.

The Learner-Informants

At the time of the data elicitation, the learner-informants of all of the studies were university students, that is to say, second and third year Irish-English-speaking students specialising in French as part of their undergraduate degree programme. The speakers can be categorised into two groups. On the one hand, data were collected from second year learners who, at the time of the data elicitation, had chosen to go to a French-speaking community in the following academic year as part of a study abroad programme. On the other hand, data were collected from third-year students who had returned from France following a study abroad programme during which they had spent an academic year at a French host university. The data were based on two cross-sectional studies and one longitudinal study. The longitudinal study (Regan, 1996, 2002, 2005) followed one group of six speakers during a three-phase longitudinal investigation, involving data collected before the year abroad, after the year abroad and also from a year after return from year abroad. This had the benefit of not only providing data on immediate effects of the year abroad but also long term effects which, so far, are very scarce in the area of the acquisition of sociolinguistic competence. (See Howard, 2009 for an example of a longitudinal study in the area of grammatical development.)

Prior to their university course all of the learners had studied French at secondary school for between five and six years. Thus, formal instruction was the principal means of access to the target language. Formal grammar analysis was an integral part of the course of instruction followed by the learners at university, although this was supplemented by more informal input through conversation classes with native speakers, as well as the use of authentic materials throughout the course. Apart from learning French, the learners also had a varying knowledge of other languages, primarily Irish which they had learnt at both primary and secondary school. It is therefore possible that these speakers could be categorised as relatively multilingual and were therefore perhaps more linguistically 'aware' (Singleton, 1996) than other monolingual Anglophone learners.

The year abroad programme in which the learners participated was part of a European exchange programme (Erasmus) between the Irish university and a number of host universities in French-speaking countries, mainly France. Participation in the programme was not obligatory, and involved students applying for a limited number of places. Participation was therefore competitive, and places were attributed on the basis of the learners' academic attributes. As such, the learners can be considered to be highly motivated.

Whilst abroad, the learners attended a French university, where they pursued a course of study agreed with their home institution. In order to successfully complete the programme, the students were required to fulfil a number of criteria with regard to their course work. Instruction was content-based whereby the learners followed the same courses as the native speaker students, and did not receive any formal language instruction at all. Whilst abroad, the students lived in the *cité universitaire*, the French halls of residence. On completion of their course of study, some students were engaged in employment by a local enterprise. Jobs varied from working as secretaries in local companies to waitressing and working in shops.

In all cases, learners volunteered to partake in the study. They also provided of their services freely. Whilst the learners were aware of the fact that they were taking part in a research project, they were not aware of the nature or aims of the project. Prior to the study the learners did not know the researchers, except in their capacity as members of the teaching team of the department in which they were students.

The learners' L2 proficiency level

The sociobiographic characteristics of the learners, as well as their linguistic characteristics correspond to the defining characteristics of the advanced learner variety, as defined by Bartning (1997a, 1997b). Given the time necessary to pass through the various preceding stages of interlanguage grammaticalisation, Bartning suggests that the instructed learner demonstrating the advanced variety is typically an adult third-level learner, specialising in a particular L2 as part of a programme of study outside the target language community. Having chosen to specialise in the study of a particular L2 at tertiary level, the advanced instructed learner is typically highly motivated, learning the L2 for particular reasons, quite likely to be professional. These conditions of acquisition contrast with those of other L2 speakers, for example, the immigrant learners who participated in the large-scale European projects investigating L2 acquisition in the early stages, such as the European Science Foundation (ESF) Project, the Zweitspracherwerb Italienischer und Spanischer Arbeiter (ZISA) Projekt and the Heidelberger Projekt.

Bartning suggests that the more intensive investigation of the advanced instructed learner has occurred due to a recent need in SLA research to focus on the typical university language learner outside the target language

(TL) community, in the same way as the less-advanced naturalistic learner within the TL community has been previously investigated by the large-scale European projects referred to.[3]

On a linguistic level, Bartning notes that a distinguishing characteristic of the advanced learner concerns this learner's metalinguistic knowledge. Having spent a number of years learning the L2, the advanced learner's metalinguistic knowledge is highly developed, as a result of a focus on the formal aspects of the L2 during instruction, leading to extensive declarative knowledge – knowledge of the L2. On the other hand, the learner's procedural knowledge – knowledge used for speech production in real time – is less developed, in spite of a considerable amount of spoken fluency possibly resulting from a period of residence in the TL community: difficulty in automatising declarative knowledge in real time is common.[4] Towell *et al.* (1996) suggest that difficulties in real time planning are the single most important stumbling block to fluent speech, whereby the learner has difficulty in accessing the knowledge (s)he holds in declarative terms. Rather, the advanced learner's recourse to automatised forms, or 'frozen chunks' in the language, often conceals this learner's difficulties in making creative use of the L2 morphology.[5] Although the learner may 'know' the various creative linguistic possibilities of the L2, their ability to access such knowledge and to convert it into on-line speech production may indicate various areas of linguistic difficulty, as outlined below.

Bartning (1997a, 1997b) considers the manifestation of such difficulties in use of the target language morphology to be 'fragile zones' particular to the advanced variety, which define this variety as against preceding and subsequent stages. Inflectional morphology is therefore seen to have generally emerged in this learner variety, insofar as the advanced learner generally makes productive, albeit variable use of such morphology. This is unlike in the case of the learner in the early stages of acquisition, when the learner's language use is largely based on pragmatic means in view of the absence of grammatical morphology in the learner's language, and also in the case of the pre-advanced learner. The latter must firstly pass through a stage of creative grammaticalisation, whereby a linguistic form that formerly had lexical status, acquires grammatical status in the learner's interlanguage, and thereafter a stage of adaptive grammaticalisation follows, involving the change in functional value that such a grammatical form, already existing in the learner's interlanguage, may express, as a result of a discovery by the learner of another functional value that such a form can express in the target language.[6] Put another way, the process of grammaticalisation involves, on the one hand, acquiring a larger range of linguistic forms to express different values which were previously expressed by a single form. On the other hand, however, a single form expressing a single value may assume other values, as the learner discovers the full range of values expressed by that single form in the target language. Form–function relations in relation to acquisition of structural elements are fluid at this stage.

Having generally passed through such stages of grammaticalisation, the advanced learner's language use is still characterised by considerable linguistic variation, where the learner must establish greater control in real time over his/her variable use of the target language forms. In Bartning's terms, such variation constitutes a range of 'fragile zones' in the advanced learner, and are particularly evident in the area of the L2 morphology and syntax, verb morphology being by far the most important.[7] For example, in the case of past time marking in target language French, the learner alternates between use of the PC and the IMP in similar linguistic contexts.[8] Similarly, in the case of the marking of number, the learner alternates between singular and plural marking on verbs.[9] Such fragile zones demonstrate areas of variation, which have not yet stabilised, and which underlie a tendency to alternate with varying degrees of correctness between different linguistic forms in similar functional contexts. Thus, inflectional morphology is no longer emerging in this learner variety, insofar as the advanced learner generally makes productive, albeit variable use of such morphology. Other common fragile zones, apart from verb morphology, but still in the area of morphosyntax, concern nominal morphology in the areas of gender, adjectival agreement, nominal agreement, as well as pronominal reference. For example, in the case of gender, the learner of French alternates between use of masculine and feminine forms with individual nouns. Such variation is also characteristic in the case of adjectival agreement, where the marking of plurality also constitutes an area of variation. Similar fragile zones have been noted across a range of target-languages by learners of differing second languages, as reviewed by Bartning (1997a, 1997b).

The lack of control in the fragile zones mentioned points to the particular areas in which development within the advanced variety must occur before the subsequent stage of acquisition can be attained, namely near-native competence, where the learner demonstrates greater control in the aforementioned fragile zones. That is to say, within near-native competence, the fragile zones previously mentioned are generally less conspicuous, due to increased fluency. The near-native speaker is therefore often indistinguishable from the native speaker, insofar as the learner's use of the TL grammar is generally quite target-like.

However, some studies point to certain important differences which clearly distinguish the near-native speaker and the native speaker, in relation to more subtle aspects of the target language. For example, Coppieters (1987), in his study of learners of French at the near-native level, finds differences between the learner's reaction on grammatical judgement tests and those of the native speaker, in spite of the fact that his learners had been living in the target language community for many years. Such differences of linguistic intuition notably occur in areas where functional distinction is important, such as in the area of tense and aspect on such forms as the *passé composé* and the *imparfait* in French. However, Birdsong (1992) offers opposing evidence, by suggesting that native and non-native speaker intuitions do not differ drastically. These findings suggest that the notion of a 'critical period' in L2 acquisition, after which the attainment of native-speaker norms is out of reach of the adult L2 learner, is less important than Coppieter's study might suggest.[10]

While such studies focus on morpho-syntactic issues, other studies such as Perdue (1993b) suggest that it is on the level of discourse organisation that differences primarily remain, distinguishing the near-native speaker from the native speaker. Perdue suggests that the grammaticalisation process in late acquisition interacts with the learner's L1 discourse organisation, whereby the near-native speaker's interlanguage is resistant to the discourse organisation features of the L2. For example, from a discursive perspective, Carroll *et al.* (2000) note important differences between the spatial descriptions produced by their learners of German and native German speakers: whilst the near-native speaker may be highly proficient in the area of morphosyntax, the learner's L1 has a strong influence on the discourse structure through which such morphosyntax is expressed.

The previous section has detailed the learner-informants by situating their advanced learner status in relation to the early and pre-advanced stages of acquisition, as well to the following and final stage, namely that of near-native competence. The following section will outline the data collection procedures in which the learners participated.

Data Collection

The learners participated in the classic Labovian sociolinguistic interview with the researchers (Labov, 1984). As has been pointed out, the word 'interview' is perhaps not the best for describing what is in fact an informal chat, where the speaker is ideally as relaxed as possible. Variationist research methodology and interview techniques have been variously described in Poplack (2000), Tagliamonte (2006), Feagin (2002), and Paollilo

(2002). We conducted the interviews in French and recorded them onto a cassette using a Coomber tape recorder. In some cases microphones were not used as it was felt that the learners were sufficiently audible, which reduced the formality of the situation. The learners were specifically told that the form of their language was not important.[11] Although native speakers of English, the first two author/interviewers demonstrated near-native competence in the target language, whilst the third is a native speaker from France.

According to Labovian principles, our aim was that the interviews should be as informal as possible. As such, the observer's paradox, namely the learners' awareness of being observed, was minimised as much as possible. Although the interviews were held in a room at the university, they were often held over coffee. Prior to the actual interview, a general period of 'getting to know you' was allowed for in an attempt to make the learners feel comfortable with their surroundings, rather than 'jumping right in' once they arrived. As regards the tape recorder, this was placed to the side on a table between the interviewer and the informant. In all cases the informants were aware that they were being recorded.

Each interview followed a similar interview format, with the general aim of encouraging the speakers to produce spontaneous speech, in order that we could 'tap into' their vernacular style. The conversational modules proposed by Labov (1984) were used and adapted to suit these speakers' particular interests. The modules chosen were common to all interviews. Each module consisted of a standard group of questions focusing on a particular topic. Topics were chosen to elicit both formal and informal speech. Any questions on language were reserved for the end of the interview to avoid the speaker monitoring their speech during the conversation. Formal modules dealt principally with the learners' language learning background and experience, as well as with professional topics relating to their studies and to employment. Informal topics dealt with everyday topics such as holidays, experiences of being in France, pastimes, as well as Labov's classic modules, the 'Danger of Death', 'Fate' and 'Premonitions' modules.

In general, interviews lasted approximately one hour, at the end of which the informants completed an ethnographic questionnaire, with the aim of providing information about themselves as well as about their language learning background, for example, type and level of contact with the language in the target language community, attitudes towards the target language and language learning, and so on. This information provided a check on the authenticity of similar information provided in the oral interviews. A pseudonym was provided for each speaker.

When all the interviews were completed, the data were transcribed into standard orthography following the transcription conventions proposed for French by Blanche-Benveniste and Jeanjean (1987). For the purposes of this book, the data formed the basis of a number of quantitative analyses of a range of sociolinguistic variables in the learners' speech. As the analysis of each variable will be presented in the chapters to follow, the following section will be restricted to a global overview of the application of variationist methods to the study of sociolinguistic variation under investigation here.

Data Analysis Within the Variationist Paradigm

Labov's variationist model of language is explicitly a probabilistic, as opposed to a deterministic, one. Its purpose is to account for the dynamic nature of language. It is a particularly useful model for the representation and explanation of interlanguage, which is generally agreed to be inherently variable and also systematic (Adamson, 1988; Bayley & Preston, 1996; Bayley & Regan, 2004; Ellis, 1994; Young, 1991). Labov's description of native speech as 'orderly heterogeneity' can also be applied to interlanguage. The method used in the analysis of linguistic variation is variable rule analysis. The analysis of the L2 data in the present study was carried out using the Varbrul computer program. This is a set of programmes designed to analyse variable data by using the 'maximum likelihood' method of estimating probabilities. It controls for skewing resulting from unevenness in factor distribution and resulting empty cells. The analysis is a procedure for discovering the relative influence of various factors simultaneously on the production of a particular variant in speech. Data on each particular combination of factors are input into the Varbrul program and by estimating a maximum likelihood, the programme calculates the conditional probabilities for each factor. Each factor has a coefficient (p) attached to it. A p-value greater than 0.50 indicates that the factor favours the production of a variable, whereas a p-value less than 0.50 indicates that the factor disfavours it. The resulting figures in relation to our interlanguage data can show trends in the language development of the speakers, and thus provide reliable evidence for changes due to the period of time spent abroad.

A variation analysis involves a number of procedural measures, including establishing the 'envelope of variation', hypothesising the factors – linguistic and extralinguistic or social – believed to constrain the variation, coding the data, inputting the data into the Varbrul computer program, and interpreting the results. The variables studied in the speech of our year abroad speakers were *ne* deletion, /l/ deletion, *nous/on* alternation and variable use of future tense. Excellent accounts of variationist analysis can be found in Guy (1993), Poplack and Tagliamonte (2001), Tagliamonte (2006) and Bayley and Lucas (2007).

One of the defining characteristics to emerge from the range of studies which have previously investigated interlanguage variation is identified by Young and Bayley (1996) in their principle of multiple causes: in contrast to early research by variationists in second language acquisition which tended to identify solely one factor as causing the variation, the causes of variation in SLA are manifold and can rarely be attributed to only one factor. The factors contributing to variation in L2 speech are wide-ranging, but can be categorised as linguistic, extralinguistic and stylistic. As well as demonstrating that variation in L2 speech was caused by multiple factors, early work by variationists in SLA showed that, contrary to what was previously supposed, this variability was also systematic. Now variationist research in relation to L1 speech had developed research tools which modelled the systematic variability of native speaker speech (Sankoff, 1987, 1988; Labov, 1984) and the computer program, Varbrul, evolved to do this by carrying out a multivariate analysis which attempts to model the variation by finding the 'best fit'. Varbrul carries out a multivariate analysis which, through progressive iterations, finds the most parsimonious model of the variation in the data. Details of the mathematical underpinning of the program can be found notably in Rousseau and Sankoff (1978), Pintzuk (1987), Robinson *et al.* (2001).

Variationist researchers in SLA found that the same models and research tools were appropriate for modelling variation in L2 speech. As with L1 speech many versions of the Varbrul program have been used. But they are similar insofar as they all calculate the likelihood of the variant being produced taking into account the multiple constraining factors. The program is ideally constructed for natural speech data which, unlike data produced in controlled laboratory conditions, for instance, gives rise to many empty cells. The coded data is fed into the computer program which, through successive iterations eventually finds the 'best fit'. This can involve several 'recodings' on the part of the analyst. The effect of several simultaneous factors is calculated. Where there is interaction, this must be eliminated. Results show which factors (known as 'factor groups') are significant in affecting the variation, but also a range of probability figures for the 'factors' within these groups, in order of importance. This range of figures is known as the 'constraint order' and can tell us an enormous amount regarding the relative importance of the factors which affect the variation. Through this process we can hold a very accurate 'lens' up to the L2 speech and examine its detail and texture in a way which would be impossible by other methods. We have also found that it permits us to examine the detail of L2 speech as it evolves over time.

The multivariate analysis thus captures the underlying system of constraints in quantitative terms regarding the relative influence of each factor on the speaker's choice. As Young and Bayley (1996: 253) write: 'we are able to make statements about the likelihood of co-occurrence of a variable form and any one of the contextual features in which we are interested. These statements express in quantitative terms the strength of association between a contextual feature and the linguistic variable.'[12]

Having presented a general overview of the research project from which our studies emanate, the following chapter is the first in a series of four which will present our findings concerning the acquisition of four different sociolinguistic variables in L2 French.

Notes

1. See, for example, Devitt (1995).
2. See, for example, Singleton (1996).
3. See, for example, Perdue (1993a) in the case of the ESF Project, Klein and Dittmar (1979) in the case of the Heidelberger Projekt and Clahsen et al. (1983) in the case of the ZISA Projekt.
4. For a review of such concepts, see McLaughlin (1987).
5. See, for example, Raupach (1984) and Myles and Mitchell (1999) for a discussion of the role of formulae in procedural learning. Regan (1997) also suggests that recourse to chunking by the advanced learner allows him/her to sound more native-like.
6. See, in particular, the collection of papers in Dittmar (1992), including the paper by Anna Giacalone Ramat for a detailed discussion of the process of interlanguage grammaticalisation.
7. See Bartning (1989, 1990a, 1990b, 1993, 1994, 2000) for particular examples, as well as Bartning (1997a, 1997b) for a synthesis of the studies. Coleman and Towell (1987) equally provide a collection of papers concerning the advanced learner.
8. For discussion, see for example Howard (2002a, 2004).
9. For discussion, see for example Howard (2006).
10. For discussion of the notion of a 'critical period', see for example Birdsong (1999), Hyltenstam and Abrahamsson (2000) and Schachter (1990).
11. It was not a test!
12. See Young and Bayley (1996) who provide an overview of the programme as it is used for L2 data.

Chapter 5
The Acquisition of ne deletion by Irish-English speakers of French L2 during the Year Abroad

In this chapter, we report the results of our investigations of *ne* deletion in French by Irish-English speakers. We chose this variable as the first in our investigations for two main reasons: (1) its frequency in native speaker speech and therefore in the input that L2 speakers receive, both in the formal and the naturalistic milieu; (2) the fact that *ne* deletion is a stable, long-standing sociolinguistic variable in French. As we have noted earlier, we wished to investigate the production of the L2 speakers in relation to both stable, well established variables as well as newer incoming ones and to see whether the learners of French L2 seem to be aware of the L1 speaker variation patterns in relation to variation and change in the language they are acquiring.

Negation in French

In modern French, negation is based on two particles, the pre-verbal *ne* which is variably realised, and a post-verbal particle, such as *pas*, a general marker of negation, or another marker such as *plus, jamais, rien, point, aucun, guère, personne,* amongst others. As the first of two particles, *ne* comes between the subject and the following constituent, which can be a verb or pronoun in affirmative sentences (ex. *Je ne vois pas*). In the case of the post-verbal particles, these had a positive semantic value in Old French – *pas* meant a step, *goutte*, a drop, *personne*, a person, *mie*, a crumb, and so on – but these lexemes were emptied of their semantic content over time. Nyrop (1925) sees them as acquiring a negative value, as they began to be used in negative expressions.[1] *Ne*, the first particle is deleted at varying rates within the speech community. In addition, deletion of *ne* is a very mildly marked variant of the variable. This is an additional reason for its frequency in the input which L2 speakers are exposed to.

Ashby (1981) notes that the grammaticalisation of a second marker of general negation is an innovation in French, and that in the other Romance languages, Latin *non* and its descendants are only sporadically reinforced. This strengthening of the negative is common to many languages, but only became common in French from the 17th century on, where it began to be seen as obligatory. The later grammaticalisation of *pas* resulted in *ne* being, in fact, redundant. Throughout the history of the language, there has been a shifting from one particle to the other, and between the use of one only or both negative particles. Latin *non* became Old and Middle French *ne*, with *pas* optionally, which became *ne* with obligatory *pas* in Classical French and in contemporary written French. Modern spoken French uses, formally, *ne ... pas*, and informally, simply *pas*. Written French still uses *ne ... pas*. It seems possible (Ashby, 1981, 2001; Harris & Vincent, 1988; Kayne, 1975) that French today is undergoing a process of cliticisation, whereby the loss of *ne* between the subject and the finite verb is leading to a fusing of the clitic pronoun and the verb into one form consisting of prefix and stem. For example, *je* would be fused to *vois*[2]: *j'vois pas*. For the purposes of our work here, we will focus on the variable deletion of the first particle in contemporary spoken French and investigate whether this variable pattern is acquired and, if so, how by L2 speakers.

Variable Use of *ne* in Spoken French

Ne deletion or omission is a widespread and well-documented phenomenon in contemporary spoken French throughout the world. Native speakers of French produce the following utterances variably:

Je ne vois pas ⇨ *Je vois pas.*

Ne is deleted at extremely high rates in almost all varieties of spontaneous spoken French, in all French-speaking communities today. Gadet (1989) notes that *ne* deletion is an excellent indicator of register, formality, hierarchy and solidarity.

Ne deletion in France

The rates of *ne* deletion seem to have increased recently in France, if we compare the rates reported by Ashby (1981, 2001). Ashby (1981) found that speakers in France produced rates of deletion of 40% for formal speech and 61% for informal speech. However, in 2001, he finds that speakers he interviewed in 1995 were omitting *ne* at 80%. Coveney (1996) found a rate of deletion of 81.2% in speakers in Picardie. He found an important effect for formality with a formal context producing 50% deletion and an informal, 88.6% (Coveney, 1996: 89–90). Given evidence from age grading (younger speakers were using less *ne* than older ones) and indeed a gender variation pattern in the expected direction (women use less of the informal variant), Ashby advances an argument for a change in progress which would see the ultimate disappearance of the particle *ne* from French.

It is possible to interpret the variable behaviour of *ne* deletion in native speaker French in two ways. On the one hand, as outlined above, a strong case can be made for seeing the variable behaviour of *ne* deletion as a change in progress, where the clitic subject is becoming part of the verb stem. In support of this, apparent time analyses show the requisite age-grading (young people delete more than older ones in the French of France). Armstrong and Smith (2002) reported in Dewaele and Regan (2002) show that *ne* deletion is becoming a feature even of formal radio interviews. On the other hand, however, a strong case has been made for *ne* deletion as a stable sociolinguistic variable (Blanche-Benveniste, 1985). This variable is seen as one which has been around for a long time and which, because of its symbolic value, is likely to be retained in its variable state. *Ne* is maintained as a syntactic and stylistic resource. Whether it is interpreted as a change in progress in French or a stable sociolinguistic variable, it is a productive and highly sensitive item in sociolinguistic terms.

Ne deletion in Canada

Rates of *ne* deletion in Canada have always been higher than in France. In Quebec and Ontario, deletion rates were reported as almost categorical, approaching 100%, by Sankoff and Vincent as early as 1977, and more recently by Sandy (1997). Sankoff and Vincent (1977(1980)) show that the very few tokens of *ne* which were found in their corpus correlated with stylistic register and topic. Sankoff and Vincent (1977(1980)) see *ne* deletion as available to speakers of Montreal French for their use as they find appropriate. Poplack (1989) finds *ne* deletion rates of 99% in the Ottawa Hull corpus.

Variation in relation to *ne* usage has been shown to be highly constrained by linguistic and extralinguistic factors in studies of varieties of both Metropolitan and Canadian French (Ashby, 1981; Coveney, 1997; Armstrong, 2002). Ashby's (1976) study of Malécot's Paris corpus shows that deletion is conditioned by grammatical, stylistic and social factors. In his own study, Ashby (1981) shows similar conditioning. Linguistic factors include the type of verb, type of subject, presence or absence of a clitic, co-occurrence with lexicalised phrases, preceding and following phonological segments. Extralinguistic factors found to constrain the variation include formality of style, age, social class and gender.

Ne Deletion in Non-native Speaker French: Advanced vs Early and Intermediate Learners

Level of proficiency is an important feature of the acquisition of variation patterns in an L2. In relation to *ne* deletion, advanced learners' linguistic behaviour is very different from that of earlier learners. The factors which affect *ne* deletion in the speech of low proficiency learners are more likely to involve developmental ones than is the case in higher proficiency speakers. Low proficiency Anglophone speakers of French L2, for instance, may use only the first of the two negative particles: *je ne vois* or they may indeed produce *je vois pas*, but not because they have learnt the sociolinguistic significance of this, rather for developmental reasons, such as the use of unanalysed chunks which is a characteristic of low proficiency speakers.[3] Eventually in a U-shaped trough configuration in a later stage they may revert to using *je vois pas* but this time similarly to the way L1 speakers use it. As the focus of our work is on sociolinguistic competence and the acquisition of L1 variation patterns by the L2 speaker, we will only briefly outline previous work on *ne* deletion in low to middle proficiency learners. Sanell (2007), for example, presents a detailed and subtle account of the acquisition of negation in French and finds that there is a correlation between the use of negation and additive adverbs (*aussi*) and restrictives (*seulement*) and the grammatical development of the learner. Here we will describe in greater detail previous work on *ne* deletion in advanced learners.

In relation to variation specifically, a useful construct was first proposed by Corder (1981) as described in Chapter 1. He saw variation in learner language as being represented on two axes, the vertical and the horizontal. This construct continues to be a useful one, and has been used by Ellis (1985), Young (1988), Adamson (1988), Adamson and Regan (1991) and Regan (1996). This model sees progress along the vertical axis as developmental progress and progress along the horizontal axis as constituting the acquisition of sociolinguistic competence. This representation is, however, a simplified one and it is reasonable to suppose that the acquisition of sociolinguistic competence is, in fact, progressing from a relatively early point on the vertical axis. That is, while developmental progress is taking place, sociolinguistic competence is being acquired simultaneously, at least after the very early stages of development or what is referred to sometimes as the *basic variety* (Perdue, 1993a, 1993b). It has already been observed that the acquisition of sociolinguistic competence in the L1 takes place at a very early stage. Very young children have been seen to have acquired the vernacular norms of the linguistic community they are living in. Roberts and Labov (1995) and Roberts (1997), for instance, found that three-year-old children had already acquired the *in/ing* as well as t/d deletion variables in English. Payne (1980), interestingly, found that while children and adolescents (from 8 to 20 years of age) who moved to the Philadelphia area after the early language acquisition period had difficulty acquiring some aspects of the phonology, by and large they acquired the Philadelphia dialect. It may well be that L2 speakers also begin to acquire sociolinguistic competence relatively early. However, for the purposes of studying the acquisition of sociolinguistic competence, we preferred to look only at advanced learners, as this allows us to disentangle developmental and sociolinguistic competences and facilitates the task of tracking and describing the acquisition of sociolinguistic competence.

Early and intermediate L2 speakers and *ne* deletion

Trévise and Noyau (1984) examined the French L2 of eight adult Spanish speakers living in Paris. They hypothesised that formality would have the greatest effect on *ne* deletion and interviewed the speakers twice. The first interview was the classic sociolinguistic interview designed to elicit spontaneous speech. The second interview was focused on metalinguistic awareness on the part of the speakers and the authors expected that this second interview would most favour retention of *ne*. In fact, they found that those who deleted most were those who had lived longest in Paris, whose age of arrival was earliest, who had studied there longest, had most contact with native speakers and had the most positive attitudes towards French speakers. In sum, the effect of greater contact with native speakers was more significant in *ne* deletion than that of style.

The speakers in the study were divided into several groups in relation to *ne* deletion: some used *pas* exclusively, often in chunks such as *moi sais pas, y a pas*. Others used *ne* with *pas*, or in four cases out of 202, *ne* was used alone in pre-verbal position. The authors interpret the pre-verbal *ne* as evidence of a basilect and also of transfer from their L1. Other studies have also found examples of this pre-verbal *ne* alone (Benazzo & Giuliano, 1998; Goldfine, 1987; Klein & Perdue, 1997). Others, however, have found no examples of this pre-verbal *ne* in Arabic L1 speakers, for example Véronique and Stoffel (2003). Meisel (1997) suggests that rather than a basilectal form, this pre-verbal *ne*, which does not appear in the input the L2 speakers receive, in any case, may be due rather to the influence of formal instruction reinforced by similarities between the L1 and the L2.

Advanced L2 speaker, *ne* deletion and different contexts of acquisition

In this section we consider evidence from advanced L2 speakers in different contexts of acquisition: the traditional classroom, the immersion classroom, living in the native speech community (e.g. the case of naturalistic Anglophone speakers living in Montreal), and during study abroad. We compare the use of *ne* deletion by groups of speakers in each of these different language use and learning situations.

Ne Deletion and the Classroom Learner

Dewaele (1992, 2004) and Dewaele and Regan (2002) studied the omission rates of *ne* in informal and formal styles in the interlanguage of advanced Dutch learners of French in a Flemish region of Belgium, mainly in the classroom. Variation between formal and informal styles was limited, and the degree of omission was much lower than that of native French speakers. Dewaele concludes in relation to the Dutch speakers that the variable rule used by natives is also used by non-natives, but to a lesser degree. That is to say, factors such as style, the speaker's personality, and the speaker's gender determined the extent of *ne* deletion in their speech. He also finds that the use the speaker makes of French influences the use of *ne*, in terms of the type and frequency of their contacts in the language – those speakers who limited themselves to the language learnt in the classroom, were limited to the formal register learnt in the classroom and mostly retained *ne*. Thomas (2002) also finds that Canadian Anglophone learners in a foreign language classroom context delete *ne* much less than L1 speakers.

Ne Deletion in the Native Speech Community by L2 Speakers

Devaluy (1993b) and Nagy *et al.* (2003) who study Anglophone and Francophone behaviour in relation to *ne* deletion in Montreal French show that while infrequent, the use of the complete negative in spoken French is maintained in the community. Nagy *et al.* looked at the effect of style and found that both Anglophone and Francophone speakers when reading aloud from a text produce 90% of negatives with *ne* as they appear in the text. In a sociolinguistic interview, however, where the speech was relaxed, the Francophones omit *ne* 99% of the time. While lower, the rates of the Anglophones were found to reflect their integration pattern within the Francophone community. They did, however, reproduce the variation pattern of negation of the Francophone speakers such that there was a concordance of patterns of variation in negation among Francophones and Anglophones.

Ne Deletion and French Immersion Learners in Canada

Rehner and Mougeon (1999) carried out a variationist study of *ne* deletion in the spoken French of 40 English-speaking students in French immersion programmes in Ontario. They examined a possible total occurrence of 2163 and found a deletion rate of 28%. As with the Flemish classroom learners, the Canadian immersion classroom learners delete at a much lower rate than native speakers do. The Varbrul study carried out by Rehner and Mougeon showed that significant factors affecting the variation included home language – many of these speakers came from multilingual backgrounds – the students whose home language was English deleted *ne* more than those with other home languages. The speakers who deleted *ne* more were also those who had spent a period of time in a francophone family in a home-stay situation, who had more contact with francophone speakers, who had more exposure to the French media and who had had more French classes. Middle class speakers tended to delete a little less than working class speakers. Sex of speaker and formality of subject matter were not shown to be significant by the Varbrul analysis. Only one linguistic factor was significant: *ne* itself was deleted more than any of the post-verbal negators. Twenty-eight of the 40 speakers omitted the second negator in 78 instances. Example: *je n'allais ø à l'école* (Renner & Mougeon, 1999: 144). The authors propose a transfer explanation for this phenomenon.

Ne Deletion and Irish Year Abroad Learners

Bayley and Regan (2004) and Regan (1995, 1996, 2005) carried out a longitudinal study of the acquisition of sociolinguistic competence by Irish English speakers of French L2. This study was carried out over three calendar years and included a prolonged stay in a French-speaking country as well as a year of further language learning in the university classroom in Ireland. The subjects of this study form a subset of five informants from a larger longitudinal study of the acquisition of sociolinguistic competence by seven Irish learner learners of French L2. The study is still one of the few longitudinal studies in study abroad research, and also one of the few longitudinal studies of the acquisition of native speech variation by L2 learners. Most work in this area is cross-sectional, comparing either a group of 'before' learners with a different group of 'after' learners or comparing a group of 'stay-at-home' learners with a different 'away' group. An innovative aspect of the longitudinal design of this study is that it does not confine itself simply to the more typical pre- and post-year abroad analysis, but it also follows the same speakers for a further phase in their development, so that they were interviewed a year after their return from the year abroad and had spent a further year in the classroom. From this study, we can begin to draw conclusions for the first time regarding possible long term benefits of year abroad in relation to the acquisition of native speaker variation patterns.

Thus, the speakers were interviewed at three different points in time during the three years of the study: the first when they had studied French for two years at university and were about to leave for their year abroad after the second year of their studies; the second interview took place immediately after their return from France and before they started their final year at university and finally the students were interviewed for the third time a year later at the end of their last year of the BA degree. The principal aim of the study was to chart the development of the acquisition of sociolinguistic competence by these speakers as represented by their acquisition of the variable use of *ne* in spoken French.

Firstly the study set out to compare the resulting probability figures from before and after the stay abroad (the two times represented as factors in the analysis), to see if reweightings of these probability figures took place, and if so, which ones. The resulting figures would reflect developmental trends in the language of the speakers.

Following Ashby (1981, 2001) and Sankoff and Vincent (1977(1980)) for native speech variation in relation to *ne* and observations of the L2 speech of Irish learners in a previous pilot study (Regan, 1990), the following factors were proposed: style, lexicalisation, following phonological environment, preceding phonological environment, clause type, subject of verb, verb tense, presence of object clitic between *ne* and *pas*, syntactic structure of the verb. Table 5.1 shows the factor groups with their constituent factors and examples of each factor with tokens taken from the corpus. Every token of negation in the data was recorded and coded in a string which was then fed into the Varbrul program. Tokens in a phonologically ambiguous environment were omitted. For example, *on n'était pas bien payé*. Also omitted were frozen forms such as *pas mal, pas maintenant, pas du tout*.

Research Questions in Relation to *Ne* Deletion by Irish L2 Speakers in a Study Abroad Context

The principal research question of the project was: What was the effect of the year abroad on the acquisition of sociolinguistic competence,

Table 5.1 The factor groups for *ne* deletion in the speech of Irish L2 speakers of French

Groups and factors	Examples
Style	
Formal	
Informal	
Following phonological segment	
Vowel	Je n'ai aucune idée
Consonant	Elle ne travaille pas
Preceding phonological segment	
Vowel	Je n'allais pas
Consonant	Elle ne va pas en France
Syntactical structure of the verb	
Modal	Elle ne pouvait pas trouver
Auxiliary	J'ai entendu rien d'elle
Copule	C'est pas moi
Main	J'aimais pas
Time of the interview	
Interview 1	Before Study Abroad
Interview 2	After Study Abroad
Clause	
Main	Je dis rien contre elle
Subordinate	Tout est bien s'il n'y a rien
Subject	
Pronoun	Je pourrais pas
Noun	Les gens n'étaient pas contents
Presence of clitic object	
Absent	Je ne travaillais pas
Present	Je ne l'aimais pas
Lexicalisation	
Nonlexicalised	Je ne voudrais pas sourire
Lexicalised phrase	Il n'y a pas / il y a pas / je ne sais pas / je sais pas

The Acquisition of ne Deletion

specifically on the acquisition of native speaker variation patterns in relation to *ne* deletion? Taking the use of *ne* deletion in the speech of the L2 speakers as an indication of this area of acquisition, what were the rates of deletion before and after the year abroad? However, it was not simply a question of examining rates of deletion. As we have seen, variation analysis seeks to discover patterns of use in the relative frequency of occurrence of structures and not just the fact of these structures. The detail of the grammar of these speakers was the focus of inquiry. What was the constraint ordering of the factors affecting the deletion. Did the constraint order change over the three years of the study? Was there a different constraint order, for instance, before the year abroad and after? For example, if an unmonitored style causes more deletion than a casual one before the year abroad and still causes more deletion afterwards, we can say the constraint ordering remains the same. If there is a difference, it would suggest that there is a change in the grammar of the speakers. Were there factor groups or factors which significantly influence the 'before' but not the 'after' data (or vice-versa)? Or is the constraint ordering the same but the rate (expressed by the probabilistic weight) different? By these means the study aimed to examine close-up the detail of the grammar of the speakers and to describe the changes resulting from the year abroad experience.

Results

The Varbrul analysis of variable *ne* deletion in the speech of L2 Irish speakers revealed several interesting features. One of the main findings is that the rates of deletion changed significantly after the year abroad, all of the speakers deleting more but the least proficient making the most striking increase in deletion.

Variation in Time 1 and Time 2 (before and after year abroad)

When the data are divided into two separate sets (Time 1 and Time 2 presented in Table 5.2 we can see even more clearly the generalisation and

Table 5.2 Varbrul results for the combined data for before and after the year abroad interviews

	Factor weight
Time 1 (before year abroad)	0.32
Time 2 (after year abroad)	0.67

strengthening of the native grammar-like rule at Time 2 which was already in place in Time 1 (in the same way as it was for the classroom speakers as well as the L2 speakers in the native speech community of the studies mentioned earlier). In relation to the effect of the year abroad, a striking finding therefore is the effect for 'Time of interview', where the probability figures for deletion from before and after France significantly increase from 0.32 for Time 1 to 0.67 for Time 2. Clearly rates of deletion between the before and after data are very different, with speakers deleting *ne* in their speech far more after the year abroad.

Results show a picture of a grammar which is evolving, where the rule regarding *ne* deletion is generalising and strengthening from Time 1 to Time 2, and appears to maintain itself on return from the target language community. In the case of most of the factor groups investigated, these also become more like the native speaker grammar, as we will outline in the following.

The L2 speakers have clearly discovered several crucial things about the deletion of *ne* in spoken French. They know (even from Time 1 before they go to France for the year abroad) that *ne* is deleted much more in casual speech than formal speech. In relation to style, the L2 speakers show the same constraint ordering as native speakers. Interestingly, although their experience in France confirms their hypothesis that *ne* is retained more in formal style, after the year abroad, style makes slightly less of a difference to deletion rates than before in the speech of these learners. The L2 speakers delete more in monitored style in Time 2 than Time 1, but only slightly less in casual style in Time 2 than in Time 1. The speakers clearly know the rule 'delete more in casual than in formal style' but they have learnt that deletion is a native-like thing and they now delete more everywhere, even in monitored style. Over-generalising is a frequent phenomenon in L2 speech and here the speakers seem to be over-generalising in relation to an aspect of sociolinguistic variation.

The L2 learners have also learnt that one deletes more in 'lexicalised' phrases such as *je sais pas* or *c'est pas ça*, than in nonlexicalised ones. Ashby (1981) shows this to have a strong effect on *ne* deletion in native speaker speech, and so it is also for the L2 Irish speakers here. Given the frequency of these lexicalised phrases in the input that they are exposed to, the L2 speakers have recognised *sepa* and *chepa* and so on as popular stereotypes. In addition, their use of lexicalised phrases is probably also related to the effect of 'chunking' in their acquisition process. The range for the figures for lexicalisation, as Table 5.3 shows, is very wide, especially in Time 2.

It is true that lexicalisation is a significant factor in *ne* deletion in L1 speech but the L2 speakers seem to over-generalise their use of *ne* deletion

Table 5.3 *Ne* deletion in lexicalised phrases

	% of ne *deleted*	*Factor weight*
Nonlexicalised phrases	36	0.33
Lexicalised phrases	64	0.78

in lexicalised phrases. There may be two processes going on here in the L2 speech: (1) a strategy in which they recognise these lexicalised phrases as 'native sounding'; (2) a well-recognised developmental stage in which they use these lexicalised phrases as unanalysed chunks (Myles & Mitchell, 1999; Nattinger & De Carrico, 1992). They may well be beyond the stage at which they reanalyse the segments of chunks to work out one-to-one relationships between linguistic forms and their meanings, and they may have reached a plateau with regard to their use. Now they use them as an easy way of sounding like a native speaker following the impulse of L2 speakers to accommodate to native speakers, and thus further the goal of integration into the speech community.

As regards the other factor groups which were shown to be significant by the analysis, subject, and following phonological segment, strengthened slightly after the year in France and both showed the same constraint ordering as for L1 speech in French. In the case of the factor of subject, Ashby's (1981) findings along with those for our L2 learners are presented in Table 5.4.

The L2 learners' pattern is broadly similar to the native pattern. As we saw earlier there is an ongoing process in French whereby the subject clitics are being bound to the verb and where clitic and verb become increasingly bound, and *ne* 'may be progressively squeezed out' (Ashby, 1981: 681). For these reasons and for reasons of fast speech reduction, the effect of the preceding pronoun is to delete *ne*. The L2 speakers, like the L1 speakers, also show a preference for prosodic reduction: where the subject

Table 5.4 Varbrul analysis for *ne* deletion: Ashby (1981) and L2 learners

	Ashby (1981)	*L2 learners*
Full noun phrases	0.28	0.02
Nonclitic pronouns	0.57	0.21
Clitic pronouns	0.64	0.53

Table 5.5 Varbrul analysis for *ne* deletion: Ashby (1976) and L2 learners in Time 1 and Time 2

	Ashby (1976)	L2 learners – Time 1	L2 learners – Time 2
Main clause	0.70	0.52	0.64
Subordinate clause	0.40	0.36	0.32

tends to bind to the verb, and the presence of *ne* would prevent this, it tends to be deleted. The year in France seems to have little effect on this prosodically-induced reduction which seems to be a more universal phenomenon; however, contact with native speakers has decreased the rate of deletion after Full noun phrases, perhaps a result of strengthening an interlanguage rule which (mistakenly) allows reduction only after pronominal subjects.

In relation to the factor group of following segment, a following vowel disfavours deletion as would accord with the universal preference for CV structure in phonology. This has been noted in L1 French speech. As regards object clitic, for these L2 speakers, the presence or absence of the clitic does affect whether they delete *ne* or not – in contrast it does not affect *ne* deletion in native speaker speech (Ashby, 1976). The L2 speakers, however, are more likely to retain *ne* in *il ne le comprend pas* than *il ne comprend pas la leçon*. This is very likely due to processing complexity for the L2 speaker who is focusing on complex word order issues in the L2, and therefore more likely to monitor their speech and so retain *ne*. Tarone and Swain (1995) find evidence for monitoring by the speaker resulting in more target-like forms – it may be that the more standard *ne* retention falls into this category of target-like forms for the L2 speakers who clearly understand *ne* deletion to be casual. Clause type was not shown to be significant. However, this was almost certainly due to a small number of tokens of this factor group. However, in an early run of the data, the effect of clause type was very strong, as Table 5.5 presents.

The L2 speakers after the year in France, slightly strengthened their rule and roughly mimicked the native speaker pattern.

Individual variation

As with other studies of L2 speakers, there was much individual variation found in the study of these Irish speakers. There has been some debate as to the validity of reporting group results for L2 speakers.[4] Bayley (1994) studied Chinese and Hungarian speakers of English L2, using a substantial number of speakers, while Regan (2005) studied Irish speakers of French L2 using a small number of speakers. In both studies, similar patterns are found for both group and individual speakers.

As regards individual variation in the present study, it is interesting to piece together from the ethnographic data gathered from both the interviews and from questionnaires, the individual experiences of the speakers. As regards individual differences in the speakers of the present study, it appears that the *ne* deletion rates of those who had previously spent little or no time in a Francophone country increased the most.

The third phase: Long term gains

After studying Irish learners of French L2 before and after the period of study abroad, Regan (2005) continues the investigation of the acquisition of variation patterns by the same speakers through a third phase (Time 3), that is, a year later, back in the classroom where input is more formal. Contrary to the hypothesis that the speakers once back in the classroom for a year would show signs of 'decolloquialisation', results of the third phase show that the hypothesis was not supported. The rate of *ne* deletion was maintained a full year after the stay in France. As Table 5.6 below shows, the speakers have acquired the native speech pattern of variation in relation to *ne* deletion after a year in France (though at slightly different rates). And further, a year later (Time 3), they are still holding on firmly to this pattern.

One individual, Sally, on the contrary, had spent quite a bit of time prior to the study in France (mainly on exchange holidays with a French

Table 5.6 Rates of *ne* deletion for individual speakers in Time 1, Time 2 and Time 3

Speakers	Time 1	Time 2	Time 3
Judy	0.79	0.93	0.85
Cathy	0.08	0.36	0.44
Sally	0.46	0.30	0.38
Donna	0.00	0.22	0.14
Miles	0.15	0.39	0.56

correspondent and during Club Med holidays where the language used was French by native French organisers). This speaker, who deleted quite a bit (0.46) before the year abroad, actually dropped her deletion rates to 0.30 after the year in France. This speaker reported her frustration at lack of contact with native speakers during the academic year in France, and felt she spent too much time with non-French-speaking students. For the Time 1 data, the individuals were categorised into three groups, depending on the amount of time spent in France prior to the study. The first group had spent virtually no time in France previously, the second had spent slightly more (holidays with parents of short duration, two or three weeks), the third group had spent slightly more time in France and had more contact with native speakers. For instance, Judy had spent two months as a 'jeune fille au-pair'. None of the speakers, however, had spent as much as three months. In Time 1, the probability figures for *ne* deletion for Group 1 was 0.02. In fact, one speaker who had never been to France, retained *ne* categorically – there was not a single case of *ne* deletion in the interview for this speaker at Time 1. For Group 2, the deletion rate was 0.65 and for Group 3, it was 0.72. Clearly, even a very short stay in France resulted in increased deletion rates. After the year abroad, Group 1 went from 0.02 as a group to 0.21, 0.37 and 0.48 as individuals. Donna, who had zero deletion before France, now has 0.21. Group 2 also had an increase in deletion rates. Group 3, whose rates were relatively high before France, retained these high rates or increased them slightly. The results of the Varbrul analysis, as they relate to individual speakers, appear to confirm, for the acquisition of sociolinguistic competence, what has previously been proposed by many studies for other areas of second language acquisition: that the least proficient speakers make the greatest gains during a year abroad (Freed, 1995a; and others).

Ne deletion and different contexts of acquisition

In this chapter we have looked at four different contexts for the acquisition of sociolinguistic competence in French L2. We have focused on the same sociolinguistic variable in all cases: the deletion of the pre-verbal negative particle *ne*.

We have reported evidence of variation in *ne* deletion from the traditional classroom for Dutch L1 learners of French L2, from the immersion classroom for Canadian learners, from the Year in France for Irish learners and from Anglophone speakers living in a Francophone community in Montreal (for a further discussion of these contexts see Regan, 2008). While the research on these four different contexts was carried out by different researchers and research teams, there are nevertheless many points in common to all of these variation studies which make a comparison of great interest.

In relation to the classroom Dutch L1 learners of French L2, the learners' speech showed some sociostylistic variation, but this was nevertheless much less than that of native speakers. The Canadian immersion learners had acquired sociolinguistic variation in relation to *ne* deletion, but were still not deleting at native speaker rates. Irish learners who spent a year abroad increased their rates dramatically but deleted still slightly less than L1 speakers. Anglophone Canadian speakers living permanently in a francophone community deleted *ne* at practically native speaker rates. It seems as though we can conclude that in a continuum of contexts from least contact with native speakers to most contact, acquisition of sociolinguistic competence as represented by native speech variation takes place most effectively in the native speech community and with the most contact with native speakers.

The overall findings of this study in relation to *ne* deletion can be resumed in general terms:

- after a year abroad, the overall rate of *ne* deletion increases dramatically;
- the deletion rule strengthens for nearly all of the conditioning factor groups after the year abroad;
- the constraint ordering for the factors tends to remain consistent for these advanced learners;
- also the constraint ordering is very similar to that of native speaker speech and becomes even more so after the year abroad;
- the least proficient speakers make the greatest gains;
- as regards long term effect, it appears that the gains in sociolinguistic variation patterns are retained a year later.

The study shows that contact with native speakers is crucial for the acquisition of native speaker variation patterns by the L2 speakers in relation to *ne* deletion in French. Those who had some contact with native speakers before the study began already deleted *ne* more than those who had had no contact with native speakers. Also the grammar of the speakers in the study, when looked at close-up, was similar in structure, in relation to *ne* deletion to that of native speakers. In addition, the effect of a full academic year in France resulted in a dramatic rise in *ne* deletion rates for the group of speakers. Individually, those who had the most contact with native speakers did best in relation to *ne* deletion.

Notes

1. For a full discussion of *ne* deletion, see Gaatone (1971), Sankoff and Vincent (1977) and Armstrong (2002).
2. For a more detailed account of issues of particle use in French negation in relation to topic scope and focus, see Sanell (2007).
3. Although these chunks are also used as a strategy by advanced learners.
4. For discussion, see Bayley (1994) and Bayley and Regan (2004).

Chapter 6
The Variable Use of Nous/On during the Year Abroad

In contrast to *ne* deletion, *nous/on* alternation is a relatively less long established variable in spoken French. For this reason it gives us an opportunity to investigate the behaviour of L2 speakers in relation to another type of variable in L1 speech: do they acquire this in the same way as the well established *ne* deletion; at the same rates; do they have the same constraint ordering as that of L1 speakers?

The variable use of *nous/on* is common to a large number of varieties of contemporary spoken French. This variable has been frequently studied and analysed since the 1900s (Bollack, 1903; Damourette & Pichon, 1911–1940; Doppagne, 1966; Togeby, 1974). Bollack (1903) predicted that in 2003, the first person plural form would have completely disappeared and that French native speakers would only use forms like *nous aime*. Even though, a century later, this is not quite the case, variation in *nous/on* has undergone considerable change in spoken French, worldwide.

Natural French discourse reveals the remarkable range of referential meanings conveyed by the subject clitic *on*. Laberge (1977, 1978) identifies eight functions of *on* in Montreal French:

(1) the indefinite *personne*   (5) *il/elle*
(2) non identified agent   (6) *nous*
(3) *je*   (7) *vous*
(4) *tu*   (8) *ils/elles*

Studies by Ashby (1992) have established correlations between, on the one hand, *on* and its paradigmatic equivalents *tu/vous* and, on the other, a number of linguistic, discourse and social variables (see Table 6.1).

In the following example, found in Ashby's corpus of Tourangeaux speech, the pronoun *on* is used to refer to the speaker herself along with the rest of her fellow Tourangeaux:

> … tandis que *nous*, quand même pas. *On* sent qu'*on* est pas de la région, mais *on* peut pas savoir d'où qu'*on* vient.[1] (Ashby, 1992)

Table 6.1 Typology of *on* and its possible variants (Ashby, 1992: 138)

Variants	Identification of the reference	Discursive function
ils/elles	indefinite	divergence of the reference
tu/vous	indefinite	generalisation
je/nous	definite	mutation of the pronoun

Atlani characterises this with particular relevance:

> *On*, parce qu'il est frontière entre la personne et la non-personne ... est aussi frontière entre ce qui est identifiable, etdonc nommable, et ce qui ne l'est pas.[2] (Atlani, 1984: 26)

Most such studies focus on the identifiability of a single referent of *on* by hearer inference and on the discourse function (for example, generalisation) which this pronoun may fulfil. Indeed prototypically the subject clitic *on* is an indefinite pronoun whose function is to convey a generalisation. *On* is attested as early as the *Serments de Strasbourg*, where one finds 'sim cum OM per dreit son fradra salvar dift', translated by Rickard (1974) as 'as *one* ought by right to help one's brother'.

Stewart (1995) shows the markedness of the subject pronouns and underlines the fact that *on* is least marked of all the subject pronouns:

+ marked   *je*
⇑   *nous*
              tu
              vous
⇓
− marked   *on*

Stewart demonstrated how such indeterminacy can be exploited by speakers for specific face-saving purposes.

Grevisse (1982) describes the sporadic use of *on* for definite reference in place of the personal pronouns *je, tu, vous, il(s), elle(s)*, where it refers to modesty, discretion, irony, contempt, pride, and so on. Atlani (1984) describes the uses of *on* in journalistic prose, some of which are anaphoric. According to Boutet (1986) and Atlani (1984), the French speaker may use *on* with deliberately ambiguous reference. As such the clitic pronoun *on* is often perceived – and still is by some – as a lack of 'responsibility' of the speakers towards their own speech. *On* allows a certain level of ambiguity in the reference, it defocuses the referent (Chafe, 1993).

Boutet hypothesises that:

> l'incompréhension n'est pas [toujours] révélée, et (…) chaque participant de l'échange poursuit son discours en ayant attribué à *on* un sens, une interprétation, distinct de ceux attribués par le (ou les) autres participants.³ (Boutet, 1986: 49)

Togeby (1974) finds that the use of *on* instead of *nous* was favoured in Old and Middle French, and Grevisse (1993) suggests that this use might have spread during the 19th century. Cook (1994) notes that during the French Revolution it was quite common to find sketches where the authentic language spoken in Paris at the time was represented. Brunot quotes the following example from *Cahiers révolutionnaires*:

> *Nous*, pour les prendre, on mettait le feu dans leurs villages.⁴ (Brunot, 1966: 333)

The clitic pronoun *on* has been condemned by grammarians, teachers and educators in general as incorrect because it was perceived as originating in working-class speech, then because of its wide range of referential values, and its lack of semantic accuracy (Doppagne, 1966). Damourette and Pichon cite the following exchange:

> M. (17 years old) – En classe, on était vingt-huit.⁵
> Mme (his mother) – *On* était ! … "*Nous* étions vingt-huit."⁶ (Damourette & Pichon, 1911–1940: 293–294)

Today the pronoun *on* is widely used in the spoken language by native speakers of all social backgrounds.

Several researchers have agreed that there is a certain degree of semantic similarity between *nous* and *on* (Grafström, 1969; Mühlhäusler & Harré, 1990; Muller, 1970; Posner, 1996; Thomas, 1956), which justifies their alternate use. However although it is common to switch from *nous* to *on*, it is quite unusual to switch from *on* to *nous*. Coveney (2000) argues that the use of *nous* rather than *on* is motivated primarily by style-related factors, rather than by a semantic distinction or a theme-changing situation. It may well be that there is a natural progression from the more formal *nous* to the less formal *on* as conversation progresses, rather as one moves from *vous* to *tu* in an analogous stylistic progression.

The Variable Use of Nous/On: Stable Variation or Change in Progress?

In French L1, the use of *on* instead of *nous* has frequently been seen as a change in progress. For example, Fonseca-Greber and Waugh (2002) and Waugh and Fonseca-Greber (2002) studied a corpus of Metropolitan and Swiss French. They analysed the speech of 27 upper-class speakers (11 men and 16 women) during informal conversations. Results showed a high frequency rate of *on* (99%). Fonseca-Greber and Waugh (2002) concluded that the change was near completion in this variety of French. The rare occurrences of *nous* were found in the speech of speakers from the Metropolitan French corpus – since *nous* has already totally disappeared from Swiss spoken French – and in the speech of teachers who also belonged to the more conservative group of the 40 years plus. Fonseca-Greber and Waugh also held that speakers were hyper-correcting. They attributed the more conservative and hyper-correct French to the educational system, to the forces of standardisation and to the prestige of literary language. Furthermore, the results of this study on Swiss French showed that the meaning associated with the subject clitic *on* has dramatically changed. While in the past the subject clitic *on* had the function of an indefinite pronoun, it is nowadays used more and more as a personal pronoun with the meaning of *nous*. Indeed, their results showed that 5.7% of the pronouns *on* used in the interviews were indefinite pronouns while 76.3% had the meaning of first person plural. The indefinite meaning is now conveyed through the use of the personal pronouns *tu* or *vous* in spoken French. The researchers conclude that Swiss French is further advanced than Metropolitan French as far as grammatical-semantic changes are concerned in relation to *nous/on*.

However other researchers such as Blanche-Benveniste (1997a, 1997b) have stressed the stable nature of variation in the use of *on* versus *nous*. Blanche-Benveniste (1997a: 40) points out that most people use the subject clitic *on*, even politicians. But few studies of Metropolitan French have tried to quantify precisely the variation in *nous/on*.

The Variable Use of *Nous/On* in Metropolitan French

Boutet (1986) analysed the influence of linguistic factors on the variable use of *on* versus *nous* in Metropolitan French. In her study, she used three categories to distinguish the specificity and restrictiveness of the referent in order to account for the alternate use of *on* and *nous*. Her categories comprise of (1) a group whose reference is specific and restrictive – in this first category, it refers to a group of people that the speaker can name and count, like members of the speaker's family; (2) a group that is specific and nonrestrictive – that is, a cohesive group of people that cannot all necessarily be identified but share something in common, like people who work in the same company as the speaker; (3) a group that is nonspecific and nonrestrictive – like 'humanity', a group that cannot be identified in full, but that the speaker is part of. On the basis of an extensive analysis of her corpus of 30 interviews conducted with workers from a steel factory in Nanterre (on the west coast of France), Boutet showed that the more specific and restrictive the reference is, the more likely speakers use *nous*, and the less specific and restrictive the reference is, the more likely speakers use *on*. In another study, Boutet (1994) reported that *nous* was totally absent from her corpus of 44 interviews conducted with factory workers in Metropolitan French.

Coveney (2000) also conducted a study on Metropolitan French. He conducted informal, conversational interviews with 30 adult speakers from Picardy (Northern France) working in a summer camp, and the results showed that the subject clitic pronoun *on* was very frequently used (95.6%) while *nous* was only used 4.4% of the time. He took into consideration the possibility that a certain number of linguistic factors influenced the choice between *on* and *nous*. These factors would be inclusion or exclusion of the addressee, reference to a group 'seen from the outside' compared to a group 'seen from within'. This follows Blanche-Benveniste's (1987: 208) suggestion of a more subtle semantic difference whereby *nous* is often 'used to refer to a group "seen from outside" and facing or confronted with others external to this group, whereas on is used for the group "seen from within"' (cited in Coveney, 2000: 465). Here is an example taken from Coveney illustrating this definition:

> alors à c moment-là *on* explique aux parents voilà/euh nous *nous* n vérifions ni euh comment – ce que écrivent les enfants/et on ne/on – on ne vérifie pas combien de lettres ils écrivent.[7] (Coveney, 2000: 472)

One could perhaps claim that, in this example of *nous*, the speaker is referring to the group of people running the centre as seen from the outside. But this interpretation would imply that in switching to *on* a few seconds later, the meaning changes, and that now the group is suddenly – and inexplicably – being seen from within. Coveney (2000: 472) interprets this data in the context of Bell's (1984) theory of speech style as audience design. Speaking on the telephone, and speaking to an addressee that one does not know personally, means that one is more distant in both social and spatial terms from the addressee, and these are factors which regularly trigger greater formality.

While speech style appeared to be a crucial factor, Coveney (2000: 477) found that *nous* was barely present in his corpus. He notes that 'in variationist terms, the *nous/on* alternation is what Bell (1984) has referred to as a "hyper-style variable", in that the stylistic (intrapersonal) variation massively outweighs that of the social (interpersonal) dimension'.

This variable use of *nous/on* has also been noted in another study of the speech of children. Sanz Lecina and Nespoulous (1995) studied the discourse of 20 primary school pupils in France. They found that unlike adults, children used *on* primarily to signal 'I and the other(s)', but never as an equivalent of 'someone' like in the following example: 'Avec mes copains, on va souvent à la piscine'. Results showed that *on* was more frequent than *nous* in children's speech. The authors explained it in terms of the order of acquisition of pronouns. Personal pronouns are acquired much later than singular personal pronouns in French. In child language acquisition, French plural person pronouns are learnt later than the singular ones (Clark, 1985). Coveney suggests

> one might suppose then that the vast numbers of French children who had to learn French as their second language (or dialect) in the nineteenth and early twentieth centuries, would have cheerfully made their task easier by avoiding nous +4p verb whenever possible. (Coveney, 2000: 449)

In a study conducted by Söll (1983b) with nine-year-old children, no occurrences at all of *nous* were found compared to a frequent use of *on*, hence correlating with Sanz Lecina and Nespoulous's (1995) study. The subject clitic *on* is acquired earlier which suggests that it may be easier than *nous*.

Frequency of use in the input is often an important factor in the acquisition of a variant. Mougeon (1995) has argued that *on* is generally used with imperative intention when speaking to a child. She provides the following examples: 'on se tait, on obéit, on se calme'[8] (Mougeon, 1995: 116). This may partially explain the frequency of *on* in children's speech found in the studies above.

The Variable Use of *Nous/On* in Canadian French

The variable use of *on* and *nous* was firstly studied in the L1 of native speakers of French from Quebec by Laberge (1977). Based on the Sankoff and Cedergren (1976) corpus of 120 speakers of Montreal French, Laberge found that *nous* (e.g. *ma soeur et moi,* **nous** *avons fait des courses en ville*) was hardly used (1.6% of the time) while *on* (e.g. *mon équipe et moi,* **on** *a fait la troisième mi-temps au bar du coin*) was frequently used (98.4% of the time). As far as effects of extra-linguistic parameters on the alternation between *on* and *nous* were concerned, gender, social class and age proved to be very significant for the use of *nous*. Indeed, the speakers who used *nous* belonged to the age group of 50 years and over. Furthermore, the results showed that twice as many women as men used *nous* and that there were almost three times as many middle-class as working-class speakers who used *nous*. These results can be explained by well-documented research on L1 variation which states that working-class speakers as well as female speakers show a clear preference for standard variants.[9]

Furthermore, Laberge noticed that the use of *nous* correlated with the use of other formal variants such as the retention of *ne* in negative constructions. She also stressed the fact that formal variants occurred during the most formal part of the interview. Laberge's results relating to the variable *nous/on* were confirmed by Deshaies's (1985a, 1986) study of French spoken in Quebec city. The results showed that the competition between *nous/on* was nearly non-existent as there were only 31 occurrences of the subject pronoun *nous* versus 6561 occurrences of *on* in the collected data. Hence Deshaies concludes that *on* is nearly categorically used in Montreal when the reference is specific and restricted.

Style proved to be a crucial factor in the choice between *nous/on* in Canada as in France. Three studies analysed this aspect of *nous/on* alternation (Brunelle & Tousignant, 1981; Deshaies, 1986; Laberge, 1977). Laberge found that in the first part of the interview, which focused on formal topics,[10] there was a significantly higher frequency of *nous* (5.6%) than in the rest of the interview (1.3%) which dealt with more informal topics. The Varbrul probabilities of 0.269 and 0.731 for the first and second parts of the interviews respectively confirmed that this difference in use of *nous* is both a substantial one, and attributable to when it happens in the interview, that is, at the beginning or in the second part of the interview (Laberge, 1977: 134–140).

Brunelle and Tousignant (1981) reported some evidence that in Montreal *nous* was frequently used when speaking in a formal style. They gave the example where the change was most advanced of a 46-year-old woman who was recorded in two styles, spontaneous conversation and interview, and had frequencies for *nous* of 0/10 in the former, but 7/9 in the latter.

In Deshaies's (1981, 1985b, 1985c) study of French in Quebec City, one speaker out of 53 – a 46-year-old woman – produced 13/29 of her occurrences of *nous* at the start of the interview, which, as we have seen, generally elicits a more formal speech style.

In all of these studies on Canadian spoken French, the subject pronoun *nous* appears to be a stylistically marked variant.

The Variable Use of *Nous/On* in Canadian Immersion L2 Speakers' Speech

Many researchers who have studied Canadian immersion programmes in the last couple of decades (Swain & Lapkin, 1990, 1998; Harley, 1992a, 1992b) have shown that learners in immersion programmes in French were generally found to attain scores in reading and listening that approached those of native speakers of the same age. As far as their speaking and writing skills were concerned, immersion learners were found to outdo their counterparts on regular French programmes, but were yet not quite reaching native-like competence.

Mougeon and his colleagues, as we have already mentioned (Mougeon & Rehner, 2001; Mougeon *et al.*, 2001, 2002; Nadasdi *et al.*, 2001; Rehner & Mougeon, 1999; Rehner *et al.*, 2003) have researched extensively the acquisition of variation patterns in immersion schools in Greater Toronto, Ontario in Canada. For the variable we are concerned with in this chapter, Rehner *et al.* (2003)[11] found that learners did not use the formal variant *nous* more than the informal variant *on* (44% *nous* vs 56% *on*) contrary to their expectations.[12] An analysis of extralinguistic factors showed that use of the variant *on* increased with extracurricular French language exposure, including stays with Francophone families and stays in a Francophone environment. This confirms the positive impact of exposure to native speakers outside the classroom on the acquisition of an informal variant such as *on* which is widely used by native speakers of Quebecois French. The positive effect of more exposure experienced by immersion learners is further emphasised when we compare their results to formal learners in a traditional classroom setting. In relation to Irish learners who have had no naturalistic exposure but only learnt French in the formal setting, Lemée (2002) showed that learners who had never spent any time in the country of the target language only used *on* 50% of the time. Other studies have already documented a similar positive effect of exposure on the speech of other learners of French L2 (Blondeau & Nagy, 1995, in relation to exposure to naturalistic milieu; Regan, 1995, 1996 for the year abroad experience) and for other L2 learners (Bayley, 1996).

In relation to immersion learners, Rehner *et al.* (2003) found that gender and social class exerted the expected effect with female and middle-class learners more likely to use the more socially and stylistically prestigious *nous*. These results were similar in direction to those of Blondeau and Nagy (1998) on Anglophone learners of French L2 in Montreal. Learners seem to have inferred that subject clitic *nous* was a more standard form than *on*. In their study, the results showed that as in native speech non-specific and nonrestricted referents tended to promote the use of *on* (0.85), whereas the specific and restricted referents favoured *nous* (0.47). The researchers concluded that in this case of variation, immersion learners observed the patterns of constraints used by L1 speakers of Canadian French (Laberge, 1977).

Mougeon and his colleagues found that learners from a Romance language background (Italian or Spanish) displayed the highest level of *nous* usage. This may be due to the fact that these languages use similar first person plural subject pronouns (*noi* and *nosotros* respectively), but also to the absence of a variant similar to the pronoun *on*. Rehner *et al.* (2003) speculated that Anglophone learners might have preferred the use of *on* because of its morphological and phonological closeness to *one* in English, a subject pronoun which is semantically linked to the French pronoun *on*. The researchers also hypothesised that these Anglophone learners simply had no other variant available in their L1 that could have led them to the use of *nous*.

Findings concerning the positive impact of naturalistic contact for the acquisition of sociolinguistic variation are further evidenced in work by Blondeau *et al.* (2002) and Nagy *et al.* (1996) who found significant use of informal sociolinguistic markers by naturalistic informants living in Montreal.

Acquisition of Variable *Nous/On* in L2 Speakers and the Year Abroad

We will now briefly review research done on L2 *nous/on* variation and consider this research in relation to the year abroad.

Sax (2003) analysed the speech of 30 female American learners of French regarding the use of *on* versus *nous* in formal and informal situations.[13] Her participants consisted of 10 learners in second year university French who had never spent time abroad, 10 learners in fourth year French, half of whom had spent from several weeks to a year in France, and 10 graduate students, who had all spent at least between a year and four years abroad. She found that time spent in the country of the target language strongly correlated with the use of the informal variant *on*: learners who had gone abroad extensively favoured *on* (0.83[14]) while learners who spent less than two weeks or between two and 5.25 months disfavoured *on* (0.10 and 0.28, respectively). In a previous study, Sax (2001) stressed that learners who spent a year abroad used *on* considerably more than those who had never been or who had gone for less than 16 weeks. The level of nonspecificity and nonrestriction of the referent only favoured *on* at 0.61, and when the referent was restricted and specific, they favoured *nous* (0.46). The constraint ordering was similar to native speaker order.

For the learners who had spent most time abroad, Sax's results showed that the level of use of *on* was closet to native-like levels, and some stylistic variation was evident with 91% use of *on* in the formal context, versus 94% use of *on* in the informal context. As regards proficiency level, Sax showed that at the second year level, there was emergent use of *on* and perhaps incipient awareness of stylistic variation, since there were more occurrences of *on* in the informal setting (1% vs 4%). By fourth year, use of *on* was decidedly stronger and learners seemed to have had a much stronger sense of a stylistic correlation between *on* and *nous* (47% *on* in formal vs 65% in informal situations).

Dewaele (2002) reported on a corpus of advanced oral and written French interlanguage[15] produced by 32 university students (13 females and 19 males, aged between 18 and 21) from the Flemish part of Brussels.[16] He found that the amount of authentic interaction with native speakers of French, but not the amount of formal instruction, was significantly related to the learners' use of *on* in oral production (79.4% use of *on* vs 20.6% of *nous*). The use of *on* is correlated with the rates of morpho-lexical accuracy, a higher speech rate, *ne* deletion in negative constructions and use of more colloquial vocabulary. Interestingly, analysis of the written data showed proportions of *on* equal to those produced by the learners in the spoken data (78.1% of *on* vs 21.9% of *nous*). This led Dewaele to conclude that as a group, the L2 learners had not yet acquired the stylistic factors affecting the variation under study. In more formal situations and in written work, it would have been expected that the learners would use more frequently the formal variant *nous*. Furthermore, the learners who displayed a high rate of *nous* usage in the written corpus turned out to be grammatically less advanced. According to Dewaele (2002: 219), the presence of *nous* in his written corpus seemed to indicate 'an earlier stage in the participants' interlanguage rather than an indication of a newly acquired sociostylistic competence'. Dewaele's results corresponded with those of Sax (2003) in relation to the importance of the length of exposure to the target language in the use of *on*.

Acquisition of the Variable Use of *Nous/On* by Irish Learners of French L2

The speakers selected for this part of the study are a subset of a larger study analysing the speech of Irish learners of French L2.[17] This subset has been described extensively in Chapter 4. In this section we provide empirical evidence relating to the acquisition of sociolinguistic competence by 20 Irish learners who spent a year abroad in relation to the alternating use of *nous/on*.[18] There was an equal number of male and female informants.

In addition to the more usual sociolinguistic factors, six factor groups were selected: specificity and restriction of the referent, preceding and following segment, type of verbs, third language studied and style.

The specificity and restriction of the reference was hypothesised to be an influencing factor for the use of *on*. Our previous studies on the acquisition of sociostylistic variation by L2 speakers (Lemée, 2002, 2003, 2005, 2006b; Lemée *et al.*, 2007) showed that L2 learners tended to mirror native speakers variation patterns. Hence, studies on L1 have shown that the more specific the reference, the more *on* is used.

In terms of style, we expected the L2 learners to use *nous* during the formal part of the interview and when talking about 'formal' topics such as 'the advantages of the euro'. Labov's modules designed to elicit spontaneous speech such as 'premonitions' or 'danger of death' were expected to trigger a more frequent use of the informal variant *on*.

Results

The Varbrul analysis reveals considerable variability in relation to *nous/on* alternation (69% vs 30%). Table 6.2[19] presents below the factors calculated as being significant in the use of *nous/on*.

Male speakers favour *on* much more than *nous*, compared to female speakers (0.648 vs 0.220). Female speakers stay much closer to the standard and formal style by using *nous* more often than male speakers (37% vs 28%, respectively in the use of *nous*).[20]

Interestingly, results show that middle-class speakers tend to use *on* more frequently than upper-middle class speakers. When cross-tabulating with gender, it appears that upper-middle class female speakers use the more formal variant *nous* in the same way as do L1 speakers (see Table 6.3).

A possible explanation is that *nous* is seen as prestigious socially and stylistically. The students who come back from a year of exposure to French would receive confirmation of the sociostylistic value they had inferred from the educational treatment of the variants (see Table 6.4).

Table 6.2 Results for the use of *on* by Irish L2 speakers of French

Groups and factors	% on	Factor weight
Gender		
Male	72	**0.648**
Female	63	0.220
Social status		
Upper	58	0.332
Middle	73	**0.569**
Third language		
Spanish/Italian	63	0.509
German	63	0.204
Latin	70	0.515
Gaelic	93	**0.989**
Specificity and restriction of referent		
Specific and restrictive	37	0.076
Specific and nonrestrictive	93	0.820
Nonspecific and nonrestrictive	99	**0.964**
Preceding segment *on/nous*		
Hesitation	67	0.497
Pause	71	0.329
Vowel	65	0.425
Consonant	84	**0.793**
Glide	72	0.374
Type of verbs		
State	62	0.370
Modal	89	**0.634**
Action/movement	64	0.533
Achievement	65	0.550
Accomplishment	88	0.506
Input 0.857 Log likelihood = –242,292 Significance = 0.224		

Table 6.3 Cross-tabulations: gender and social class in the speech of Irish speakers of French L2[21]

Social class	Female		Male	
	On	*Nous*	*On*	*Nous*
Middle	69%	31%	76%	24%
Upper	46%	54%	63%	37%

Table 6.4 Cross-tabulations: social class and style in the speech of Irish learners of French L2

Style	Middle class		Upper class	
	On	*Nous*	*On*	*Nous*
Formal	66%	34%	47%	53%
Informal	90%	10%	87%	13%

These results are similar to Rehner *et al.*'s (2003) findings on immersion learners of French in Canada. In Quebec French, the use of *nous* is strongly associated with upper-middle class and formal speech, so students who have had extracurricular exposure to French have had this inference reinforced. Consequently depending on their social class background and gender, the students will display variable preference for the prestige variant *nous*.

The Irish informants have studied Irish from an early age, and the results show that knowledge of Irish favours *on* (0.964) more than any other foreign language that is being studied. While Spanish/Italian and Latin also tend to favour *on* to a lesser degree, German seems to favour *nous*. One possible explanation for this is the fact that Irish has always tended to be less hierarchical in its forms of address and lacks a strict *tu/vous* opposition. In addition, it may well be that the fact that the speakers are more or less bilingual or at least a knowledge of an L2 from preschool age may have encouraged a greater degree of sensitivity to sociolinguistic nuances in variation patterns in the language.

When the referent is nonspecific and nonrestrictive, as when referring to humanity, or people in general, the use of the informal pronoun *on* is favoured by the Irish L2 speakers. These results are in line with Boutet's (1986) and Coveney's (2000) findings on the speech of native speakers of Metropolitan French. These researchers note the fact that French native speakers rarely use *nous* in their speech.

Irish speakers of French L2 use *on* categorically when the reference is nonspecific and nonrestrictive. Men seem to find a happy medium in the use of the variant when the reference is specific and restrictive, while using *on* nearly categorically when the reference is nonspecific and nonrestrictive. Results also show that L2 women use *nous* more frequently than men when the reference is specific and restrictive (see Table 6.5).

Results on the effects of the segment preceding the variant show that a word finishing with a consonant strongly favours the use of *on* (0.793) while when dealing with hesitation, pause, vowel or glide, *nous* is the favoured pronoun (hesitation: 0.503; pause: 0.671; vowel: 0.575; glide: 0.626).

While *nous* is usually followed by stative verbs that imply a duration without an implicit end, the pronoun *on* is triggered when verbs of action, achievement or realisation are used. More interestingly modals strongly favour the use of the informal variant *on* (0.634).

It is interesting to see the real impact of the year abroad as far as sociolinguistic competence relating to this particular variable is concerned compared to the learners who have not been to the country of the target language. Table 6.6 below presents the results found in a bigger corpus of 48 speakers (Lemée, 2003) on the effect of native contact on the use of *nous/on*.

Table 6.5 Cross-tabulations: gender and specificity/restriction of the reference in the speech of Irish speakers of French L2

	Female		Male	
Specificity/restriction	*On*	*Nous*	*On*	*Nous*
Specific/restrictive[22]	22%	78%	44%	56%
Specific/nonrestrictive[23]	90%	10%	96%	4%
Nonspecific/nonrestrictive[24]	100%	0%	99%	1%

Table 6.6 Impact of time abroad on the use of *on* by Irish L2 learners of French

Factors	*% of* on	*Factor weight*
Time abroad		
0–6 days	63	0.249
7–20 days	63	0.494
1 year	69	**0.515**
Input 0.897 Log likelihood = –422,884 Significance = 0.000		

It seems that spending any period of time in the country of the target language has a positive effect on the acquisition of sociolinguistic competence. Learning the language in the classroom triggers mainly the formal variant *nous*. But as the learners' linguistic competence develops, they need more authentic interactions which allow them then to use the informal variant *on*.

Conclusion

Our research reveals that in relation to *nous/on* alternation after the year abroad experience the L2 speakers rates are still considerably below that of native speakers. while generally following the same patterns of native speech for gender style and some linguistic factors such as specificity and restriction. So even though there is some stylistic variation in the use of the mildly marked pronoun *on* compared to the more formal *nous*, it does not reach the near-categorical use of *on* instead of *nous* that French native speakers display. These findings relating to a relatively 'new' variable in spoken French as opposed to the much 'older' and more established *ne* deletion, are interesting in their possible implications.

It could be that the generally all pervasive, productive and stable nature of the older variable *ne* is more available on many levels to the L2 speaker. A frequency of input argument could be made for the near native rates of *ne* deletion in the L2 speech, whereas the slightly less frequent and less stable *nous/on* alternation may be less salient for the L2 speaker. L1 influence has also been seen to play a role in *nous/on* alternation, whereas this is much less the case in *ne* deletion.

At least we can conclude that behaviour in L2 speech in relation to the old and the newer variables is different whatever the reasons.

Notes

1. As for us, not really. We feel that we are not from the region, even though they can't say where we come from.
2. *On*, because it is the border between the person and the non-person ... is also at the border with what is identifiable, what is not.
3. Misunderstanding is not [always] apparent, and (...) each participant to the discourse carries on with his/her speech having attributing to *on* a meaning, an interpretation which are different from what the other participants have understood.
4. In order to catch them, we used to set fire to their village.

5. In class, there were twenty-eight of us.
6. We were! ... There were twenty-eight of us.
7. 'so then you/we explain to the parents "well/er we do not check either er how – what the children write/and we do not/we – we do not check how many letters they write."'
8. 'Be quiet, do as you're told, calm down'.
9. See Chapter 9 on Gender in this volume, Trudgill (1972, 1984), Labov (1990), and for a general sociolinguistic account, see Coates (1993, 1998).
10. These topics dealt with the informant's social background, school, geographical mobility and jobs.
11. They analysed three corpora: (1) a corpus of oral speech of 41 immersion learners of French L2 (30 females and 11 males). The participants were middle and upper-middle class learners. There were 21 learners from Grade 9, and 20 from Grade 12; (2) a corpus of oral speech from seven teachers of French who were recorded while teaching immersion students; (3) written material – that is, two series of text books (one with dialogues, another with written texts) and accompanying exercise books – used by the learners during their French immersion programme.
12. Results also showed that the teachers used *on* more frequently than *nous* (83% *on* vs 17% *nous*). In the class material, the learners' books revealed 52% of *nous* vs 48% of *on*, while books containing literary work as well as journalistic articles produced 83% of *nous* versus 17% of *on*.
13. The formal situation was a mock job interview and the informal one was an imagined conversation with a new French roommate. Interlocutors were two different native speakers of French.
14. These are Varbrul probabilities.
15. For more details about the definition of advanced learners, see Bartning (1997b).
16. The learners had all been exposed to vernacular French through songs, cartoons and film extracts during the course of the university's language institute. The oral corpus consisted of one-to-one conversations between the researcher and each participant with no time restriction. The written corpus consisted of 32 essays either on a political or a philosophical topic produced by the same participants under exam conditions.
17. For more details, see Lemée (2002, 2003).
18. We excluded from our study occurrences when on could not be replaced by nous, for example, 'on dit que', 'comment on dit', all repetitions of *on* and *nous* not followed by a verb, quotes like '*on* verra bien', all the *nous* pronouns which are not subject pronouns, for example, when it is an object pronoun (il *nous* a fallu partir), the object of a preposition (viens avec *nous*!), when used in comparative structures (leur équipe était plus forte que *nous*), in dislocated structures (*nous*, c'est pas comme ça) or as a disjunctive *nous* (*nous*, on voulait toujours aller nager).
19. The results should be read as follows: first column presents the factors, second column presents the percentage of *on* occurrences and finally the probability calculated by Goldvarb (2001).
20. For more details, see Chapter 9 on Gender in this volume.
21. For these cross-tabulations, there was an equal number of male and female informants.

22. This refers to a group of people that the speaker knows and can count, for example, members of his/her family: 'Avec mon équipe, *on* a gagné beaucoup de matches' (With my team, *we* won a lot of matches).
23. This refers to a group of individuals who cannot all be identified, for example, all the pupils in a school: 'A l'université, *on* doit acheter beaucoup de livres' (At university, *we* have to buy a lot of books).
24. This refers to humanity, people in general: 'Au Canada, *on* ne peut plus nager dans ce lac' (In Canada, no one can swim in this lake anymore).

Chapter 7
The Acquisition of /l/ Deletion in French by Irish Study Abroad Speakers

Like *ne* deletion, /l/ deletion as a variable has existed in French for many centuries (although some aspects seem to be undergoing changes recently). Also, like *ne* deletion, /l/ deletion is frequent in the input which L2 speakers have available to them in the speech community during the Year Abroad. In contrast to *ne* deletion and *nous/on* alternation which constitute examples of variability at the morphological and morphosyntactic level, /l/ deletion is an example of phonological variation.

/l/ deletion is found to occur in the subject clitic pronouns, *il, ils, elle* and *elles*, as exemplified in the following.

il va [ilva] → [iva]
il y a [ilija] → [ija] ou [ja]

It also occurs in full lexical items, notably before a glide and also intervocally, such as in the case of *table* and *escalier*. Other contexts include its generally less frequent occurrence in word-initial position in the pronouns *le, la, les, lui* and *leur*, as well as in the definite articles *le, la* and *les*.

/l/ Deletion in Metropolitan French L1

The phenomenon of /l/ deletion in the masculine subject pronouns *il* and *ils* before consonants has been attested since the latter part of the 12th century (Pope, 1934). More recent studies of contemporary spoken French have also found it to occur in other contexts. Armstrong (1996) analysed the variable in the definite articles and subject clitic pronouns and in one frequent phonolexical context – obstruent +/l/ in a word-final syllable such as 'table' or 'ronfle' – in the speech of secondary schoolchildren from Lorraine in north-eastern France (Armstrong's Dieuze corpus). He found that adolescent informants had rates of deletion ranging from 15% in the case of *'elle'* to near-categorical levels in the case of *'il'*. He reports speech style as an important variable influencing such deletion. In casual speech, results show that faster speech rates and lower degrees of self-monitoring favour the elision of weak segments, /l/ in this case, while in more formal styles, the opposite process applies. Armstrong (1996: 17) concludes that, in the latter case, the 'speakers' consciousness of the stylistic salience of these phonolexical contexts' leads to greater levels of retention. These findings are all the more interesting, as the speech of young speakers often indicates the direction of change for the language. So characteristics of the speech of children or adolescents can often point to the future state of the variable in the language.

Earlier, Ashby's (1984) study of speakers in Tours found that rates of deletion occurred within a range of 63% in the case of *'elle'*, and 88% in the case of 'impersonal *il'* such as in *'il faut'*. Laks (1980) for his Parisian speakers reports differential rates of deletion across pronouns with rates ranging from 33% in the case of *'elle'*, and 94% in the case of 'impersonal *il'*. Regarding preconsonantal *'il'* in particular, Blanche-Benveniste (1997a) writes that some current ways of pronouncing, which are different from a more received pronunciation, are so widespread that they cannot be considered marginalised phenomena any more.

/l/ Deletion in Canadian French L1

Levels of /l/ deletion are found to be higher in Canadian French than in Metropolitan French. Poplack and Walker (1986) studied /l/ deletion in French in Ottawa-Hull. They find that /l/ is categorically deleted in the case of *'il'* and *'ils'*. The feminine subject pronoun, *'elle'*, shows deletion rates reaching 84%, while 33% of *'elles'* are deleted. Similar levels of deletion are also found by Sankoff and Cedergren (1976) in a study in Montreal. Deletion ranges from 98% for impersonal *'il'* to 63% for *'elle'*.

/l/ Deletion in L2 Speech: The Case of French Immersion Speakers in Canada, L2 Canadian and American Year Abroad Speakers

Mougeon *et al.* (2001) studied /l/ deletion by classroom immersion learners in Ontario. They found that overall these speakers deleted /l/ less than 2% of the time. The context most favourable to deletion is the expression *'il y a'* (a phonetically natural context for /l/ deletion since /l/ is followed by a glide). *'Elle'* is completely impervious to deletion. Also, these immersion speakers delete more in the context of impersonal *'il'* than plural *'ils'* or singular personal *'il'*. While the immersion students' deletion rates are low, the constraint-ordering in this regard is similar to those of L1 speech. On the whole, however, the immersion speakers delete very infrequently.

In contrast, in a study of the speech of Canadian university learners who spent an academic year in France, Thomas (2002) finds significantly higher rates of /l/ deletion. In addition, he finds that similar to the native speaker norms reported by Poplack and Walker (1986), there was little difference in levels of deletion between personal *'il/ils'* and 'impersonal' *il* (77.2% vs 77.9%, respectively). Thomas notes the impact of contact with native speakers for study abroad speakers who demonstrate similar variation patterns to native speakers, but at different rates.

A further study is that by Sax (2000) who investigated /l/ deletion by American L2 speakers. Time spent abroad in Sax's study emerged as the strongest predictor of /l/ deletion. Learners who had spent either no time or up to two weeks abroad did not delete /l/ frequently (0.14)[1] compared to learners who had spent between two and five months abroad (0.36). The American learners who had been abroad for between eight months and four years deleted /l/ most frequently (0.78).

Acquisition of Variable /l/ Deletion by Irish L2 Speakers of French

The speakers of this part of the study are a subset of a larger study analysing the speech of Irish learners of French L2 (Howard *et al.*, 2006). The study is based on an analysis of the spoken data produced by 19 speakers, nine male and 10 female who had returned from France following a period of residence of one year.

The data[2] were coded for a range of factors predicted to constrain the use of this variable by L2 speakers. The seven factor groups selected for this study are listed with examples in Table 7.1.

Results

Our Varbrul analysis indicates an overall deletion rate of 33%. This rate is considerably inferior to the rates observed in the case of native speakers, as near-categorical levels of deletion are observed in the native speaker's use of some of these pronouns, particularly in the case of the use of *'il'*.

Table 7.1 Factor groups for /l/ deletion in the speech of Irish L2 speakers of French

Groups and factors	Examples
Following phonological segment	
Vowel	Il est retourné
Consonants	Elle parlait
Preceding phonological segment	
Vowel	Où elle travaillait
Consonant	Parce qu'il est revenu
Pause	Ø elles sont arrivées
Following grammatical category	
Verb	Elles travaillaient
Pronoun	Il y est allé
Other	Il ne comprend pas
Pronoun	
Il (impersonal)	Il pleuvait
Il (personal)	Il sortait tout le temps
Elle	Elle va en partis le trois juin
Ils	Ils sont partis le trois juin
Elles	Elles pensent étudier l'anglais
Position and distance of co-referent	
No co-referent	Il s'agit d'une difficulté énorme
Following	Il est intéressant, ce prof
Preceding	Ce mec, il est chouette
1 clause, right	Il est mal à l'aise, quand on parle, cet homme
1 clause, left	L'enfant, quand nous sommes sortis, elle a pleuré
2 or more clauses away, right or left	Mes amis qui étaient à Paris ont décidé de revenir
Unknown	Ils sont retournés le 4 août
Gender	
Male	
Female	
Style	
Formal	
Informal	

Table 7.2 Goldvarb 2001 results[3] for the deletion of /l/ by Irish L2 speakers of French

Groups and factors	% deleted tokens	Factor weight
Gender		
Female	45	**0.630**
Male	22	0.386
Pronoun		
il impersonal	45	**0.632**
il personal	20	0.353
ils/elles	29	**0.520**
elle	6	0.151
Following phonological segment		
Vowel	34	0.441
Consonant	32	**0.546**
Preceding phonological segment		
Vowel	38	**0.524**
Consonant	27	0.441
Pause	33	**0.521**
Following grammatical category		
Verb	23	0.405
Pronoun	47	**0.639**
Other	31	**0.513**
Input = 0.264 Log likelihood = –984,607 Significance = 0.085		

Indeed, Ashby's (1984) native speakers from Tours produced a rate of 88% in such a context, while Armstrong's (1996) results suggest near-categorical levels in the Dieuze corpus. With this type of input available to the L2 speakers of the study, it is interesting to see that they only reach 33% of deletion. Table 7.2 details the results for our L2 speakers.

The results show that female L2 speakers tend to delete /l/ much more frequently than their male counterparts (0.630 vs 0.386, respectively). This would suggest that Irish L2 female learners follow variation patterns similar to those of L1 female speakers. It has frequently been found that new linguistic changes are often carried out by women and especially by young women. For example, Armstrong (1996) and Armstrong *et al.* (2001) observe a general rate of /l/ deletion of 35.2% amongst adolescent male informants aged 16–19, as opposed to a rate of 54.2% among female counterparts in the same age group.[4] The Irish L2 speakers after their year abroad follow generally the same gender pattern.

We also found that these post-year abroad speakers demonstrate similar constraint-orderings to those observed in native speaker studies in the case of the following factor groups: preceding phonological segment, following grammatical segment, type of pronoun and following phonological segment. In the case of individual pronouns, our learners delete /l/ most frequently in the case of impersonal *'il'* with a probability of 0.632. They similarly delete quite frequently in the case of the plural pronouns *'ils'* and *'elles'* (0.520). In contrast, the other pronoun types disfavour deletion (the respective *p*-values for *'il'* and *'elle'* are 0.353 and 0.151).

The distinction made by the Irish L2 speakers in their level of deletion with impersonal *'il'* and personal *'il'* is in line with the pattern of use observed in the case of the native speaker.[5] In contrast, in the case of Canadian French speakers, Poplack and Walker (1986) report categorical levels of deletion in both personal and impersonal *'il'*, such that no effect is noted for the personal or impersonal value that this pronoun may assume. Like native speakers, the higher rate of deletion of /l/ with impersonal *'il'* reflects the learners' tendency to use this variable in lexicalised chunks such as *'il y a'* and *'il faut'*, where *'il'* carries an impersonal value. Interestingly, this use of lexicalised phrases has been found to be a common feature of L2 speech at both low proficiency (Myles & Mitchell, 1999) and high proficiency levels (see Chapter 5 for a presentation of Regan's findings in the case of her *ne* deletion study). The L2 speakers also demonstrate a lower /l/ deletion rate in contexts where the pronoun assumes a personal value, reflecting a similar tendency among native speakers.

Just as Armstrong (1996) observes in relation to his native speaker informants in the case of *'ils'*, our L2 speakers delete this pronoun more than in the case of the other pronouns with a personal value. Finally, with regard to *'elle'*, the lower rate of deletion reflects a similar native speaker tendency. However, we cannot ignore the fact that the low level of deletion with *'elle'* may also reflect an effect for the pronunciation of *'elle'* with or without final schwa, such that a consonant cluster may or may not arise when the following sound is a consonant. This is also similar to native speaker behaviour in this phonological context.

In the case of the factor of the following phonological segment, we observed that the Irish L2 speakers follow the usual tendency for consonants (as opposed to vowels) to favour /l/ deletion. For the Irish L2 speakers, the factor weight is 0.555 for consonants as opposed to 0.451 for vowels.

The preceding phonological segment was also found to exert an influence, with vowels and pauses favouring /l/ deletion, while consonants disfavoured it (the p-values are 0.524 and 0.521 vs 0.441, respectively).[6]

In the case of the factor of following grammatical category, pronouns were found to favour /l/ deletion (0.639), as were certain other grammatical categories such as the negative particle *ne* (0.513). This is in contrast with verbs which are found to disfavour /l/ deletion (0.405).

Although we hypothesised that style would be significant, this was not the case. In fact, in the case of native speakers, some studies such as Laks (1980) do not report an effect for style, while others, such as Armstrong (1996), Armstrong *et al.* (2001) report a minimal effect in the case of deletion in the context of impersonal '*il*'. In that respect, our L2 speakers once again follow a similar pattern to that of native speakers.

Individual variation in the case of /l/ deletion

Apart from the linguistic, social and stylistic factors discussed so far, it must also be noted that considerable individual variation characterises the speakers' use of the variable, as we have also seen to be the case with our other variables. The individual learners' rates of deletion are presented in Table 7.3.

As Table 7.3 shows, the level of /l/ deletion across the speakers is far from being a uniform phenomenon, but rather some learners delete considerably more than others. Such individual variation has frequently been observed in studies of the L2 acquisition of sociolinguistic variation, such as Regan (1995) as well as in study abroad research.[7] As Howard *et al.* (2006) outline in relation to study abroad, such inter-learner variation may possibly reflect the effect of various extra-linguistic factors which impact on the speaker's L2 development, such as the extent of the speaker's interaction with native speakers, the speaker's integration in the L2 community, and the speaker's residence and *raison d'être* while abroad.

Conclusion

The general conclusions of this study of /l/ deletion by Irish year abroad speakers of French are that these speakers delete considerably more after a year in France but still much less than native speakers. For

Table 7.3 Individual rates of /l/ deletion for Irish L2 speakers

Factor group	Factors	% deleted tokens	Factor weight
Learners	Alan	27	0.496
	Bernie	41	**0.615**
	Cathal	7	0.122
	Danielle	7	0.126
	Eoin	5	0.106
	Fiona	6	0.127
	Gerard	30	0.490
	Henry	31	**0.562**
	June	48	**0.755**
	Kelly	39	**0.585**
	Liam	19	0.407
	Maurice	26	0.469
	Niamh	65	**0.824**
	Oran	41	**0.650**
	Siofra	40	**0.605**
Input = 0.264 Log likelihood = –984,607 Significance = –0.085			

example, we found variability in their levels of deletion even in preconsonantic position where native speaker deletion is quasi-categorical. Nonetheless, the effects of the factors found to constrain such deletion emerge as similar in relation to the constraint hierarchies observed across our L2 learners and their native speaker counterparts.

Another finding is that the gender pattern underlying such variation is more significant than style. This finding is in line with those presented by Major (2004) who, as we have already noted, found that in relation to phonology gender patterns were acquired before stylistic ones by L2 speakers.

It may be significant that though /l/ deletion has been variable for centuries in French, it is undergoing change in some new linguistic contexts where it had previously not been observed. The L2 speaker rates are less close and therefore their rates are less close to native speaker rates than those of *ne* deletion, for instance, the position of which is unambiguous in the spontaneous speech heard by the L2 speakers and which they reproduce almost at the same rates as native speakers.

In conclusion, while the rates of /l/ deletion in Irish L2 speech are less close to those of native speakers, they are considerably higher than those reported in previous studies of L2 speakers who have not spent a year abroad. This study of a phonological variable therefore gives us additional evidence that, as in the case of morphosyntactic variation, phonological variation patterns in L2 speech can be positively affected by the year abroad experience.

Notes

1. These are Varbrul probabilities.
2. We excluded from our study occurrences of the variable which were immediately followed by a word beginning with /l/ in view of the phonetic ambiguity arising. We also excluded occurrences of stressed pronouns such as 'chez elle/ chez elles'.
3. The results should be read as follows: first column presents the percentage of occurrences when /l/ is deleted, and the second one, the probability calculated by Goldvarb (2001).
4. In contrast, the informants in the much earlier Canadian study described by Poplack and Walker (1986) were found to demonstrate the opposite gender pattern.
5. See Ashby (1984); Armstrong (1996); Armstrong *et al.* (2001).
6. The difference for this factor is less than for native speakers.
7. See Chapters 2 and 3 of this volume for more detail.

Chapter 8
The Variable Use of Future Temporal Reference during the Year Abroad

The last variable we studied in the speech of L2 Irish speakers of French in the context of Year Abroad is their use of future tense. Future tense usage is variable in native French and, in fact, is probably currently undergoing change. Speakers of French all over the world are tending more and more to use the periphrastic future (*je vais le faire*) as opposed to the inflected future (*je le ferai*) which was more used in former times.

This variable in the morphology of French, like the variable use of *nous/on* is interesting in terms of seeing whether the L2 speakers' variation pattern becomes closer to native speaker usage after exposure to input during the year abroad, in the same way as older stable variables (e.g. *ne* deletion) are affected. Once again, we carried out a study of L2 speaker use of the variable before and after the Year Abroad on the speech of twelve Irish students, a subset of our larger data set.

Future Tense in French

According to prescriptive grammars, there are three major variants to express future temporal reference in French:

(1) Inflected future (IF)
    Pendant l'été, je rendrai visite à ma sœur (M – 531)
    (During the summer I will visit my sister)
(2) Periphrastic future (PF) (*aller* + infinitive verb)
    Je conseillerais à quelqu'un qui va aller en France de le faire (J – 92)
    (I would advise someone who is going to France to do it)
(3) Present tense with a future value (P)
    Ils viennent cet été avec leur fille (N – 104)
    (They are coming over this summer with their daughter)

These forms are considered as variants of the same sociogrammatical variable, with the same referential value of future time reference. Prescriptive grammars have always maintained that the inflected future refers to a distant future, while the periphrastic future is used in order to present an event in a near future. Grevisse (1993) says that the inflected future 'marque un fait à venir par rapport au moment de la parole'[1] while the periphrastic future 'marque souvent un futur proche, parfois aussi un futur relativement lointain, mais considéré comme inéluctable'.[2]

Traditional grammars also see the inflected future as referring to a less assertive force of statement which expresses a level of uncertainty on the part of the speaker on the realisation of the event. Jeanjean (1988: 241) states that 'l'idée de futur est donnée d'emblée et sans limitation dans l'à venir. C'est une sorte de futur statif'.[3]

Many linguists believe that the periphrastic and inflected forms coexist and construct distinct semantico-enunciative operations. Laurendeau (2000), for example, suggests that the fundamental distinction between these operations is not temporal but rather modal. The periphrastic form is used to increase the assertive force of the statement while the inflected form is used to decrease that assertive force. He illustrates his point with the following examples: 'je vais y aller tout à l'heure' and 'j'irai tout à l'heure', concluding that the difference is in the level of certainty or uncertainty of the speaker on the realisation itself, rather than on the proximity or nonproximity of the moment of realisation. As such the second sentence would be more likely to imply 'I might go, if I feel like it', while the first sentence tends to promise the realisation of the event. (Blanche-Benveniste *et al.* (1991: 188) tell us that 'pour le rencontrer (i.e. inflected future), il suffit de le chercher là où il se trouve, c'est-à-dire dans les situations qui correspondent à son sémantisme, comme les discussions d'un projet'.[4] Confais argues that it is important to take into consideration the pragmatic attitude of the speaker in line with the part played by his/her speech:

> The [inflected future] functions less as a vehicle of the speaker's conviction with regard to the non-verifiable content of this utterance than as a sign of his 'engagement' vis-à-vis his utterance, which is thus more action-oriented [...] The [inflected future] is used more to 'interest' the interlocutor, to console, reassure, promise, give instructions, etc.... [...] 'evokes more a preparation for an event than the event itself' [...] This is why there are so many perlocutionary uses of [inflected future] than periphrastic future. (Confais, 1995)

Fleischman (1982: 83) argues that future reference is never the exclusive property of the future tense. 'At any point in time a language can use a variety of strategies (tense forms, aspectuals, modals, temporal qualifiers, or a combination of these devices) and mobilize a number of forms to express futurity'. She is supported by Vet (1993b) who states that the only context when the inflected future does not (yet) alternate with the periphrastic future is when it is used like a modal.

Poplack and Turpin (1999) have demonstrated convincingly that accepted notions of prescriptive grammarians regarding certain linguistic variables are challenged by careful empirical work on real life speech and actual usage. Specifically in relation to future tense usage it seems that in French (as used in Francophone Canada) speakers today overwhelmingly use the periphrastic future and very rarely the inflected future. Close quantitative analyses which Poplack (2000) has carried out of very large databases of natural speech data show that the inflected future is used very rarely and in very specific contexts constrained by specific factors. Among the linguistic factors which significantly affect use of the inflected future is negation. When the speaker is using a negative phrase, the likelihood of the inflected future is much greater. Similar careful quantitative analyses of continental French do not exist yet to the same extent, but it would seem reasonable (given the direction of other variables in French) that the patterns will develop in the same way, even if at a slower rate.

We will now consider research on and perceptions of the use of future tense by linguists and prescriptive grammarians in Metropolitan French.

The Variable Use of Future Temporal Reference in Metropolitan French

Various studies have been carried out on future tense in Metropolitan French from within different frameworks. Jeanjean (1988) found that native speakers of Metropolitan French were using the periphrastic and the inflected futures with nearly the same level of frequency. She recorded a nearly even distribution of inflected and periphrastic futures in her quantitative study of Metropolitan French data collected in Aix-en-Provence. In contrast, Sundell (1991) reviewed child language corpora of the 1960s dealing with inflected and periphrastic futures, and found roughly 70% inflected future and 30% periphrastic future. Aurich (1990) suggests that there are contexts in which the inflected future and the periphrastic future are both acceptable, and where the differences are only of a stylistic, or even an idiosyncratic nature. Aurich (1990: 81) submitted pages of *Huis Clos* by J-P. Sartre to five Francophones who were at university level. The task was to decide if both IF and PF were acceptable in the segments given to them. In the following example: 'Garcin: *Il faudra bien/va bien falloir qu'ils ouvrent*', both were accepted as possible. However in *'Je vous dis qu'ils l'ouvriront/vont l'ouvrir'*, there was no clear acceptance, some favouring IF for its formality, while others favoured PF as part of the process of opening the door in the close future. Interestingly enough none of the five participants chose the same future tense reference as Sartre! In general the speakers even when asked for introspective judgements which always tend to be coloured by prescriptive norms did not give the prescriptive norm as their own usage. This would suggest that their actual usage if quantitatively analysed would be less prescriptive, i.e. they would use more of the periphrastic form.

There seems to be a clear distinction between future tense usage in spoken and written language. In relation to written French, the inflected form seems to be the firmly preferred one. Wales (2002) presented figures on the relative frequency of inflected and periphrastic future forms in *Ouest-France*, a daily newspaper. It was found that the former is dominant (90% vs 10%, respectively). Wales concludes that periphrastic future typically reports new proposals or plans as current news, while the inflected future outlines details that will be realised at the time of implementation. Both functions appear to be of importance in newspapers, but current news is more often expressed in the present tense rather than the periphrastic future. Wales (2002: 90) concludes that the inflected future continues to be productive for temporal reference in contexts where it is required. However, it seems clear that in spoken language the use of inflected future is much less common.

The Variable Use of Future Temporal Reference in Canadian French

As mentioned earlier, Canadian French shows a definite preponderance in use of the periphrastic future in speech, as exemplified by Poplack and Turpin's (1999) study in Ottawa-Hull. They found 20% of inflected futures, and 73% usage of periphrastic future, concluding that 'periphrastic future occupies a default position signalling "colourless" future'. In contrast, the inflected future is used very frequently in the context of negation where it is found to be nearly categorical (0.99 vs 0.01) – and in the presence of formal pronouns of address, like *vous*, while periphrastic future was correspondingly disfavoured (0.81 vs 0.22, respectively). The study concluded that this could be an indication of the formal nature of the inflected variant. The study also showed that the choice of the present tense was unaffected by stylistic considerations. Poplack and Turpin state that unless there is a specific adverb of time, the present tense is not found to refer to a future event.

Poplack and Turpin (1999) also showed that the inflected future was less frequent in the speech of younger speakers than in that of older ones, and suggested that inflected future is gradually disappearing in informal contexts.[5] Furthermore social class was not significant in the choice of the variants, thus implying that in spoken Canadian French, use of future tense is more of a stylistic marker than an indicator of socioeconomic class. Lesage and Gagnon (1992) found that inflected future (rather than periphrastic future form) was mainly used in written French in Quebec.

In Acadian French, which tends to behave slightly differently from other varieties of Canadian French, King and Nadasdi (2003) found a robust use of the IF (53%), compared to Poplack and Turpin (1999) who found 20% IF (73% PF, and 7% P). Nor were the factors that condition the variable in Acadian French the same as in other Canadian varieties. Temporal proximity and the level of certainty of the event favour the use of periphrastic future in Acadian French, though no such correlation was found in other Canadian varieties.[6] As King and Nadasdi (2003: 336) conclude, 'Acadian French displays different patterns of morphosyntactic variation and change than its better known neighbour, Quebec French, and here shows itself to be more conservative', hence explaining the greater frequency of the inflected future, a variant seen as more standard in other Canadian varieties, as we have seen in previous studies above.

Blondeau (2005) analysed the linguistic behaviour of a group of speakers from Montreal over a period of 24 years, in relation to future tense usage. She found that the informants used PF much more than IF. Synchronic data (Emirkanian & Sankoff, 1985; Poplack & Turpin, 1999) as well as diachronic data (Poplack, 2000) provided evidence of a differential use of the future variants depending on the generation of speakers. Consequently the work of both Poplack and Blondeau suggests that inflected future is declining. Once again, the most significant factor in the choice of inflected future was the negative context. This finding would suggest, however, the continuing role of inflected future over time even where the periphrastic form is predominant in its position as a future tense marker.

Canadian Immersion and L2 Speakers and the Future Tense

Canadian immersion classroom learners and future tense expression

In relation to future tense usage by Canadian immersion learners of French L2 Nadasdi *et al.* (2003) show that the three variants under study are used with frequency quite similar to that of native speakers from Quebec (10% IF vs 67% PF vs 10% P, respectively). They attributed these results to four factors: (1) immersion teachers use the three variants of the future with the same frequency as native speakers in Canada; (2) the variant favoured by Francophones, PF, is analytical and non synthetic (they comment that learners have a natural tendency to prefer analytical structures); (3) the English language produces what the authors called a 'convergence phenomenon' with structures like 'gonna' or use of the present tense to express future events; (4) inflected future is used more frequently in the manuals used in the immersion programme than periphrastic future. These results show that the immersion learners followed only one native speaker linguistic constraint, namely: the use of a specific adverb when using the present tense. The authors therefore conclude that the Canadian immersion learners did not master native linguistic constraints in relation to this variable.

Canadian L2 speakers in the native speech community

Variability and future temporal reference in the French of Anglo-Montrealers was analysed by Dion and Blondeau (2005). They found that the learners used the same variants as native speakers from Montreal, that is, they strongly favoured the periphrastic future over the inflected future (81% vs 10%). The rate of periphrastic future is higher for Anglo-Montrealers (81%) than it is for L1 French speakers (73%) and the Toronto immersion students (78%). In the case of inflected future, the Anglo-Montrealers had the lowest rate at 10% compared with immersion learners who rated 11%, and 20% for the native speakers of Canadian French. The authors attributed this result to the current change that has been reported to be taking place in L1 Canadian French in relation to future tense (Poplack & Turpin, 1999).

Dion and Blondeau (2005) found that the L2 French of Anglo-Montrealers followed patterns similar to those of L1 Canadian French. Indeed whether inflected future was used in an affirmative or negative sentence was found to be influential in the choice of the variant. The multivariate analysis shows a probability of 0.98 for negative sentences triggering inflected future – just as it is in L1 Canadian French, at 0.99 – even though it is not explicitly taught in the classroom.[7] Hence their conclusion that 'one can confirm that L1 patterns have a better chance of being acquired by L2 speakers who interact with L1 French speakers' (Dion & Blondeau, 2005: 88).[8]

Acquisition of the Future Temporal Reference by Irish L2 Speakers Back from a Year Abroad

In examining the use of future tense forms in Irish speakers French, we focussed on a subset of a larger study analysing the speech of Irish learners of French L2 (Lemée, 2003).[9] For the present study, we analysed the speech of 12 informants – six male and six female, aged between 19 and 28 years of age who were just back from a year in France. Seven factor groups were selected for our purpose.

Linguistic factors

The linguistic factors hypothesised to affect use of future tense forms were: temporal distance, type of adverbial specification, polarity of the speech, style, type of phrase and grammatical person that we now describe below.

The temporal distance was divided into three sections: (1) Proximal – for an event happening during the day: *Je vais aller chez ma sœur ce soir*;[10] (2) Distal – for an event occurring within a week, a month, one year or at a precise moment in the near future: *Après le Leaving Cert., j'étudierai le commerce à UCD*;[11] (3) Indeterminate – for an event occurring in the future but at no precise time: *J'espère que j'aurai les points*.[12] Prescriptive grammars claim that 'le futur périphrastique est un futur immédiat: 'Attention, tu vas tomber!' Si il est accompagné d'un complément de temps, il devient alors un futur plus ou moins lointain: 'Je vais partir en septembre'[13] (Grégoire & Thiévenaz, 1995). However, IF is thought to be used when you imagine the future or when you make plans for the future, according to the same grammars.

Adverbial specification has a ternary evaluation: (1) specific (*Ils viennent à Pâques*[14]); (2) nonspecific (*Je pense qu'ils vont me visiter dans l'avenir*[15]); (3) no adverbial specification (*J'aurai à y aller*[16]).

Recent grammar books (Grégoire & Thiévenaz, 1995) for L2 learners of French put the emphasis on using IF in more formal contexts. 'On utilise de préférence le futur proche (périphrastique) à l'oral (plus dynamique) et le futur simple à l'écrit (plus économique et plus élégant).'[17] The manuals used for teaching French in classroom also stress the fact that:

> The future tense is used after **quand** in French when the action is expected to occur in the future. In English, the present is used. Note the use of the future to indicate what will happen if something else occurs: **si+ present/future:** Si il fait beau, nous irons nager. (*Voilà!*, 5th édn, 2005: 452)

Finally like Poplack and Turpin (1999) and Nadasdi et al. (2003), we coded our tokens for grammatical person. These studies have shown that first person favours PF since this tense is considered more subjective than the other variants.

Extralinguistic factors

As with several of the variables that we studied, gender was hypothesised to be a possible influencing factor. Our previous studies on the acquisition of sociostylistic variation by L2 speakers (Lemée, 2002, 2003, 2005, 2006b) showed that women favoured the more formal variants compared to men.

Results

The quantitative variationist analysis of the L2 French speech of Irish speakers after year abroad reports significant stylistic variation in the use of future temporal reference. The results show that Irish L2 learners tend to use the IF more frequently than the PF and the P is used the least of the three variants (see Table 8.1).

These results show that Irish L2 speakers tend to use the inflected future, the more formal variant, more frequently than the other variants. Contrary to Canadian immersion learners, Irish learners who have spent a year abroad do not seem to use the more analytical structure that the periphrastic future represents. We saw earlier in this chapter that immersion learners of French in Canada used the periphrastic future with a level of frequency that was closer to that found in the speech of native speakers of Canadian French.

The results also show that female L2 Irish speakers strongly favour the use of the inflected future with a probability of 0.586, vs 0.376 for their male counterparts who tend to use the periphrastic form or the present tense to express the future more frequently (see Table 8.2).

Table 8.1 Frequency use of the future tense variants by Irish L2 speakers

	%	Number of tokens
Inflected future (IF)	55	194
Periphrastic future (PF)	26	93
Present tense (P)	17	60
Total		347

Table 8.2 Gender factor effect on the use of future tense variants by Irish L2 speakers

Factor group	Factors	No.	Inflected future %	Factor weight	Periphrastic future %	Factor weight	Present tense %	Factor weight
Gender	Male	93	43	0.376	18	NS	38	NS
	Female	127	70	**0.586**	12	NS	25	NS
		Input 0.753	Log likelihood = −91,587		Sig. = 0.029			

Female L2 speakers in our study used the more conservative inflected future tense, which also reflects a generally strong tendency in the case of native female speakers. These findings are in line with what Nadasdi et al. (2003) found in relation to gender in the speech of immersion learners of French in Canada (see Table 8.3).

Inflected and periphrastic futures are both used by the Irish L2 speakers when the sentence is in the affirmative form. However negative sentences seem to strongly favour use of the present tense. For example, 'Ce soir, je ne fais pas la cuisine'. This might be explained by the fact that the present tense conveys a certain level of certainty about the realisation of the event announced. 'Tonight I am not cooking' and that is a certainty.

Style appears to produce the expected results with the inflected future being favoured in formal contexts (0.636), while periphrastic future and present tense are favoured in informal contexts (0.519 and 0.509, respectively). When looking at the relationship between gender and formality, the results show that women tend to use the more formal variant in formal contexts (70%), while men do not seem to have any real preference.

Temporal distance seems to significantly influence use of the variants. When distal, the present is used, while proximal and indeterminate reference of the event favour the periphrastic future. This phenomenon may be explained by the fact that grammar books used by L2 learners clearly indicate the 'versatile' nature of the periphrastic future which is normally a *'futur immédiat'*,[19] but accompanied by a specific adverb becomes then *'un futur plus ou moins lointain'*[20] (Grégoire & Thiévenaz, 1995).

As we saw earlier, the use of inflected future in negative sentences is especially attested in Canadian French. Interestingly, the Irish female L2 speakers use this variant in negative contexts too, contrary to their male counterparts who seem to use the three variants without a strong preference for any one in particular. Perhaps the female L2 Irish speakers are picking up on native speaker constraints more quickly than male speakers (see Table 8.4).

Table 8.3 Goldvarb 2001 results for the linguistic factors

Linguistic factors	Inflected future	Periphrastic future	Present
Adverbial specification[18]			
Specific	0.311	NS*	**0.689**
Nonspecific	**0.774**	NS	0.326
No adverb	0.591	NS	0.409
Polarity			
Affirmative	**0.539**	**0.547**	0.453
Negative	0.301	0.258	**0.742**
Style			
Formal	**0.636**	0.458	0.476
Informal	0.458	**0.519**	**0.509**
Temporal distance			
Proximal	NS	**0.680**	0.32
Distal	NS	0.303	**0.697**
Indeterminate	NS	0.529	0.371
Type of phrase	NS	NS	NS
Grammatical person	NS	NS	NS
*NS = nonsignifiant	Input 0.685 Log likelihood = –173,600 Sig. = 0.027	Input 0.787 Log likelihood = –128,129 Sig. = 0.015	Input 0.620 Log likelihood = –92,600 Sig. = 0.172

Table 8.4 Cross-tabulation between gender and polarity in the use of future tense variants by Irish speakers of French L2

Polarity		*Male*	%	*Female*	%
Affirmative	IF		47	IF	61
	PF		36	PF	24
	P		16	P	28
Negative	IF		36	IF	67
	PF		36	PF	4
	P		18	P	30

Conclusion

It appears that in relation to this less stable variable which is undergoing change in progress in native speaker French, the response of the year abroad speakers is more ambiguous than to *ne* deletion, the more stable variable. Instead of using more periphrastic future forms in general than inflected forms, they do the opposite and use more inflected forms. However, the gender pattern which we have seen in relation to other variables is also strong in relation to future tense, with female speakers using more of the formal variant than the informal. They use more inflected forms than do male speakers in formal contexts. Female Irish speakers seem to have understood the native norms here in relation to formality.

It may be that in a new change, the L2 speakers feel less secure in using what they hear in the input, and fall back more on what they have learnt in their prescriptive grammars in relation to future tense and so use more of the inflected future.

However, despite the fact that the L1 variation pattern in relation to periphrastic vs. inflected is not quite grasped here by the year abroad learners, other aspects of the L1 grammar in relation to future tense have been acquired such as gender patterns and formality/informality patterns. So once again even here we can say that the Year Abroad experience has been positive in relation to the acquisition of sociolinguistic variation patterns.

Notes

1. Marks an event to come at the time of speech.
2. Often marks a near future, sometimes a fairly distant future too, but considered as inevitable.
3. The idea of future is given straight away in the time to come. It is a state future.
4. To find it you have to look for it in places corresponding to its semantics, that is, in discussions about projects.
5. This brings to mind what happened to the '*passé simple*' and what is happening to the subjunctive forms.
6. This difference between Acadian varieties of Canadian French has been remarked elsewhere, for example, Conrick and Regan (2007).
7. This differs from the results found in the speech of immersion learners in Toronto.
8. For more details about this research, see Blondeau *et al.* (2002) and Nagy *et al.* (2003).
9. We excluded from the multivariate analysis all tokens not referring to a future event including habitual reference tokens as exemplified in (a) or proverbial sentences such as in (b).

(a) *je crois que d'habitude ce **sera** difficile de rencontrer des gens à UCD.* (I think usually it will be difficult to meet people in UCD)
(b) *qui **vivra verra**.* (Who will live will see)
'Repair' sentences such as *'c'est que ça **pourra** ça pourrait être'* were also excluded because of the ambiguity displayed. We also excluded occurrences of non-native use of future tense or of non-native forms of future.
10. I am going to my sister tonight.
11. After the Leaving Cert, I will study Commerce in UCD.
12. I hope I will get the points.
13. The periphrastic future is an immediate future: 'Watch out, you are going to fall!' If accompanied by an adverb of time, then it becomes a distant future: 'I am going to go in September'.
14. They come at Easter.
15. I think that they will come and visit in the future.
16. I will have to go there.
17. Periphrastic future is preferably used in the oral (more dynamic) and the inflected future when writing (more economical and more elegant) (Grégoire & Thiévenaz, 1995).
18. This table shows that as far as adverbial specification is concerned, the more specific adverbs strongly favour the use of the present tense. The use of inflected future does not appear to require a specific adverb as such. It is found without any adverb or with nonspecific adverbs. This might be explained by its specific inflected form. For example, *J'irai en vacances en France*. This factor group does not seem to play a significant role in the case of the periphrastic future.
19. Immediate future.
20. More or less distant future.

Chapter 9
The Role of Gender in the Acquisition of Sociolinguistic Competence in an L2 During the Year Abroad

Gender has been shown by recent research to have been one of the most important factors in language acquisition during the year abroad. Gender impacts on many aspects of the experience of year abroad, such as practical issues of young womens' lack of freedom to move about physically and varying culture specific attitudes towards women in different host countries; identities which women feel they should adopt or which, on the contrary, they refuse to adopt as Western women in one study (Marriott, 1995) refused to adopt the behaviour of native female Japanese speakers, which they felt to be too much at variance with their identity as independent Western females. This is exemplified as Kinginger (2004) analyses the experiences of American students in France and identity issues in relation to year abroad.[1] The role of gender in second language acquisition in a year abroad setting is interesting not only for what it adds to what we know about women's use of language in general, but because it is an important causal variable in the process of language acquisition, successful or otherwise, during this time. As several recent studies have shown gender has directly affected access to input which clearly affects outcomes.

Women and Language

The study of language and women has undergone many transformations in the past hundred years. Interest in gender as a conditioning factor in language is not new. Women linguists, in particular, have been interested in the effect of gender on language use. Roszak and Roszak (1969) signals the start of a period of more intense speculation about gender differences in language. Morgan (1970) and Troth (1970) also testify to the emerging feminist critique of language usage. The 1970s see a substantial amount of work carried out on women's use of language (Firestone, 1971;

Gornick & Moran, 1971; Hole & Levine, 1971). This work was mostly placed within a dominance paradigm, and written from a feminist perspective. Then a substantial body of research on the use of language by women began to emerge from a variationist tradition (often criticised by feminist linguistics for its use of the gender variable in its investigations, for instance, Freed & Greenwood, 1996), although these criticisms have been addressed in the 'later Labovian' research on language and gender. Differences are justified by the fact that previous studies suggested that there was good reason to expect that gender differences were likely to be important, and so there was strong justification for carrying out empirical studies of language use in relation to gender. Previous studies in relation both to L1 and to L2 strongly indicated that gender differences were important so it was reasonable for variationist linguists to collect data with a view to further investigating these findings. Clearly, the interpretation of the results revealed by quantitative analysis is where issues of the social construction of gender becomes important as well as issues of communities of practice. We will outline both data from variationist studies in relation to gender as well as varying interpretations of these data.

Quantitative Findings on Language and Gender

Variationist studies of English speech found that women speakers consistently used prestige variants where a choice existed, whereas men speakers tended to use nonprestige variants. For example, in an early quantitative study, Fischer (1958) found, in relation to *in/ing* use by school children, that girls used more of the prestige variant velar *-ing* and boys used more of the nonprestige apical *-in'*. Labovian analysis found detailed quantitative evidence for the same configuration of womens' speech. The earliest studies were of US English, but soon, similar variation patterns were found in relation to other Englishes.[2] In England and Scotland, Trudgill (1974b) and Macaulay (1978), respectively found differences between the sexes in the lower middle class. Women were less likely to use the nonprestige glottal stop than men in Glasgow. In a study of sociolinguistic variation in Norwich, Trudgill (1974b) proposed the notion of 'covert' prestige, which men try to acquire by using nonprestige variants which are seen as more male and tough.

Subsequently to the patterns for *in/ing* variation, variationist research found similar patterns for numerous other variables: Wolfram (1969) found that women used less double negation, less copula deletion and more postvocalic *r*. Labov's (1966) study of the social stratification of English in

New York city found that women speakers use more of the prestige variant, in this case, the interdental [θ] as in *these, them* than men who used more of the nonprestige dental fricative [d]. As for in/ing, the tendency for women to choose the prestige variant was found not to be confined to American English. Robust results confirmed over and over that certain patterns were part of what was considered women's language.

Such seemingly convincing evidence that women use more prestige variants than men was variously ascribed to conservative use of language by women because of their role as caretakers passing on prescribed linguistic forms to their children, or 'linguistic insecurity' on women's part which makes them compensate for their relatively powerless position in society by using prestigious speech forms.

However, the picture turned out to be more complicated than had appeared initially. Different evidence subsequently emerged which seemed to contradict the initial conclusion that women are more conservative in their use of language than men. A study of a French-speaking village, Charmey, Switzerland by Gauchat (1905) from 1899 to 1904, found that in relation to ongoing sound changes there, women were, in fact, leading and that it was they who tended to forget the old sounds more quickly than the men in the village. This first truly sociolinguistic study of its kind, where male and female use is clearly divergent remains unique for its time, a period of classical dialectology when variation was assumed to obey rigid laws and only men spoke true dialect. A second study of the same community in 1929 found that women were still leading in ongoing changes. Later, Lenning (1977) studied vowel shifts in Parisian French and found that men were remaining stable with respect to these changes and that new changes were being carried by women. Ashby (1976, 1984) found in a study of French in Tours, that women were again leading in what he considered ongoing sound changes, *ne* deletion in negative constructions and /l/ deletion in clitic pronouns. Gal (1978, 1979) studied the Hungarian-German community of Oberwart in Austria. She found that language choice was part of a life choice and identity choice on the part of young women in Hungary. The young women were leading in the shift from Hungarian to German because these young women associated peasant life from which they wished to escape with Hungarian. The young women refused to mediate between two languages and cultures and strategically adopted German in order precisely to escape the social position as peasants. Similarly, Feagin (1979) found that women were leading in sound changes in vowels in all classes in Alabama English. And Milroy (1988), in addition, found that women in Belfast who worked in 'male' workplaces such as docklands used some nonprestige variants more than men.

Another body of evidence emerged which ran counter to the presumption that women used prestige forms more than men. Sociolinguistic studies in the Middle East and South Asia showed that men used prestige forms more than women did. In fact the pattern here was reversed. Abdel-Jawad (1981) found that women in Amman had lower use of the classical standard /q/ than men. Bakir (1986) examined the distribution of Classical Arabic variants and local Iraqi variants, and found similarly that women used less of the prestige variants. In addition, similar patterns emerged in Cairo, Damascus and Syria. Haeri (1994, 1996, 2003) did an ethnographic study of the relationship between Classical Arabic and Cairene Arabic. One of the findings was that given men's use of the prestige language, they had better access to jobs which required use of Classical Arabic. Conclusions generally drawn from these studies were that men have more access to Classical Arabic in educational and other contexts and therefore show greater use of prestige forms than women.

These seemingly contradictory patterns contribute to what has been called the 'gender paradox' and for which Labov (1990) posits three principles:

Principle 1. For stable sociolinguistic variables, men use a higher frequency of nonstandard forms than women.

Principle 1a. In change from above, women favour the incoming prestige form more than men.

Principle 2. In change from below, women are most often the innovators.

The Second or 'Later' Wave of Labovian Research on Women's Use of Language

Evidence of linguistic behaviour which seemed indeed to run counter to earlier results of variationist work led to a new generation of linguists who turned a critical attention to aspects of Labov's principles. This new generation of variationist researchers began to differentiate between the mainly biological category 'sex' and the more differentiated concept of gender as social construct. One of the earliest studies which impacted significantly on and changed the direction of research approaches to gender and language was Eckert (1988). This study of adolescent language practices in an American high school adopted an ethnographic approach. The researcher spent over two years in the community and explored what it meant to be male or female in that community. She found in relation to the adolescents that membership of their particular social group (Jocks or Burnouts[3]) was more important than sex in relation to the use of some language features. Subsequent research has tended to take into account the social and political context of the linguistic situation and tries to avoid an overly simplistic view of sex as a discrete factor in language use.

All these studies show that in language practices, no simplistic notion of sex as a discrete factor in variation will suffice in an analysis of language use. An example of this, for instance, is Nichols (1983), which showed that the choice of use of creole or nonstandard forms in the speech of Gullah speakers was significantly influenced by the fact that women's social networks brought them into contact with more standard English speakers, and so they used less nonstandard forms than men speakers whose employment kept them more in the same groups of people. Other factors were acting along with that of sex in producing language variation.

Many more ethnographic and anthropological studies of speech communities with the researcher as participant-observer demonstrated the importance of gender as a social construct and also gender as practice in studies of communities of practice (Eckert, 2000; Eckert & McConnell-Ginet, 2003; Holmes, 1999; Holmes & Meyerhoff, 2003). Holmes and Marra (2004), in an interesting study, examined workplace practices where relational practice largely goes unrecognised and unrewarded. The study shows how a range of different ways in which people avoid performing such relational practice and how this is considered 'women's work'. It is also made clear that this can be different in different communities of practice. Cameron (2005) carried out a detailed study of issues of aging and gender and the relationship between the two in relation to three sociolinguistic variables of Puerto Rican Spanish. In addition, Cameron studies the question in relation to other varieties of Spanish, German and English, focusing on variables that are stable, undergoing change or in the end stage of loss. In short, a wider interpretation of the role of gender in language use in society is now generally accepted, studies having been carried out now not only on English but on many language types, and in relation to many different age groups, from small children to elderly people. Holmes and Meyerhoff (2003) talk of a shift in the field of language and gender best described as a movement away from 'essentialist and dichotomous conceptions of gender to a differentiated, contextualized, and performative model which question generalized claims about gender'. This 'second phase' work highlighted the fact that sex is a biological concept and gender is a social construct arising out of social interaction. Research now avoids reducing the interpretation of a person's gender to a biological reality but rather analyses how this comes to be built up through social relationships with others. This is what defines our social identity and our gender, not simply physical or biological characteristics. Gender can no longer be adequately analysed as a simple dichotomy, but as 'the accomplishment and product of social interaction. Language is a resource which can be drawn on creatively to perform different aspects of one's social identity at different points in an interaction' (Holmes & Meyerhoff, 2003: 11). Gender is something you 'do' or perform.[4]

Gender and L2 Acquisition

As we have seen, a considerable amount of research in recent years has been done on how speakers use linguistic variants to express gendered identities in different contexts in native speaker speech. Keeping in mind the important body of recent research (Coates, 1993; Ehrlich, 2001; Holmes, 1994, 1995, 1997, 1998; Mendoza-Denton, 2004) which cogently demonstrated the dangers and limitations of an overly simplistic interpretation of the category of sex in investigations of the role of gender in language, there is nevertheless much evidence that speakers use language to mark their gender in different contexts or types of talk (Freed, 1996). People make linguistic choices and even seem to be aware from a very early age that language behaviour is gendered. In relation to L1 acquisition, variationist studies have found that children, even at a very young age, seem to be conscious of and are capable of adopting the gendered variation patterns of the context in which they find themselves. For instance Roberts and Labov (1995) and Roberts (1997) found that American English-speaking children as young as three years old were using the adult speech patterns in relation to *t/d* deletion and *in/ing* variation. Payne (1980) also discovered that young children coming into a new community very soon adopted the sociolinguistic norms and variation patterns of that community.

Now while the role of gender in L1 speech has been the subject of numerous investigations and from within many different paradigms, the same cannot be said of how gender relates to language use in the case of the multilingual or second language speaker. Although research in second language acquisition and multilingualism is by now well developed, with a rich literature investigating the acquisition of other languages from multiple perspectives, sociolinguistic and psycholinguistic. In effect, interest in gender as a variable in second language learning has gained momentum only relatively recently, although there does exist an early study as far back as the 1960s which recognised the issue. Scherer and Wertheimer comment:

> the validity analyses indicated that sex and age, and to some degree, year in college, do seem to be factors important in ability to profit from a course in German. (Scherer & Wertheimer, 1964: 51)

Given the strongly psycholinguistic tendency of SLA in its earlier stages during the 1960s and 1970s, there was often a strong universalistic underpinning to SLA research. The individual psycholinguistic aspects of acquisition were focused on by a 20th century linguistic tradition which was concerned to search only for the invariant in language. The learning process in its social context was virtually ignored and with it individual variables. Gender, as one of these variables, was almost never considered. However, more recently, as sociolinguistic and sociocultural approaches have increasingly begun to throw light on central themes and topics in SLA, more attention has been focused on gender as an influencing variable in the acquisition and use of second, third and other languages by speakers from all sorts of view, from access to input, to acquisition of speech norms (Regan, 1998b). Studies of SLA from within a social context perspective began to look more closely at the detail of the acquisition process, and discovered that only by examining this within the social context could one begin to provide a richer, more fully-rounded picture of what was actually going on during the process of L2 acquisition. Notions of gender were found to be very different depending on where the language was being spoken, in which community, which country, the relationship of the L2 speaker to the speakers within that community; in fact, a picture was emerging which was less essentialist and more relative. SLA was intricately involved with issues such as the degree of access the speaker had to speech and speakers of the other language, relations of power and solidarity between the L2 speaker and the majority language.

An early example of a study which was more sensitive to issues of gender in its interrelations with other social relations was that of Siegal (1995) who studied the acquisition of sociolinguistic competence by two women, English L1 speakers, in Japanese. It was found that even after a year living and studying in Japan, proficiency was still quite low in general for learners who spent a year in Japan, and particularly in relation to sociolinguistic competence. In a wider study, Siegal (1996) undertook to study four individual women speakers in their everyday interactional encounters while they studied and lived in Japan. Results indicate that the women found themselves in a conflict where they were trying to use honorific Japanese language as Japanese women did and at the same time trying to 'maintain face', especially in relation to their own image of themselves as Western women. This was one of the first studies of what it was like to be a woman trying to 'do things' in the L2 community, with L2 language: what it was like to be a woman in the L2 country, in this case Japan, and how the L2 speaker reacted to this. Since this work, there has been a general attempt to understand gender and its relationship between SLA and multilingualism in a more nuanced way. Recent volumes such as Pavlenko (2001, 2005), Pavlenko *et al.* (2001), Pavlenko and Dewaele (2004), Bayley and Schecter (2003) have provided further research on the area of gender, multilingualism and second language learning.

Studies in SLA, taking a broader approach to the issue of gender as a social and cultural variable, have found some significant effects (Romaine, 2003a, b). Gass and Varonis (1986), while studying sex differences in conversational interactions among Japanese speakers of English, found that mixed-sex dyads showed a greater number of negotiations than single-sex dyads. They also found that women speakers were responsible for twice as many such negotiations as men. Their study also showed that male speakers had a greater number of conversational turns in mixed-sex dyads, and that men also tended to lead the conversation in a picture-description task even when women were assigned the role of describing the picture to the male who could not see it. All these findings replicate patterns found in the speech of native speakers (Holmes, 1994).

Gender may be an important factor affecting the outcome of the SLA process (Siegal & Okamoto, 1996). A survey among Dutch students of English (Broeders, 1982) revealed that women L2 speakers tended to use prestige pronunciation more than their male counterparts. This seems to suggest that women tend to favour prestige speech when learning other languages as they do in their L1. Chavez (2001) researched on gender in the classroom and maintains that (1) gender as a learner variable interacts with additional learner characteristics, in the case of instructed learners, such as age, personality type, other academic subjects studied and language learning motivation; (2) gender, influenced by both biological and environmental, including cultural and social constraints cannot be conceived of as simply a binary variable, very much as researchers in relation to L1 speech had posited; (3) gender in second language learning must be viewed in the context of language and cultural contact, and as such gender-linked learner behaviour may vary according to the context in which the language is being learnt and used, the availability and explicitness of input, and the relationship of the learner to the potential new identity or identities they may be confronted with when they learn another language;[5] (4) when we study gender as a learner variable we can better understand how men and women set about learning another language, perhaps how likely either is to succeed in a certain context, in relation to a particular task because these vary and may significantly affect outcomes.

Since the mid-1990s there has been an increasing amount of research dealing with gender and second language acquisition. L2 gender studies have found quantitative and qualitative differences between males and females in such diverse phenomena as the relationship between gender and acquisition in classrooms and communities (Pavlenko et al., 2001), rate of interaction (Kasanga, 1996), age and rate of learning (Slavoff & Johnson, 1995), acculturation (Jewell, 1992), pragmatics (Kaspar & Schmidt, 1996), motivation (Dörnyei & Clement, 2001), gender as social practice (Ehrlich, 1997), gain during study abroad (Pica et al., 1989; Brecht et al., 1995), comprehensible output (Gass & Varonis, 1986; Pica et al., 1989), NNS/NNS interactions (Gass & Varonis, 1986).[6] All these studies have underlined the complexity of gender as a social construct and the variation that gender categories and gender relations can exhibit across speech communities and social contexts (Ellis, 1994).

Variationist Perspectives on Gender and Second Language Acquisition

Specifically within the variationist paradigm, a steady emergence of data regarding second language acquisition and gender has been apparent since the 1990s. We will briefly review research in this area and then consider this research and the issue of study abroad or year abroad. As we have seen previously in Chapter 1, research which took a sociolinguistic or particularly variationist approach to second language acquisition began only in the 1970s. Gender was identified as a significant factor in a study of second language acquisition which looked at the acquisition of community speech norms by Vietnamese and Cambodian speakers of English L2 (Adamson & Regan, 1991). Among the findings of this study was an interesting one regarding the behaviour of men and women L2 speakers in relation to L1 variation patterns. Using a detailed Varbrul analysis, the authors found that male speakers went to great lengths to approximate what they saw as male native speaker patterns in relation to *in/ing* alternation in English. The male speakers used *-in* more frequently than women speakers especially, curiously, in monitored speech. We interpreted this as a reflection of their wish to accommodate to a male native speaker norm rather than an overall native speaker norm. In fact, gender norms for these speakers was a more important feature than style (where in monitored style one would expect more use of the prestige variant *-ing*. In fact, in light of the speakers' L1s, it would have been easier in production terms for the speakers to use *-ing*. So, in fact, the speakers were working quite hard to approximate gender norms in the L2 community in which they were now living in Philadelphia. For these male L2 speakers, they were being 'male' in their new community. '[T]hese two groups of speakers may be accommodating toward different targets: non-native females toward native females and non-native males toward native males' (Adamson & Regan, 1991: 13). This was probably among the first variationist studies of second language acquisition to focus on gender as playing a central role. In fact it showed the speakers constructing their identity partly through their awareness and use of gendered language.

A second significant variationist study which shows the importance of gender as a feature of identity construction is Major (2004). This research examined variation in native-like forms by investigating gender and stylistic differences in the English of native speakers and native speakers of Japanese and Spanish, with equal numbers of men and women in each L1 group. Major studied four phonological processes which are widespread in all varieties of American English: (1) palatalisation in four environments (e.g. *got you* → *go*[č] *you*, *did you* → *di*[ĵ] *you*, *this year* → *thi*[š] *year*, *raise your* → *rai*[ž] *your*), (2) deletion of *v* in *of* (e.g. *can o' beans*), (3) -*ing* pronounced *in'* (e.g. *runnin'*),[7] and (4) *n* assimilation in *can* (e.g. [n] → [m] in *I ca*[m] *be here*, [n] → [ń] in *she ca*[ń] *go*). The results from native speaker speech demonstrated that there were significant differences based on gender and style. Both groups of non-native speakers showed significant differences based on gender but only one group showed significant stylistic differences. The results of both groups clearly indicated that for these four phonological processes, gender differences were acquired before stylistic differences. One of Major's interesting conclusions is that where some gender differences can reflect pejorative stereotypes about men and women (especially in the areas of sexist language and semantic, pragmatic and discourse differences), in the area of phonology, there seems less likelihood of differences being due to negative stereotyping. He concludes that 'gender differences are indeed salient and should be included in any full description of interlanguage' (Major, 2004: 180).

Adamson and Regan (1991) and Major (2004), both variationist studies which revealed gender difference in L2 language use, were studies of speakers in naturalistic contexts. There is, however, also evidence of gender differences in L2 speech in instructed contexts. An interesting context for second language acquisition is that of the immersion classroom. Numerous accounts are available of the effects throughout the world of immersion education on second language acquisition.[8]

A wealth of material has emerged in recent years from the work of Mougeon and his colleagues on the acquisition of variation patterns in immersion schools in Canada. This work has resulted in a better understanding of how sociolinguistic competence is acquired during the immersion experience thanks to numerous detailed quantitative studies of this aspect of second language acquisition. By considering in their analysis the many factors hypothesised to account for variation in the speech of the immersion learners, the researchers built up a picture of the sociolinguistic competence of these speakers in an instructed setting.

In relation specifically to gender and the acquisition of sociolinguistic competence in French, Mougeon *et al.* (2001), Mougeon and Rehner (2001) and Rehner *et al.* (2003) studied 41 immersion students from three Greater Toronto area high schools and found that female speakers tend to favour variants that are typical of standard usage (as opposed to more vernacular variants) (for instance, *ne* maintenance, use of *seulement* (only), and the inflected future: *demain, j'irai à la piscine*). Mougeon and his colleagues suggested that the reason for this is that in the classroom speech of immersion teachers and in the course materials used in the immersion context, the formal variants are used frequently if not all the time. The students then are led to infer that the favoured variants are standard and prestigious or associated with formal register. This would then explain why the female students favour the standard variants more than male students do. Rehner *et al.* (2003) in their study of the alternate use of *nous/on*, show that male speakers use *on* (the less prestige variant) slightly more than their female counterparts. The authors conclude that the students have inferred that *nous* is more standard than *on*. The study also showed that since the use of *nous* is highly marked, both socially and stylistically in spoken Canadian French, the students who had increased extracurricular exposure to this variety of French would have received confirmation of the sociostylistic value they had inferred from the treatment of the variants in the immersion context. Mougeon and Rehner (2001) found that female learners used the restrictive adverb *seulement* (only) more than male learners, and Nadasdi *et al.* (2001) showed that inflected future (e.g. *je lui parlerai demain*) was more frequent in the speech of female learners.[9]

Rehner *et al.*'s (2003) findings with regard to gender are consistent with those of Blondeau and Nagy (1998) for Anglophone speakers of French L2 in Montreal, this time in uninstructed or naturalistic settings. In their study of nondoubled subjects (e.g. *Pierre parle* vs *Pierre, il parle*), Blondeau and Nagy found that female L2 speakers used the formal variant more often than male speakers.

In general, although there were exceptions in relation to certain variables, Mougeon and his colleagues found that of L2 speakers in immersion programmes in Canada female speakers tended to choose the prestige forms where there was a choice and where they perceived the variant to be prestigious; and to this extent, were replicating the classic L1 behaviour in relation to prestige variants.

The Acquisition of Sociolinguistic Variation Patterns: Gender and the Year Abroad

We have seen that after a lengthy period of monolingual bias in relation to gender in second language acquisition more research is recently being carried out in this area. For instance, despite calls for such, less attention has been paid to the issue of context, gender and second language acquisition. While scholars insist on the importance of context as an influencing factor in the role of gender in SLA, there is still little real empirical research which investigates this in any detailed way. We will now focus on research we have carried out on study abroad as a context of acquisition and we will analyse the role of gender in this particular context.

As with the issue of gender and second language acquisition, in relation to context specifically, we need to ask the following questions:

- How do L2 speakers, whether in instructed or in natural settings, use the sometimes limited L2 resources at their command to enact gendered identities and how does this affect their acquisition of the target?
- How do the gendered identities of target-language societies in which the L2 speakers are living and the L2 speakers' acceptance or rejection of these identities for themselves affect the way they acquire and use the L2? Which role models do they have in terms of being male or female in the L2 community?
- How does the amount of participation which male and female speakers have in the L2 community affect learners' access to the sociolinguistic norms of that speech community? Regan (1995, 1998b) for instance, found that contact with native speakers was a significant feature in the acquisition of sociolinguistic competence during a year abroad.

While currently there is a substantial amount of qualitative work being carried out from various perspectives in relation to sociolinguistic competence in L2 acquisition, it is important also to provide empirical data from detailed linguistic studies on the actual language of L2 users. Only by having this empirical data can we hope to approach the full picture of this aspect of acquisition. In the following section we will provide close-up, detailed, quantitative data from our projects on the acquisition of sociolinguistic competence during a year abroad by Irish English speakers of French. While carrying out Varbrul multifactorial analyses of the four variables previously presented (/l/ deletion, *nous/on* alternation, *ne* retention and the expression of the future), we focused on gender as a factor in their language use, with the wider aim of investigating the role of gender in the acquisition of sociolinguistic competence during a year abroad.

Gender as a Factor in Relation to Four Linguistic Variables in French L2: /l/ Deletion, *Nous/On* Alternation, *Ne* Retention and the Expression of the Future

/l/ deletion

An earlier study (Howard *et al.*, 2006) showed that female learners favoured /l/ deletion in clitic subject pronouns to a much greater extent than male speakers (see Table 9.1).

These results suggest that these second language female speakers have a similar pattern to the variation patterns produced by native female speakers. They are similar to the patterns found by Armstrong (1996) for L1 speakers. He showed that the female speakers produced the newer, incoming variant more than male speakers in relation to deletion of /l/ (the classic Labovian pattern). Armstrong observed a deletion rate of 35.2% amongst his adolescent male informants aged 16–19, as opposed to a rate of 54.2% amongst their female counterparts in the same age group. /l/ deletion rates for Irish L2 speakers of French suggest that female L2 speakers behave in the same way as native female speakers. These findings in relation to French L2 are similar to the earlier studies by Adamson and Regan (1991) and that of Major (2004) which showed that L2 male and female speakers approximated native speaker norms. The findings that female speakers are leading in newer changes are similar to many other studies which find that new changes are often carried by women and especially by young women.

Nous/On alternation

Behaviour in relation to *nous/on* alternation by L2 speakers also follows the same patterns as that of native speakers. In her study of the

Table 9.1 /l/ deletion by L2 speakers after year abroad

Factors	No. deleted	% deleted	Factor weight
Male	242	22	0.386
Female	413	45	0.630

Table 9.2 *Nous /on* alternation by L2 speakers after year abroad

Factors	No. on	% on	Factor weight
Male	368	72	0.585
Female	163	63	0.336

alternate use of *nous/on* by Irish-English learners of French, Lemée (2003) finds that male speakers, after a year abroad, use the informal pronoun *on* much more frequently than their female counterparts (see Table 9.2).

These results show that female learners stay much closer to the more formal and standard style with a higher frequency of *nous* (37% vs 28%). Mougeon *et al.* (2003) found a similar pattern in relation to the speech of immersion learners of French in Ontario. In both cases female speakers seem to realise that *nous* is socially and stylistically marked. Coveney (2000), in relation to French L1 in France, and Laberge (1977), in relation to French L1 in Canada, found that style is a crucial factor in the choice between *nous* and *on*. It seems that as regards *nous/on* alternate use, Irish L2 speakers, after their stay in France, seem to approximate what native speakers do in relation to gender patterns.

Ne retention

We find that in relation also to a stable sociolinguistic variable (*ne* deletion) as opposed to ongoing changes, L2 speakers follow the gendered patterns of L1 speakers of French, after being exposed to native speaker input during the Year Abroad. As we have seen earlier women tend to retain *ne* more than men (see Table 9.3).

In a study of *ne* retention and gender by Lemée and Regan (2008), results show that *ne* retention is reasonably high for both male and female

Table 9.3 Retention of *ne* by L2 speakers after year abroad

Factors	No. ne	% ne	Factor weight
Male	191	52	0.424
Female	171	65	0.576
Input = 0.603 Log likelihood = −305,7567 Significance = 0.044			

L2 speakers, with a higher rate for women (65% vs 52%). This is in line with the expected direction for female native speakers who favour the prestige form in general in the case of a stable variable.

The expression of the future

In the use of future tense, Lemée (2006a) finds that female L2 speakers strongly favour the use of the inflected future (e.g. *j'irai à l'université demain*), unlike their male counterparts who tend to use the periphrastic form to express the future (e.g. *l'année prochaine je vais aller à l'université*) or the present tense (e.g. *demain, c'est moi qui fait les courses*) to express the future more frequently, as the percentages show.[10] The use of the inflected future is the more conservative variant in this case (see Table 9.4).

Conclusion

Recent variationist research, and in particular the research we have carried out on year abroad as a setting for acquisition, by looking closely at the detail of what speakers actually do, suggests that context is crucial to the acquisition of L1 variation patterns by L2 speakers – and especially the issue of whether L2 speakers have access to native speaker speech. In relation to gender, these detailed empirical studies provide compelling evidence that recent claims for the importance of carrying out ethnographic work are indeed justified. Carrying out detailed quantitative studies which focuses on language but is informed by contextual ethnographic and anthropological knowledge promises to provide the fullest and richest picture of the acquisition of sociolinguistic variation patterns by L2 speakers.

Based on these data on year abroad and gender, all of them produced by Varbrul, multivariate analyses, we can draw certain conclusions in

Table 9.4 The future tense by L2 speakers after year abroad

Factors	No. IF	%	Factor weight	No. PF	%	Factor weight	No. Pr	%	Factor weight
Male	40	43	0.376	17	18	NS	36	38	NS
Female	90	70	0.586	16	12	NS	57	25	NS

Input = 0.753
Log likelihood = –91,587
Sig. = 0.029

relation to male/female variation patterns and Year Abroad as a causal variable. It appears, at least for the population we studied of Irish students and their stay in France, that, both in relation to stable sociolinguistic variables and also to ongoing changes in French, the L2 speakers after exposure to L1 input in France, have a strong tendency to emulate native speaker variation patterns. It appears that these advanced learners have 'noticed' gender patterns in native speech and, consciously or unconsciously, tend to reproduce them. Our findings concur with those of Adamson and Regan (1991) and Major (2004), in relation to the acquisition of L1 sociolinguistic variation patterns and the crucial role of gender as a factor in this area of acquisition. It also appears from research in language and gender in general, that gender is an important element in the L2 speaker's construction of his/her identity in another community.

Notes

1. See also Kinginger and Farrell Whitworth (2005) and Kinginger and Blattner (2008).
2. See also Horvath (1985) for Australia.
3. These categories refer to two distinct social groups towards which adolescents gravitate in the United States; the Jocks tending to be more middle class and focused on school and sports, the Burnouts more working class and focused on the town.
4. For an outline of the history of the treatment of gender in relation to language use, see Regan (1992).
5. Very much as in the case of the women in Marriot's (1995) study of the Anglophone learners of Japanese.
6. For a more comprehensive list, see Major (2004).
7. This process should properly be considered a morpho-phonological process since it is limited to the -*ing* morpheme, whereas the other three processes are strictly phonological, since they are not morpheme-dependent.
8. See, for example, Conrick and Regan (2007) on immersion in Canada, de Courcy (2002) in Australia, Hickey (1997) in Ireland.
9. However some studies have shown either no gender effect [Dewaele and Regan (2002) on *ne* deletion; Nadasdi *et al.* (2001) on third person plural subject-verb agreement] or they find the opposite pattern (Nagy *et al.*, 1996), in relation to [t^s] as an allophone of /t/ and [d^z] as an allophone of /d/ as in *tu dis* [t^syd^{z}i].
10. All these findings are in line with what Nadasdi *et al.* (2003) found in the speech of immersion learners of French in Canada.

Chapter 10
Spending a Year Abroad: Do We Acquire Sociolinguistic Competence?

Introduction: Findings from our Research

In this chapter we summarise what we have learnt about second language acquisition and the year abroad experience, in particular, the acquisition of sociolinguistic competence. We will also present some theoretical issues raised by our research. We show how the approach we use involving detailed fine-grained empirical analyses of the speech elicited from our study abroad speakers has helped us to shine light on areas of second language acquisition, the detail of which might otherwise have been difficult to access. The variationist paradigm within which we have constructed our databases, analysed our data and interpreted our results, has permitted us to have a close picture of the texture of variation in the evolving speech of speakers in the year abroad experience and to determine in quantitative terms the multiple factors (as well as the constraint hierarchies) relating to these variants.

Research Questions

Our research aims in studying the year abroad using a variationist perspective and quantitative analysis were to investigate precisely how the L2 speaker acquires new variation patterns, how this is affected by social context, whether the gains made on the level of variation patterns are maintained in the longer term, whether gender plays a role in this process of acquisition and if so, what role does it play, and how the acquisition of native speaker patterns relates to identity construction on the part of the L2 speaker.

In order to describe and analyse the process and product of acquiring sociolinguistic competence, as this is instantiated by the acquisition of native speaker variation patterns, we chose variables for investigation each of which, in different ways, illustrated aspects of this domain of acquisition. The variables we analysed are all sociolinguistically sensitive ones in native speaker speech and frequent in the input to which the L2 speaker had access. Some are phonological variables, some related to morphosyntax or even lexical items, some are stable variables in L1 speech, some are newer changes. We carried out multivariate analyses on the occurrences of variants of these variables in the speech of the L2 speakers in our year abroad studies.

What have we Learnt about Sociolinguistic Competence and Study Abroad?

We will now summarise what we have learnt in relation to these specific research questions. We discovered that after a year abroad, the L2 speakers approximate L1 variation speech patterns. This approximation is closer in relation to some variables than others, but in general, the speakers are using variation patterns which are significantly more similar to those of native speakers than before they went abroad and more than those of speakers who do not go abroad.

L2 speakers, L1 variation patterns and language change in the L1 speech community

In a related issue we discovered, by tracking constraint hierarchies, that L2 speakers participate in phonological and other changes which are taking place in the speech community of which they are temporarily members. In general we found that on contact with native speakers during the year abroad the L2 speakers were very sensitive to general variation patterns. They seem to react differently to the old and the new changes. On closely examining the more subtle aspects of the Varbrul data for all four variables which we studied, we found that the L2 speakers had reacted slightly differently according to whether the variable under discussion was a long standing stable sociolinguistic variable like *ne* deletion, or a long standing, but less stable one, like /l/ deletion or, on the other hand, the newer incoming variables which we looked at, *nous/on* alternation and variable use of future tense. The L2 speakers firmly grasped the stable variable, *ne* deletion, but were less certain in relation to the newer or incoming ones like variable use of future patterns, where they did not altogether have the same rates or patterns as L1 speakers. In all cases, the L2 speakers moved towards native speaker usage to some extent on contact with native speakers – in terms not only of rates, but also of variation patterns as revealed by constraint orders. They do seem to be sensitive to a difference in native speaker variation patterns in the different types of variation in L1 speech. So we can conclude that advanced speakers are indeed sensitive to native speaker variation patterns on exposure during year abroad.

Context of acquisition

Context of acquisition is crucial for the acquisition of this area of language for advanced learners (and for lower proficiency learners also, although we examined these in less detail). We found a cline in gains in sociolinguistic competence in the four contexts which we compared. Along with a study abroad context, we systematically compared research on three other contexts. We compared (1) the traditional classroom, (2) Canadian immersion education programmes, (3) naturalistic acquisition, and (4) a year abroad following extensive classroom learning. There was a consistent pattern in relation to the four variables studied, going from least gains being made in the traditional classroom and most in the naturalistic setting. So it appears from our results that context of acquisition is crucial, and along with learning in the classroom, a stay in the native speech community is essential for a better grasp of sociolinguistic norms.

Contact with native speakers

It appears that contact with native speakers is also a positive factor in the acquisition of native speaker variation patterns; simply going abroad is not in itself sufficient. Contact is crucial in that it provides both quantity of input and also, given naturalistic interactions with native speakers, the type of modified input which is best for acquisition. Contact with native speakers was related to the length of stay abroad. We found that length of stay in the speech community is correlated in most cases with the acquisition of native speaker variation patterns. If a speaker stays for a year, for instance, gains are considerably more than if the stay is only for two months. Research in Canada with immersion students found, similarly, that these students' sociolinguistic competence increased with extra-curricular French language exposure, including stays with Francophone families and in a Francophone environment.

The role gender plays during the year abroad

In addition, it appears that male and female speakers react to old and new sound changes in ways which parallel those of native speakers.

Gender plays a very important role in the acquisition of this area of sociolinguistic competence and it is frequently bound up with issues of identity construction in the L2 speech community: how the L2 speaker perceives gendered norms in the target community and uses their choice of variant to relate to these norms in whichever way the speaker wishes. In most of the variables we analysed, gender emerged as a major influencing factor, which correlates with Major's (2004) findings that gender is acquired earlier than style.

Long term benefits?

In relation to long term effects, indications from a detailed analysis of one of the variables (*ne* deletion) are that these linguistic gains are not lost but maintained a year later (Regan, 2005). The L2 speakers do not 'decolloquialise', but have very clearly understood the sociolinguistic implications of the vernacular variants and continue to use them even a year later when the native speaker input is no longer daily available.[1]

SLA of the variable rather than the categorical

Our study has focused on how what is variable in the grammar is acquired, as opposed to what is categorical, which had been the unique focus previously in sociolinguistic approaches to second language research. This new research thread has turned attention to the fact that many forms which are thought to be categorical in native speaker speech are in fact variable (as numerous variationist studies since the 1960s have demonstrated). In this book, we wanted to demonstrate precisely how L2 speakers acquire this variation as it appears in native speech. We saw that the particular learning context of year abroad is especially successful for the acquisition of the variable in native speaker speech. The acquisition of sociolinguistic competence seems to be particularly susceptible to the year abroad experience, and clearly so, as opposed to other areas of acquisition where research findings can seem more ambiguous. (Researchers do not seem to find that grammatical structures always improve after a year abroad, for instance.) As we have already noted, we made comparisons between the language use of speakers in the context of year abroad in SLA, and those in the traditional classroom, the immersion classroom, as well as the naturalistic setting. Quantitative evidence, as represented by both rates and constraint hierarchies of variants, reveals that the year abroad causes significant changes in variation patterns.

In general, these seem to move considerably closer to native speaker variable patterns during the year abroad experience (although still less so than naturalistic learners). Classroom learners, on the other hand, show a distinctly lesser approximation to native speaker rates and patterns of variation.

Implications of the Research

The research we have carried out on language acquisition during the year abroad has implications at the basic research level and also at political and programmatic levels. From the results of our study of sociolinguistic competence and the year abroad, we can draw some broader conclusions. Context of acquisition has important implications for the acquisition of what is variable in native speaker speech. There is much evidence to suggest that a formal context is generally successful in helping the L2 speaker with learning what is categorical in the target language. What does not appear to be available to the learner in this context is knowledge (conscious or unconscious) of what is variable in NS speech. Dewaele and Regan (2001) find, for example, that learners who experienced only classroom learning used far fewer colloquial words than those who had spent time in the native speech community. Dewaele (1992) finds that active interaction with native speakers has the most significant effect of various factors he studied. Regan (1996) similarly found that contact with native speakers has an important effect on the acquisition of sociolinguistic norms. Our research (and that of others whom we have discussed earlier, see Chapters 2 and 3) reveals that those who have spent time in the native speaker community seem to have a grasp of how native speakers behave linguistically in relation to variation. Similar to native speakers, they are using knowledge of the probabilities of the appearance of one variant as opposed to another (Adamson, 1988). And recent research seems to indicate that they replicate the patterns of native speakers more closely than those speakers who learn in a classroom. Lemée (2002) finds that Irish speaking learners who have spent a year in France use the informal variant *on* in continental French significantly more than those who have not. Preston and Yamagata (2004) show that learners can acquire native speaker rates in relation to categorical phenomena in the classroom. But acquiring variation patterns in native speaker speech seems to need contact with the community.

In the studies we have carried out on the acquisition of native speech variation patterns, we show that classroom learning is not sufficient for learners to acquire target-like variation patterns. It may indeed be that what is categorical in native speaker speech can be acquired in the classroom. However, the acquisition of native speaker patterns of variation appears to require prolonged contact with native speakers. Mougeon's Canadian immersion classroom learners and Dewaele and Regan (2001) in relation to Dutch and Irish learners found that classroom learners did not appropriate native speaker variation to any great extent. It would seem therefore that second only to being a naturalistic learner, study abroad is the optimum context for this domain of SLA. Effectively it is necessary to be in the native speaker community to learn this type of variation successfully, probably due to prolonged contact with native speakers. This is yet another piece of evidence that context is a crucial causal variable. We can now add sociolinguistic competence to the other modules of language acquisition as depending centrally on context and the input it affords. It should here be noted that this research will increasingly involve the important work being carried out currently in the area of pragmatics, as there is considerable and increasing overlap between sociolinguistics and sociopragmatic competence (see Barron & Warga, 2007; Warga, 2007; Warga & Schölmberger, 2007).

It is important to point out that while common sense would indicate that 'going abroad' would be good for language learning, and indeed that folk wisdom, as we pointed out in Chapters 1 and 2, has always maintained the benefits of going abroad. Why then research what seemed obvious? It is because folk wisdom should always be examined and challenged. In addition, we now know far more than before about the detail of many aspects of this context of L2 acquisition. We have quantitative detail to demonstrate the finer points of different aspects of language acquisition and year abroad: we know the rates of acquisition of L1 variation patterns at different linguistic levels: phonological, morphological, morphosyntactic and lexical. And we know more about the social factors which affect this process, as we have already outlined.

Theoretical Implications: Research Issues

The role of input

The variationist sociolinguistic approach to SLA research which we have taken in this book has revealed a number of interesting research issues in the course of our investigation of the topic of year abroad. At the outset of this volume we reflected on a few of the major issues and themes interrogated by second language researchers. One of these was the role of input. The results of our research tell us more about input and about the relationship between the role of input and context of acquisition. Previous research in SLA from different perspectives had found that opportunities for informal contact with native speakers probably contributes to improvement as it can profoundly affect access to input. Polanyi (1995), for instance, in a diary study, shows that female students in Russia dealing with aggressive Russian males in unpleasant interactions had less access to input than their male counterparts, and so the linguistic gains of these young women were less than they might otherwise have been. Research in general has found that more informal interactive contact with native speakers is related to gains in nativeness.

Through our various analyses of year abroad speech, we have quantitative evidence which confirms these general findings insofar as one particular aspect of acquisition, sociolinguistic competence, is concerned. We found robust evidence that the acquisition of variation patterns of the L2 speech community, was significantly positively affected by contact with native speakers (which we interpreted from amount of time spent in the community as well as ethnographic information regarding time spent with native speakers).

In relation to *ne* deletion, Irish learners after a year abroad, increased their rates of deletion significantly and approached those of native speakers. In addition, the constraint order became closer to that of native speakers after spending a year in a French-speaking country. The general grammar of the L2 speaker was closer to the structures of the native speaker. In relation to *nous/on* alternation, Irish L2 speakers who have spent time in the target language country appear to be more sensitive to L1 constraints than stay at home speakers when the two groups were compared. The L2 speakers, after a year abroad, are closer to native speaker patterns and rates of *nous/on* alternation. The variable use of *nous/on* by Irish L2 speakers approaches native speaker usage after a year abroad.

One of the questions we raised at the outset was whether L2 speakers reacted differentially to older more established variables as opposed to new changes. It appears that the L2 speakers were indeed sensitive to these differences and indeed even followed gender specific native speaker behaviour in relation to these two different variable types. The L2 female speakers in our study of /l/ deletion, for instance, approximated native female tendencies to carry new changes. Also, L2 speakers seemed to better approximate native norms in relation to stable variables than incoming or new ones.

Group and Individual Variation in Relation to L2 Speakers

Another theoretical issue which has been raised by SLA scholars is whether sociolinguists' practice of combining large numbers of speakers can lead to valid results, given that SLA has well-documented the individual variation that characterises SLA and normally focuses on the individual rather than the group. The relationship between group and individual has been explored within the variationist paradigm (Guy, 1980). Variationists have found, in relation to L1 use, that overall community patterns of variation are replicated by the individual. The issue of the individual L2 speaker and the group had received little attention in the SLA literature. On the one hand, SLA research is concerned with the individual learner, but, on the other hand, SLA variationist researchers tend to group learners together. There had been little empirical evidence that such grouping was valid, given the importance of individual variation in SLA. We investigated whether it is meaningful to group learners together, given individual variation. We analysed, using Varbrul, the relationship between the group and the individual in relation to *ne* deletion at three distinct phases in the year abroad process over three years and discovered that there were indeed striking similarities between the figures for the group and the individual at all three stages (Regan, 2004). An interesting picture emerges of a synchronous pattern on the part of the group of speakers and of the individuals within that group. There was a general coincidence of pattern between deletion rates for the majority of the speakers and the norms for the group. The group as a whole showed a significant increase in *ne* deletion during a stay in a Francophone country, and then a maintenance, on the whole, of these rates after returning to the classroom. This is exactly the case for each speaker but one. And even where there is individual variation, we show that where the rates may be somewhat different, the overall pattern is the same. Separate Varbrul runs were done for each individual. The constraint ordering for the group remained similar and the constraint ordering from speaker to speaker was also similar.[2] The pattern, repeated from individual to individual, replicated the pattern for the group as a whole. In all of the analyses, the same pattern emerges, whether it is a case of Varbrul runs for the group or Varbrul runs for the individual speakers. The figures go from initial low rates to rates which are significantly greater and then are basically maintained at that level. This would seem to indicate that, despite the individual variation inherent in SLA, the relationship between the group and the individual, in relation to variation patterns, is nevertheless maintained, rather in the same way as it is for L1 speakers. Similar results for group and individual in relation to sociolinguistic approaches to SLA have been found by Bayley and Langman (2004) in a cross-sectional study of Chinese, Hungarian and Spanish speakers learning English. We suggest that we now have cross-sectional as well as longitudinal linguistic evidence that it is reasonable to report group results in L2 research.

The Acquisition of Sociolinguistic Competence: Process and Product

The research we have carried out also addresses the issue of process as well as the product in SLA. We have charted in quantitative terms the progress of the acquisition and use of the variants we investigated by measuring rates of use as well as constraint hierarchies of influencing factors. We were able to track the acquisition of community norms over periods ranging from one to three years, charting which factors affected choice of variant at different stages of acquisition. This had already been successfully done by variationist SLA researchers who were investigating the acquisition of the categorical (Young, 1991). Given that beginners' production processes are more susceptible to universal constraints such as CV CV syllable structure, Young, in relation to plural -s marking on English nouns, found that learners realise -s between a word final and a word-initial vowel simply to maintain that CV alternation in nouns. More advanced learners are more in control of the L2 and, as a result, not so susceptible to universal constraints. To handle different stages of development, Young coded the stage in a separate factor group, and estimated the relative importance of stage of development. During the acquisition process learners generally restructure their language so different factors affect variation in different ways. Young found that different factors did indeed affect the learners at different stages. This is expected in earlier learners. Generally our advanced learners had the grammatical structures in place, whether negation or future tense usage, or use of *nous* and *on*. They just restructured their interlanguage so that the factors which affected variation were ever closer to those which constrain NS variation. Our analysis approached this issue of development using longitudinal data. We have effectively charted over time the acquisition of what is variable in the L1. We understand the acquisition of variation patterns to be part of linguistic competence and hence to have psycholinguistic validity. Far from being a peripheral element, we consider this knowledge to be a central part of competence for the native speaker. It would seem then that this would be part of non-native speaker competence also, insofar as L2 speakers, by and large, wish to become more native-like. As we pointed out in Chapter 1, the aims and motivations of L2 speakers of course, can vary widely. Some speakers wish to master basic grammar rules and use the language for certain restricted purposes and others may wish to become a part of the chosen language community. Knowledge of categorical rules of the L2 might seem to be enough for some speakers. In fact it is not. Speakers, however, who wish to integrate into the native speaker community, need to know more: they need knowledge of what is variable in the speech variety of this community. Our exploration of the acquisition of the variable as opposed to the categorical in L2 contributes ultimately to our understanding of the role of variation in language.

Practical Implications: Programmatic and Policy Issues

For these reasons it would appear that the debate on study abroad internationally should take into account this new research thread and its findings in relation to sociolinguistic competence. Study abroad has been the focus of much debate in language education and policy-making. Our research suggests that study abroad is extremely positive in relation to one area at least of SLA.

Such sociolinguistic benefits are in some cases at odds with the existing evidence concerning some other areas of L2 development, where the gains are less extensive. Nonetheless, as a crucial component of the L2 speaker's speech repertoire, the sociolinguistic gains demonstrated by our learners point to the highly fruitful outcomes of the investment in study abroad programmes by both education policy-makers and programme organisers and their institutions alike. Moreover, on the basis of the evidence which we have documented here, spanning 15 years of study abroad research, it is clear that study abroad is equally a highly worthwhile investment on the learner's part in his/her language learning path.

Our findings complement those concerning other aspects of the study abroad learner's L2 development – see, for example, Coleman (1997), Collentine and Freed (2004), Freed (1995a, 1998) – such that we now have a fuller picture of the L2 learner's development during study abroad, as well as a more detailed profile of his/her linguistic repertoire post-study abroad. Our research on the linguistic aspects of the year abroad with its focus on sociolinguistic competence has allowed us to understand more about SLA as well as about how people come to be sociolinguistically competent in another language and thereby manage to interact to their own satisfaction with people from the various language communities they interact with throughout their lives.

Future Research

For future research, however, in relation to the development of sociolinguistic variation, there is now scope for similar research in relation to other target languages across a similarly wide range of variables as we have presented here – unusually, much of the existing research, including our own, has focused on L2 French, such that it remains to be seen how the acquisition of such variation may be in some ways language-specific. While we have considered some extralinguistic factors in relation to language contact, such as intensity of contact, as well as degree of exposure, other outstanding issues concern the need for more ethnolinguistic research which might capture the specificity of the learner's sociolinguistic development from the learner's own perspective[3] as well as in relation to the specificity of his/her opportunities for such development from a micro-perspective. Such an approach will necessarily provide complementary insights to the fine-grained material we have provided of these learners' use of a number of sociolinguistic variables, by capturing issues, for example, to do with the learners' awareness, conscious or not, of their usage as they interact with speakers daily during the course of their study abroad programme. Final questions to be addressed in the future might also concern the relationship between other social factors and sociolinguistic development: issues such as the learner's *raison d'être* whilst abroad – whether the learner works or follows a programme of university study, and his/her residence type – whether *en famille*, in an independent residence, or in student halls of residence.[4]

While the last 15 years of research has provided pivotal insights into the relationship between study abroad and sociolinguistic development, results suggest that future research will be extremely fruitful in further consolidating and expanding these insights.

Notes

1. Clearly analysis of the other variables also in longer term studies would be necessary to confirm this.
2. See also Regan (1996).
3. See for instance de Courcy (2002).
4. In the case of our learners, they were generally housed in university residences.

References

Abdel-Jawad, H. (1981) Cross-dialectal variation in Arabic: Competing prestigious forms. *Language in Society* 16, 359–368.
Adamson, H.D. (1988) *Variation Theory and Second Language Acquisition*. Washington DC: Georgetown University Press.
Adamson, H.D. (2005) *Language Minority Students in American Schools: An Education in English*. Mahwah, NJ: Erlbaum.
Adamson, H.D. and Regan, V. (1991) The acquisition of community speech norms by Asian immigrants learning English as a second language. *Studies in Second Language Acquisition* 13, 1–22.
Armstrong, N. (1996) Variable deletion of French /l/: Linguistic, social and stylistic factors. *Journal of French Language Studies* 6, 1–21.
Armstrong, N. (1998) The sociolinguistic gender pattern in French: A comparison of two linguistic levels. *Journal of French Language Studies* 8, 139–158.
Armstrong, N. (2002) Variable deletion of French ne: A cross-stylistic perspective. *Languages Sciences* 24 (2), 153–173.
Armstrong, N. and Smith, A. (2002) The influence of linguistic and social factors on the recent decline of French ne. *Journal of French Language Studies* 12 (2), 23–41.
Armstrong, N., Bauvois, C. and Beeching, K. (2001) *La Langue Française au Féminin: Le Sexe et le Genre Affectent-ils la Variation Linguistique?* Paris: L'Harmattan.
Ashby, W. (1976) The loss of the negative particle *ne* in French: A syntactic change in progress. *Lingua* 39, 119–137.
Ashby, W. (1981) The loss of the negative particle ne in French: A syntactic change in progress. *Language* 57 (3), 674–687.
Ashby, W. (1984) The elision of /l/ in French clitic pronouns and article. In E. Pulgram (ed.) *Romanitas: Studies in Romance Linguistics*. Ann Arbor: University of Michigan Press.
Ashby, W. (1992) The variable use of *on* versus *tu/vous* for indefinite reference in spoken French. *Journal of French Language Studies* 2, 235–257.
Ashby, W. (2001) Un nouveau regard sur la chute du *ne* en français parlé tourangeau: S'agit-il d'un changement en cours? *Journal of French Language Studies* 11, 1–22.
Atlani, F. (1984) *La Langue au Ras du Texte*. Lille: Presses Universitaires de Lille.
Aurich, H.V. (1990) *Aller et Gaan: La Périphrase Futurale en Français et en Néerlandais*. MA thesis, Department of Romance Languages, University of Groningen.
Bachman, K. (1990) *Fundamental Considerations in Language Testing*. Oxford: Oxford University Press.

Bahloul, M. and Waugh, L. (1996) La différence entre le futur simple et le futur périphrastique dans le discours journalistique. *Modèles Linguistiques* 17 (1), 19–36.

Bakir, M. (1986) Sex differences in the approximation to standard Arabic: A case study in issues in Arabic sociolinguistics. *Anthropological Linguistics* 28 (1), 3–9.

Bardovi-Harlig, K. (1999) Exploring the interlanguage of interlanguage pragmatics: A research agenda for acquisitional pragmatics. *Language Learning* 49, 677–713.

Barro, A. and Grimm, H. (1993) Integrating language learning and cultural studies: An ethnographic approach to the year abroad. In J. Coleman and A. Rouxeville (eds) *Integrating New Approaches: The Teaching of French in Higher Education* (pp. 147–164). London: AFLS/CILT.

Barro, A., Jordan, S. and Roberts, C. (1998) Cultural practice in everyday life: The language learner as ethnographer. In M. Byram and M. Fleming (eds) *Language Learning in Intercultural Perspective: Approaches through Drama and Ethnography* (pp. 76–97). Cambridge: Cambridge University Press.

Barron, A. (2003) *Acquisition in Interlanguage Pragmatics. Learning How to Do Things with Words in a Study Abroad Context*. Amsterdam/Philadelphia: Benjamins.

Barron, A. and Warga, M. (2007) Acquisitional pragmatics: Focus on foreign language learners. *Intercultural Pragmatics* 4 (2), 113–127.

Bartning, I. (1989) Swedish university students' French interlanguage. *Swedish Working Papers on Bilingualism* 8, 1–10.

Bartning, I. (1990a) L'acquisition du français des apprenants universitaires suédois – quelques aspects. *Revue Romane* 25 (2), 165–80.

Bartning, I. (1990b) L'interlangue française des apprenants universitaires suédois – aspects de l'accord du verbe. In O. Halmoy, A. Halvorsen and L. Lorentzen (eds) *Actes du Onzième Congrès des Romanistes Scandinaves*. (pp. 27–38). Trondheim: Tapir.

Bartning, I. (1993) French interlanguage – development and variation. A presentation of a research project. In B. Hammarberg (ed.) *Problem, Process, Product in Language Learning* (pp. 1–11). Stockholm: Stockholm University, Department of Linguistics.

Bartning, I. (1994) Recherches sur l'acquisition des langues secondes/étrangères et du français langue *étrangère-aspects* du développement, d'interaction et de variation. In G. Boysen (ed.) *Actes du XIIe Congrès des Romanistes Scandinaves* (pp. 22–32). Aalborg: Aalborg University Press.

Bartning, I. (1997a) *C'est* in native and non-native spoken French. *Studier i modernesprak* 11.

Bartning, I. (1997b) L'apprenant dit avancé et son acquisition d'une langue étrangère. Tour d'horizon et esquisse d'une caractérisation de la variété avancée. In I. Bartning (ed.) *Les Apprenants Avancés*. Special issue of *Acquisition et Interaction en Langue Etrangère* 9, 9–50.

Bartning, I. (2000) Gender agreement in L2 French: Pre-advanced vs advanced learners. *Studia Linguistica* 54 (2), 225–237.

Batardiére, M-T. (1993) Research study on affective and environmental factors of older learners during second language immersion. *Teanga* 13, 41–53.

Batardiére, M-T. (2003) The effects of study abroad on second language grammatical development: A qualitative study of the written performance of four Irish advanced learners of French. PhD thesis, Trinity College, Dublin.

Bayley, R. (1994) Interlanguage variation and the quantitative paradigm: Past tense marking in Chinese-English. In E. Tarone, A. Cohen and S. Gass (eds) *Research Methodology in Second Language Acquisition* (pp. 157–181). Hillsdale, NJ: Lawrence Erlbaum.

Bayley, R. (1996) Competing constraints on variation in the speech of adult Chinese learners of English. In R. Bayley and D. Preston (eds) *Second Language Acquisition and Linguistic Variation* (pp. 97–120). Philadelphia: John Benjamins.

Bayley, R. and Langman, J. (2004) Variation in the group and the individual. Evidence from second language acquisition. *International Review of Applied Linguistics in Language Teaching* 42 (4), 303–318.

Bayley, R. and Preston, D. (1996) *Second Language Acquisition and Linguistic Variation*. Amsterdam/Philadelphia: Benjamins.

Bayley, R. and Schecter, S.R. (2003) *Language Socialization in Bilingual and Multilingual Societies*. Clevedon: Multilingual Matters.

Bayley, R. and Lucas, C. (2007) *Sociolinguistic Variation: Theories, Methods, and Applications*. Cambridge: Cambridge University Press.

Bayley, R. and Regan, V. (2004) The acquisition of sociolinguistic competence. *Journal of Sociolinguistics* 8 (Special Issue 3).

Bell, A. (1984) Language style as audience design. *Language in Society* 13, 145–204.

Benazzo, S. and Giuliano, P. (1998) Marqueurs de négation et particules de portée en français L2: *Où* les placer? *Acquisition et Interaction en Langue Etrangère* 11, 35–62.

Birdsong, D. (1992) Ultimate attainment in second language acquisition. *Language* 68 (4), 706–755.

Birdsong, D. (1999) *Second Language Acquisition and the Critical Period Hypothesis*. Mahwah, NJ: Erlbaum.

Blanche-Benveniste, C. (1985) *Une chose* dans la syntaxe verbale. *Recherches sur le Français Parlé* 7, 141–168.

Blanche-Benveniste, C. (1987) Le pronom *on*: Propositions pour une analyse. In C. Blanche-Benveniste (ed.) *Mélanges Offerts à Maurice Molho* (III). Paris: Les Cahiers de Fontenay.

Blanche-Benveniste, C. (1997a) *Approche de la Langue Parlée en Français*. Paris: Ophrys.

Blanche-Benveniste, C. (1997b) La notion de la variation syntaxique dans la langue parlée. *Langue Française*, 115, 19–29.

Blanche-Benveniste, C. and Jeanjean, C. (1987) *Le Français Parlé: Transcription et Édition*. Paris: Didier Erudition.

Blanche-Benveniste, C., Bilger, M., Rouget, C. and Van den Eynde, K. (1991) *Le Français Parlé: Etudes Grammaticales*. Paris: Editions du Centre National de la Recherche Scientifique.

Blondeau, H. (2005) La variation au fil du temps chez une cohorte de Montréalais francophones. Paper presented at the annual conference of the *Association of French Language Studies*, Université de Savoie, Chambéry.

Blondeau, H. and Nagy, N. (1995) Aspects of L2 competence in a bilingual setting. Paper presented at the *24th Conference of NWAV*, Philadelphia, University of Pennsylvania.

Blondeau, H. and Nagy, N. (1998) Double marquage du sujet dans le français parlé par les jeunes anglo-montréalais. *Actes du congrès annuel de l'Association canadienne de linguistique*, Université d'Ottawa, May 1998, *Cahiers Linguistiques d'Ottawa* January 1999, 59–70.

Blondeau, H., Nagy, N., Sankoff, G. and Thibault, P. (2002) La couleur locale du français L2 des Anglo-montréalais. In J-M. Dewaele and R. Mougeon (eds) *L'appropriation de la variation par les apprenants du français langue seconde*. Special issue of *Acquisition et Interaction en Langue Étrangère* 17, 73–100.

Blum-Kulka, S. (1982) Learning to say what you mean in a second language. *Applied Linguistics* 3, 29–59.

Bollack, L. (1903) La langue française en 2003. In C. Désirat and T. Hordé (eds) *La langue française au XXème siécle*. Paris: Bordas.

Boutet, J. (1986) La référence à la personne en français parlé: Le cas de *on*. *Langage et Société* 38, 19–50.

Boutet, J. (1994) *Construire le Sens*. Bern: Lang.

Brecht, R. and Davidson, D. (1992) Language assessment gains in study abroad: Assessment and feedback. In E. Shohamy and A. Walton (eds) *Language Assessment for Feedback, Testing, and Other Strategies*. Dubarque, IA: Kendall/Hunt Publishing.

Brecht, R. and Ginsberg, R. (1991) Language acquisition gains in study abroad: Program assessment and modification. Paper presented at *NFLC Conference on Language Testing*, Washington DC, March 1991.

Brecht, R., Davidson, D. and Ginsberg, R. (1993) *Predictors of Foreign Language Gain During Study Abroad*. Washington, DC: National Foreign Language Center.

Brecht, R., Davidson, D. and Ginsberg, R. (1995) Predictors of foreign language gain during study abroad. In B. Freed (ed.) *Second Language Acquisition in a Study Abroad Context* (pp. 38–66). Amsterdam/Philadelphia: Benjamins.

Brecht, R.D. and Robinson, J.L. (1995) On the value of formal instruction in study abroad: Student reactions in context. In B. Freed (ed.) *Second Language Acquisition in a Study Abroad Context*. Amsterdam/Philadelphia: John Benjamins.

Brunelle, A. and Tousignant, C. (1981) L'autocorrection chez un sujet montréalais: Étude quantitative. In D. Sankoff and H. Cedergren (eds) *Variation Omnibus*. (pp. 25–31). Edmonton: *Linguistic Research Incorporated*.

Brunot, F. (1966) *Histoire de la Langue Française*. Paris, Colin.

Bucholtz, M. (1999) Why be normal: Language and community practices in a community of nerd girls. *Language in Society* 28, 203–223.

Byon, A. (2006) Language socialization in Korean-as-a-Foreign-Language classrooms. *Bilingual Research Journal* 30 (2), 265–291.

Cameron, R. (2005) Ageing and gendering. *Language in Society* 34, 23–61.

Carlson, J., Burn, B., Unseen, J. and Yachimowicz, D. (1990) *Study Abroad. The Experience of American Undergraduates*. Westport, CT: Greenwood Press.

Carroll, J. (1967) Foreign language proficiency levels attained by language majors near graduation from college. *Foreign Language Annals* 1, 131–151.

Carroll, M., Murcia-Serra, J., Watorek, M. and Bendicioli, A. (2000) The relevance of information structure to second language acquisition studies. The descriptive discourse of advanced adult learners of German. In C. Perdue (ed.) *The Structure of Learner Language*. Special issue of *Studies in Second Language Acquisition* 22, 441–466.

Celle, A. (2005) The French future tense and English 'will' as markers of epistemic modality. *Languages in Contrast* 5 (2), 181–218.

Chafe, W. (1993) Uses of the defocusing pronominal prefixes in Caddo. In H.K. Hardy and J. Scancarelli (eds) *Native Languages of the Southwest*. Lincoln: University of Nebraska Press.

Chavez, M. (2001) *Gender in the Language Classroom*. Boston: McGraw Hill.

Clahsen, M., Meisel, J. and Pienemann, M. (1983) *Deutsch als Fremdsprache: Der Sprachenerwerb Ausländischer Arbeiter*. Tübingen: Gunter Narr Verlag.

Clark, E. (1985) The acquisition of Romance, with special reference to French. In D. Slobin (ed.) *The Cross-linguistic Study of Language Acquisition* (Vol. 1) (pp. 687–782). Hillsdale, NJ: Erlbaum.

Coates, J. (1993) *Women, Men and Language: A Sociolinguistic Account of Gender Differences in Language*. London: Pearson Education.

Coleman, J. (1995a) The current state of knowledge concerning student residence abroad. In G. Parker and A. Rouxeville (eds) *'The Year Abroad': Preparation, Monitoring, Evaluation* (pp. 17–42). London: AFLS/CILT.

Coleman, J. (1995b) A comparative survey of the proficiency and progress of language learners in British universities. In R. Grotjahn (ed.) *Der C-Test: Theoretische Grundlagen und Praktische Anwendungen Volume 3* (pp. 367–399). Bochum: Brockmeyer.

Coleman, J. (1996) *Studying Languages: A Survey of British and European Students. The Proficiency, Background, Attitudes and Motivations of Students of Foreign Languages in the United Kingdom and Europe*. London: CILT.

Coleman, J. (1997) Residence abroad within language study. *Language Teaching* 30, 1–20.

Coleman, J. (1998) Language learning and study abroad: The European perspective. In B. Freed (ed.) *Language Learning in a Study Abroad Context*. Special Issue of *Frontiers. The Interdisciplinary Journal of Study Abroad* IV, 167–205.

Coleman, J. (2001) Lessons for the future: Evaluating FDTL languages. In J. Coleman, D. Farney, D. Head and R. Rix (eds) *Language Learning Futures. Issues and Strategies for Modern Languages Provision in Higher Education*. London: CILT.

Coleman, J. and Towell, R. (1987) *The Advanced Language Learner*. London: CILT/AFLS.

Collentine, J. (2004) The effects of learning context on morphosyntactic and lexical development. In J. Collentine and B. Freed (eds) *Learning Context and its Effects on Second Language Acquisition*. Special Issue of *Studies in Second Language Acquisition* 26, 227–248.

Collentine, J. and Freed, B.F. (2004) Learning context and its effects on second language acquisition. In J. Collentine and B. Freed (eds) *Learning Context and Its Effects on Second Language Acquisition*. Special Issue of *Studies in Second Language Acquisition* 26.

Confais, J-P. (1995) *Temps Mode Aspect: Les Approches des Morphèmes Verbaux et leurs Problèmes à l'Exemple du Français et de l'Allemand*. Toulouse: Presses Universitaires du Mirail.

Conrick, M. and Regan, V. (2007) *French in Canada: Language Issues*. New York: Peter Lang.

Cook, M. (1994) *Dialogues Révolutionnaires*. Exeter: Exeter University Press.

Cook, V. (2002) *Portraits of the L2 User*. Clevedon: Multilingual Matters.

Cook, V. (2003) *Effects of the Second Language on the First*. Clevedon: Multilingual Matters.

Coppieters, R. (1987) Competence differences between native and non-native speakers. *Language* 63, 544–573.

Corder, S. (1981) Formal simplicity and functional simplification. In R.W. Andersen (ed.) *New Dimensions in Second Language Acquisition Research* (pp. 146–152). Rowley, MA: Newbury House.

Coveney, A. (1996) *Variability in Spoken French: A Sociolinguistic Study of Interrogation and Negation*. Exeter: Elm Bank Publications.

Coveney, A. (1997) Awareness of linguistic constraints on variable ne omission. *Journal of French Language Studies* 8, 159–187.

Coveney, A. (2000) Vestiges of nous and the 1st person plural verb in informal spoken French. *Language Sciences* 22, 447–481.

Cox, R. and Freed, B. (1988) The effects of study abroad on form and function: A comparison of students who have been abroad and those who have not. *Report to the Consortium for Language Learning and Teaching*. New Haven, CO: MS.

Damourette, J. and Pichon, E. (1911–1940) *Des Mots à la Pensée: Essai de Grammaire de la Langue Française*. Paris: Editions D'Artrey.

De Courcy, M. (2002) *Learners' Experiences of Immersion Education: Case Studies of French and Chinese*. Clevedon: Multilingual Matters.

DeKeyser, R. (1986) From Learning to Acquisition in a US Classroom and During a Semester Abroad. PhD thesis, Stanford University.

DeKeyser, R. (1991) Foreign language development during a semester abroad. In B. Freed (ed.) *Foreign Language Acquisition Research and the Classroom* (pp. 104–119). Lexington, MA: DC Heath and Co.

Deshaies, D. (1981) *Le Français Parlé dans la Ville de Québec: Une Étude Sociolinguistique*. Québec: Centre International de Recherche sur le Bilinguisme.

Deshaies, D. (1985a) Contribution à l'analyse du français québécois: Étude des pronoms personnels. *Revue Québécoise de Linguistique Théorique et Appliquée* 10 (3), 11–40.

Deshaies, D. (1985b) Références personnelles et types de discours en situation d'entrevue. In P.R. Léon and P. Perron (eds) *Le Dialogue* (pp. 77–91). Ottawa: Didier.

Deshaies, D. (1985c) Etude de la syntaxe des pronoms personnels en français. *Revue de l'Association Québécoise de Linguistique* 4 (4), 77–104.

Deshaies, D. (1986) Variation linguistique: Le cas des pronoms personnels du français. In D. Sankoff (ed.) *Diversity and Diachrony* (pp. 311–322). Amsterdam/Philadelphia: Benjamins.

Deshaies, D. and Laforge, E. (1981) Le futur simple et le futur proche dans le français parlé dans la ville de Québec. *Langue et Linguistique* 7, 23–37.

Devaluy, M. (1993b) *Ne* ne disparaîtra-t-il pas en français parlé à Montréal? Je sais pas. Paper presented at annual conference of *Association Canadienne Française pour l'Avancement des Sciences*, Ottawa.

Devitt, S. (1995) *French – Its Acquisition as a Second Language*. Dublin: Authentik.

Dewaele, J-M. (1992) L'omission du *ne* dans deux styles oraux d'interlangue française. *Interface. Journal of Applied Linguistics* 7, 3–17.

Dewaele, J-M. (2002) Using sociostylistic variants in advanced French interlanguage. *EUROSLA Yearbook*, II, 205–226.

Dewaele, J-M. (2004) Retention or omission of the *ne* in advanced French interlanguage: the variable effect of extralinguistic factors. In R. Bayley and V. Regan (eds) *Sociolinguistics and Second Language Acquisition*. Special issue of *Journal of Sociolinguistics* 8 (3), 433–450.

Dewaele, J-M. and Regan, V. (2001) The use of colloquial words in advanced French interlanguage. *EUROSLA Yearbook I*, 51–68.

Dewaele, J-M. and Regan, V. (2002) Maîtriser la norme sociolinguistique en interlangue française: le cas de l'omission variable de *ne*. *Journal of French Language Studies* 12 (2), 123–148.

Dewey, D. (2004) A comparison of reading development by learners of Japanese in intensive domestic immersion and study abroad contexts. In J. Collentine and B. Freed (eds) *Learning Context and its Effects on Second Language Acquisition* Special Issue of *Studies in Second Language Acquisition* 26, 303–327.

Díaz-Campos, M. (2004) Context of learning in the acquisition of Spanish second language phonology. In J. Collentine and B. Freed (eds) *Learning Context and Its Effects on Second Language Acquisition*. Special Issue of *Studies in Second Language Acquisition* 26, 249–273.

Dion, N. and Blondeau, H. (2005) Variability and future temporal reference: The French of Anglo-Montrealers. Paper presented at *NWAV* 32, University of Pennsylvania, Pennsylvania.

Dittmar, N. (1992) *Grammaticalisation in Second Language Acquisition*. Special Issue of *Studies in Second Language Acquisition* 14 (3).

Doppagne, A. (1966) *Trois Aspects du Français Contemporain*. Paris: Larousse.

Dörnyei, Z. and Clement, R. (2001) Motivational characteristics of learning different target language. Results of a nationwide survey. In Z. Dörnyei and R. Schmidt (eds) *Motivation and Second Language Acquisition* (pp. 399–432). Honolulu, HI: University of Hawaii Press.

Doughty, C. and Long, M. (2003) *The Handbook of Second Language Acquisition*. Oxford: Blackwell.

Dufon, M.A. and Churchill, E. (2006) *Language Learners in Study Abroad Contexts*. Clevedon: Multilingual Matters.

Dyson, P. (1988) *The Year Abroad*. Report for the Central Bureau for Educational Visits and Exchanges, Oxford University Language Teaching Centre.

Eckert, P. (1988) Adolescent social structure and the spread of linguistic change. *Language in Society* 17, 245–267.

Eckert, P. (1990) The whole woman: Sex and gender differences in variation. *Language Variation and Change* 1, 245–268.

Eckert, P. (1998) Gender and sociolinguistic variation. In J. Coates (ed.) *Language and Gender: A Reader* (pp. 64–75). Oxford: Blackwell.

Eckert, P. (2000) *Linguistic Variation as Social Practice: The Linguistic Construction of Identity in Belten High*. Oxford: Blackwell.

Eckert, P. and McConnell-Ginet, S. (2003) *Language and Gender*. Cambridge: Cambridge University Press.

Ehrlich, S. (1997) Gender as social practice: Implications for second language acquisition. *Studies in Second Language Acquisition* 19, 421–446.

Ehrlich, S. (2001) Gendering the 'learner': Sexual harassment and second language acquisition. In A. Pavlenko, A. Blackledge, I. Piller and M. Teutsch-Dwyer (eds) *Multilingualism, Second Language Learning, and Gender* (pp. 103–128). New York: Mouton de Gruyter.

Ellis, R. (1985) *Understanding Second Language Acquisition*. Oxford: Oxford University Press.

Ellis, R. (1994) *The Study of Second Language Acquisition*. Oxford: Oxford University Press.

Emirkanian, L. and Sankoff, D. (1985) Le futur simple et le futur périphrastique dans le français parlé. In M. Lemieux and H. Cedergren (eds) *Les Tendances*

Dynamiques du Français Parlé à Montréal (Vol. 2) (pp. 189–204). Québec: Gouvernement du Québec.

Feagin, C. (1979) *Variation and Change in Alabama English: A Sociolinguistic Study of the White Community*. Washington, DC: Georgetown University Press.

Feagin, C. (2002) Entering the community: Fieldwork. In J.K. Chambers, P. Trudgill and N. Schilling-Estes (eds) *The Handbook of Language Variation and Change* (pp. 20–39). Malden/Oxford: Blackwell.

Firestone, S. (1971) *The Dialectic of Sex*. New York: Bantam.

Firth, A. and Wagner, J. (1997) On discourse, communication and fundamental concepts in SLA research. *Modern Language Journal* 8 (3), 285–330.

Fischer, R. (1958) Social influences on the choice of a linguistic variant. *Word* 14, 47–56.

Fleischman, S. (1982) *The Future in Thought and Language: Diachronic Evidence from Romance*. Cambridge: Cambridge University Press.

Fonseca-Greber, B. and Waugh, L. (2002) The subject clitics of European conversational French: Morphologization, grammatical change, semantic change in progress. In R. Nuñez-Cedeño, L. López and R. Cameron (eds) *Proceedings of the 31st Symposium in the Romance Languages*. Amsterdam/Philadelphia: Benjamins.

Fortune, T. and Tedick, D. (2008) *Pathways to Multilingualism: Evolving Perspectives on Immersion Education*. Clevedon: Multilingual Matters.

Freed, A. and Greenwood, A. (1996) Women, men, and type of talk: What makes the difference? *Language in Society* 25, 1–26.

Freed, B. (1990) Language learning in a study abroad context: The effects of interactive and non-interactive out-of-class contact on grammatical achievement and oral proficiency. In J. Atlatis (ed.) *Linguistics, Language Teaching and Language Acquisition: The Interdependence of Theory, Practice and Research* (pp. 459–477). Georgetown University Round Table on Languages and Linguistics. Washington, DC: Georgetown University Press.

Freed, B. (1993) Assessing the linguistic impact of study abroad: What we currently know – what we need to learn. *Journal of Asian Pacific Communication* 4 (4), 151–166.

Freed, B. (1995a) *Second Language Acquisition in a Study Abroad Context*. Amsterdam/Philadelphia: Benjamins.

Freed, B. (1995b) What makes us think that students who study abroad become fluent? In B. Freed (ed.) *Second Language Acquisition in a Study Abroad Context* (pp. 123–148). Amsterdam/Philadelphia: Benjamins.

Freed, B. (1995c) Language learning and study abroad. In B. Freed (ed.) *Second Language Acquisition in a Study Abroad Context* (pp. 3–32). Amsterdam/Philadelphia: Benjamins.

Freed, B. (1996) Language and gender research in an experimental setting. In V.L. Bergvall, J. Bing and B. Freed (eds) *Rethinking Language and Gender Research: Theory and Practice* (pp. 54–76). London: Longman.

Freed, B. (1998) An overview of issues and research in language learning in a study abroad setting. In B. Freed (ed.) *Language Learning in a Study Abroad Context* Special Issue of *Frontiers* (IV), 31–60.

Freed, B., So, S. and Lazar, N. (2003) Language learning abroad: How do gains in written fluency compare with oral fluency in French as a second language? *Association of Departments of Foreign Languages Bulletin* 34, 34–40.

Freed, B., Dewey, D. Segalowitz, N. and Halter, R. (2004a) The language contact profile. In J. Collentine and B. Freed (eds) *Learning Context and Its Effects on Second Language Acquisition*. Special Issue of *Studies in Second Language Acquisition* 26, 349–356.

Freed, B., Segalowitz, N., Dewey, D. and Halter, R. (2004b) Context of learning and second language fluency in French: Comparing regular classroom, study abroad, and intensive domestic immersion programs. *Studies in Second Language Acquisition* 26 (2), 275–301.

Gaatone, D. (1971) *Etude Descriptive du Système de la Négation en Français Contemporain*. Genève: Librairie Droz.

Gadet, F. (1989) *Le Français Ordinaire*. Paris: Armand Colin.

Gal, S. (1978) Peasants can't get wives: Language change and sex roles in a bilingual community. *Language in Society* 7, 1–16.

Gal, S. (1979) *Language Shift: Social Determinants of Linguistic Change in Bilingual Austria*. New York: Academic Press.

Gass, S. (1990) Second and foreign language learning: Same, different or none of the above? In B. VanPatten, T. Dvorak and J. Lee (eds) *Foreign Language Learning: A Research Perspective* (pp. 34–44). Cambridge, MA: Newbury House.

Gass, S. (1997) *Input, Interation and the Second Language Learner*. Mahwah, NJ: Lawrence Erlbaum.

Gass, S.M. and Varonis, E.M. (1986) Sex differences in NNS/NNS interactions. In R. Day (ed.) *Talking to Learn: Conversation in Second Language Acquisition* (pp. 327–351). Rowley, MA: Newbury House.

Gass, S.M. and Varonis, E.M. (1994) Input, interaction and second language production. *Studies in Second Language Acquisition* 16, 283–301.

Gass, S., Madden, C., Preston, D. and Selinker, L. (1989) *Variation in Second Language Acquisition. Psycholinguistic Issues*. Clevedon: Multilingual Matters.

Gauchat, L. (1905) L'unité phonétique dans le patois d'une commune. In M. Niemeyer (ed.) *Aus Romanischen Sprachen und Literaturen* (pp. 175–232). Halle: Festschrift Heinrich Mort.

Giacalone Ramat, A. (1995) Tense and aspect in learner Italian. In P-M. Bertinetto, V. Bianchi, Ö. Dahl and M. Squartini (eds) *Temporal Reference, Aspect and Actionality. Vol II Typological Perspectives* (pp. 289–309). Turin: Rosenberg and Sellier.

Gillespie, S., Ford, K.L., Gillespie, R.D. and Leavell, A.G. (1996) Portfolio assessment: Some questions, some answers, some recommendations. *Journal of Adolescent and Adult Literacy* 39 (4), 480–491.

Goldfine, C. (1987) Negation in French L2 learners. *Linguistics* 23 (1), 49–77.

Gornick, V. and Moran, B. (1971) *Women in Sexist Society: Studies in Power and Powerlessness*. New York: Basic Books.

Grafström, A. (1969) On remplaçant *nous* en français contemporain. *Revue de Linguistique Romane* 33, 270–298.

Grégoire, M. and Thiévenaz, O. (1995) *Grammaire Progressive du Français*. Paris: Clé International.

Grevisse, M. (1982) *Le Français Correct*. Paris: Club France Loisirs.

Grevisse, M. (1993) *Le Bon Usage, Grammaire Française* (3rd edn). Paris: Editions Duculot.

Grusec, J.E. and Hastings, P. (2007) *The Handbook of Socialization: Theory and Research*. New York: The Guilford Press.

Guntermann, G. (1992a) An analysis of interlanguage development over time: Part I, *por* and *para*. *Hispania*, 75 (1), 177–187.

Guntermann, G. (1992b) An analysis of interlanguage development over time: Part II, *ser* and *estar*. *Hispania* 75, 1294–1303.
Guntermann, G. (1995) The peace corps experience: language learning in training and in the field. In B. Freed (ed.) *Second Language Acquisition in a Study Abroad Context* (pp. 149–169). Amsterdam/Philadelphia: John Benjamins.
Guy, G. (1980) Variation in the group and the individual. In W. Labov (ed.) *Locating Language in Time and Space* (pp. 1–36). New York: Academic Press.
Guy, G. (1993) The quantitative analysis of linguistic variation. In D. Preston (ed.) *American Dialect Research*. Amsterdam/Philadelphia: Benjamins.
Haeri, N. (1994) A linguistic innovation of women in Cairo. *Language Variation and Change* 6 (1), 87–112.
Haeri, N. (1996) *The Sociolinguistic Market of Cairo. Gender, Class and Education*. London: Kagan Paul International, New York.
Haeri, N. (2003) *Sacred Language, Ordinary People: Dilemmas of Culture and Politics in Egypt*. New York: Palgrave Macmillan.
Harley, B. (1992a) Patterns of second language development in French immersion. *Journal of French Language Studies* 2, 159–185.
Harley, B. (1992b) Aspects of the oral second language proficiency of early immersion, later immersion, and extended French students at grade 10. In R.J. Courchêne, J.I. Glidden, J.S. John and C. Thérien (eds) *Comprehension-based Second Language Teaching* (pp. 371–388). Ottawa: Ottawa University Press.
Harris, M. and Vincent, N. (1988) *The Romance Languages*. London/New York: Routledge.
Hashimoto, H. (1994) Language acquisition of an exchange student within the homestay environment. *Journal of Asian Pacific Communication* 4 (4), 209–224.
Herschensohn, J. (1998) Minimally raising the verb issue. In *Proceedings of the 22nd Annual Boston University Conference on Language Development* (pp. 325–336). Somerville, MA: Cascadilla Press.
Herschensohn, J. (2003) Verbs and rules: Two profiles of French morphology acquisition. *Journal of French Language Studies* 13 (1), 23–45.
Hickey, T. (1997) *Early Immersion Education in Ireland: Na Naíonraí*. Dublin: Linguistics Institute of Ireland.
Hole, J. and Levine, E. (1971) *Rebirth of Feminism*. New York: Quadrangle Books.
Holmes, J. (1994) *Women, Men and Politeness*. London: Longman.
Holmes, J. (1995) *Women, Men and Language*. London: Longman.
Holmes, J. (1997) Women, language and identity. *Journal of Sociolinguistics* 1, 195–224.
Holmes, J. (1998) Women's role in language change. A place for qualification. Gender and belief systems. In N. Warner, J. Ahlers, L. Bilmes, M. Oliver and S. Wertheim (eds) *Proceedings for the Fourth Berkeley Women and Language Conference* (pp. 313–330). Berkeley: Berkeley Women and Language Group.
Holmes, J. and Marra, M. (2004) Relational practice in the workplace: Women's talk or gendered discourse? *Language in Society* 33, 377–398.
Holmes, J. and Meyerhoff, M. (1999) The community of practice: Theories and methodologies in language and gender research. *Language in Society*, Special Issue, *Communities of Practice in Language and Gender Research* 28 (2), 173–183.
Holmes, J. and Meyerhoff, M. (2003) *The Handbook of Language and Gender*. Oxford: Blackwell.
Horvath, B. (1985) *Variation in Australian English: The Sociolects of Sydney*. New York: Cambridge University Press.

Howard, M. (2001) The effects of study abroad on the L2 learner's structural skills: Evidence from advanced learners of French. *Eurosla Yearbook* 1, 123–141.

Howard, M. (2002a) Prototypical and non-prototypical marking in the advanced learner's aspectuo-temporal system. *Eurosla Yearbook II* (pp. 87–113). Amsterdam/Philadelphia: John Benjamin Publishers.

Howard, M. (2002b) L'acquisition des temps du passé en français par l'apprenant dit avancé: Une approche lexicale. In E. Labeau and P. Larrivée (eds) *Les Temps du Passé Français et leur Enseignement* (pp. 181–204). Amsterdam/Atlanta: Rodopi [Cahiers Chronos 9].

Howard, M. (2004) On the interactional effect of linguistic constraints on L2 variation. The case of past time marking. *International Review of Applied Linguistics* 42 (4), 319–334.

Howard, M. (2005a) L'acquisition de la liaison en français langue seconde – une analyse quantitative d'apprenants avancés en milieu guidé et en milieu naturel. *Cognition, Représentation, Langage (Revue CORELA)*.

Howard, M. (2005b) On the role of context in the development of learner language: Insights from study abroad research. *ITL International Review of Applied Linguistics* 148, 1–20.

Howard, M. (2005c) Second language acquisition in a study abroad context: A comparative investigation of the effects of study abroad and foreign language instruction on the L2 learner's grammatical development. In A. Housen and M. Pierrard (eds) *Investigations in Instructed Second Language Acquisition* (pp. 495–530). Berlin: Mouton deGruyter [*Studies on Language Acquisition* 25].

Howard, M. (2006) The expression of number and person through verb morphology in French interlanguage. *International Review of Applied Linguistics* 44 (1), 1–22.

Howard, M. (2009) Short- versus long-term effects of naturalistic exposure on the advanced instructed learner's L2 development: A case-study. In E. Labeau and F. Myles (eds) *The Advanced Learner Variety: The Case of French* (pp. 93–123). Frankfurt. Brussels, Oxford: Bern, Wien: Peter Lang.

Howard, M., Lemée, I. and Regan, V. (2006) The L2 acquisition of a phonological variable: The case of /l/ deletion in French. *Journal of French Language Studies* 16 (1), 1–24.

Huebner, T. (1995) The effects of overseas language programs: Report on a case study of an intensive Japanese course. In B. Freed (ed.) *Second Language Acquisition in a Study Abroad Context* (pp. 171–193). Amsterdam/Philadelphia: Benjamins.

Huebner, T. (1998) Methodological considerations in data collection for language learning in a study abroad context. In B. Freed (ed.) *Language Learning in a Study Abroad Context*. Special Issue of *Frontiers* 4, 1–30.

Hyltenstam, K. and Abrahamsson, N. (2000) Who can become native-like in a second language? All, none, or some? *Studia Linguistica* 54 (2), 150–166.

Hymes, D. (1967) Models of interaction of language and social setting. *Journal of Social Issues* 33 (2), 8–28.

Hymes, D. (1971) Competence and performance in linguistic theory. In R. Huxley and E. Ingram (eds) *Language Acquisition: Models and Methods*. London: Academic Press.

Hymes, D. (1972) On communicative competence. In J.B. Pride and J. Holmes (eds) *Sociolinguistics*. Harmondsworth: Penguin Books.

Ife, A., Vives Boix, G. and Meara, P. (2000) The impact of study abroad on the vocabulary development of different proficiency groups. *Spanish Applied Linguistics* 4 (1), 55–84.

Inkster, G. (1993) Integrating the year abroad. In J. Coleman and A. Rouxeville (eds) *Integrating New Approaches* (pp. 133–145). London: Association for French Studies in association with the Center for Information on Language Teaching and Research.

Jeanjean, C. (1988) Le futur simple et le futur périphrastique en français parlé. In C. Blanche-Benveniste, Cheurel, A. and Gross, M. (eds) *Grammaire et Histoire de la Grammaire. Hommage à la Mémoire de Jean Stefanini* (pp. 235–257). Aix-en-Provence, Université de Provence.

Jewell, C.M. (1992) Gender roles and second language acquisition in Hmong acculturation. Unpublished doctoral dissertation, West Virginia University, Morgantown.

Jordan, S. and Barro, A. (1995) The effect of ethnographic training on the year abroad. In G. Parker and A. Rouxeville (eds) *The Year Abroad: Preparation, Monitoring, Evaluation: Current Research and Development* (pp. 76–90). London: CILT.

Kaplan, M. (1989) French in the community: A survey of language use abroad. *French Review* 63 (2), 290–299.

Kasanga, L.A. (1996) Effect of gender on the rate of interaction: Some implications for second language acquisition and classroom practice. *International Review of Applied Linguistics* 111–112, 155–192.

Kaspar, G. (2000) Data collection in pragmatics research. In H. Spencer-Oatey (ed.) *Culturally Speaking: Managing Rapport Through Talk Across Cultures.* London: Continuum.

Kaspar, G. and Dahl, M. (1991) Research methods in interlanguage pragmatics. *Studies in Second Language Acquisition* 13, 215–247.

Kaspar, G. and Rose, K. (1999) Pragmatics and SLA. *Studies in Second Language Acquisition* 13 (2), 215–247.

Kaspar, G. and Schmidt, R. (1996) Developmental issues in interlanguage pragmatics. *Studies in Second Language Acquisition* 18, 149–169.

Kayne, R.S. (1975) *French Syntax: The Transformational Cycle.* Boston: MIT Press.

Kielsing, S.F. (1998) Men's identities and sociolinguistic variation: The case of fraternity men. *Journal of Sociolinguistics* 2, 69–99.

Kihlstedt, M. (1994) L'emploi des temps du passé chez quelques apprenants avancés et l'effet éventuel d'un séjour en France. In G. Boysen (ed.) *Actes du Douzième Congrès des Romanistes Scandinaves* (pp. 257–267). Aalborg: Aalborg University Press.

Kihlstedt, M. (1998) La référence au passé dans le dialogue. Etude de l'acquisition de la temporalité chez des apprenants dits avancés de français. PhD thesis, Stockholm University/Akademitryk.

King, R. and Nadasdi, T. (2003) Back to the future in Acadian French. *Journal of French Language Studies* 13 (3), 323–337.

Kinginger, C. (2004) Alice doesn't live here anymore: Foreign language learning and identity reconstruction. In A. Pavlenko and A. Blackledge (eds) *Negotiation of Identities in Multilingual Contexts* (pp. 219–242). Clevedon: Multilingual Matters.

Kinginger, C. and Farrell Whitworth, K. (2005) *Gender and Emotional Investment in Language Learning during Study Abroad.* CALPER Working Papers Series 2, 1–12.

The Pennsylvania State University, Center for Advanced Language Proficiency Education and Research.

Kinginger, C. and Blattner, G. (2008) Histories of engagement and sociolinguistic awareness in study abroad. Colloquial French. In L. Ortega and H. Byrnes (eds) *The Longitudinal Study of Advanced L2 Capacities* (pp. 223–246). Mahwah, NJ: Lawrence Erlbaum.

Klein, W. and Perdue, C. (1997) The basic variety (or: Couldn't natural language be much simpler?) *Second Language Research* 4, 301–348.

Klein, W. and Dittmar, N. (1979) *Developing Grammars – The Acquisition of German Syntax by Foreign Workers*. Berlin: Springer.

Kline, R. (1998) Literacy and language learning in a study abroad context. In B. Freed (ed.) *Language Learning in a Study Abroad Context* Special Issue of *Frontiers. The Interdisciplinary Journal of Study Abroad* 4, 139–166.

Krashen, S.D. (1985) *The Input Hypothesis*. London/New York: Longman.

Laberge, S. (1977) Etude de la variation des pronoms sujets définis et indéfinis dans le français parlé à Montréal. PhD thesis, Université de Montréal Canada.

Laberge, S. (1978) The changing distribution of indeterminate pronouns in discourse. In R. Shuy and A. Shnukal (eds) *Language Use and the Uses of Language* (pp. 76–87). Washington, DC: Georgetown University Press.

Labov, W. (1966) *The Social Stratification of English in New York City*. Washington, DC: Center for Applied Linguistics.

Labov, W. (1984) Field methods of the project on language change and variation. In J. Baugh and W. Scherzer (eds) *Language in Use: Readings in Sociolinguistics* (pp. 28–53). Englewood Cliffs, NJ: Prentice Hall.

Labov, W. (1990) The intersection of sex and social class in the course of linguistic change. *Language Variation and Change* 2, 205–254.

Lafford, B. (1995) Getting into, through, and out of a situation: A comparison of communicative strategies used by students studying Spanish abroad and 'at home'. In B. Freed (ed.) *Second Language Acquisition in a Study Abroad Context* (pp. 97–121). Amsterdam/Philadelphia: Benjamins.

Lafford, B. (2004) The effect of the context of learning on the use of communication strategies by learners of Spanish as a second language. In J. Collentine and B. Freed (eds) *Learning Context and its Effects on Second Language Acquisition*. Special issue of *Studies in Second Language Acquisition* 26, 201–225.

Laks, B. (1980) Différenciation linguistique et différenciation sociale: Quelques problèmes de linguistique française. Doctoral thesis, Vincennes, Université de Paris VIII.

Lapkin, S., Hart, D. and Swain, M. (1995) A Canadian interprovincial exchange: Evaluating the linguistic impact of a three-month stay in Quebec. In B. Freed (ed.) *Second Language Acquisition in a Study Abroad Context* (pp. 67–94). Amsterdam/Philadelphia: Benjamins.

Laudet, C. (1993) Oral performance of Erasmus students: An assessment. *Teanga. Irish Yearbook of Applied Linguistics* 13, 13–28.

Laurendeau, P. (2000) L'alternance futur simple/futur périphrastique: Une hypothèse modale. *Verbum* 22–23, 277–292.

Lemée, I. (2002) Acquisition de la variation socio-stylistique dans l'interlangue d'apprenants hibernophones de français L2: Le cas de on et nous. *Marges Linguistiques* 4, 56–57.

Lemée, I. (2003) Acquisition de la variation sociostylistique par des apprenants hibernophones de français L2: Les effets d'une année à l'étranger, une perspective variationniste, le cas de *on/nous*. PhD thesis, French Department, University College, Dublin.
Lemée, I. (2005) Le sexe comme facteur sociolinguistique de variation en acquisition de langue seconde. Paper presented at the annual conference of the *Association of French Language Studies*, Chambery.
Lemée, I. (2006a) L'emploi de la référence temporelle du futur par des apprenants hibernophones. Paper presented at the annual conference of the *Association of French Language Studies*, Bristol.
Lemée, I. (2006b) Do L2 female learners differ from L2 male learners? A variationist perspective on language and gender. Research Seminar, School of Applied Language and Intercultural Studies, Dublin City University.
Lemée, I., Howard, M. and Regan, V. (2007) Canada's French immersion programs: Comparative perspectives in relation to other contexts of language learning. In M. Howard (ed.) *Language Issues in Canada: Multidisciplinary Perspectives* (pp. 186–212). Newcastle: Cambridge Scholars Press.
Lemée, I. and Regan, V. (2008) Le rôle du sexe du locuteur dans l'acquisition de la compétence sociolinguistique par des apprenants hibernophones de français L2. *Synergies Royaume-Uni et Irlande* 1, 9–20.
Lenning, O.T. (1977) *The Outcomes Structure: An Overview and Procedures for Applying it in Post-secondary Institutions*. Boulder, CO: National Center for Higher Education Management Systems.
Lennon, P. (1989) Introspection and intentionality in advanced second language acquisition. *Language Learning* 39 (3), 375–396.
Lennon, P. (1990a) Investigating fluency in EFL: A quantitative approach. *Language Learning* 40 (3), 387–417.
Lennon, P. (1990b) The advanced learner at large in the L2 community: Developments in spoken performance. *International Review of Applied Linguistics* 28 (4), 309–324.
Lennon, P. (1991) Error and the very advanced learner. *International Review of Applied Linguistics* 29 (1), 31–43.
Lennon, P. (1996) Getting easy verbs wrong at the advanced level. *International Review of Applied Linguistics* 34 (1), 23–36.
Lesage, R. and Gagnon, S. (1992) Futur simple et futur périphrastique dans la presse québécoise. In A. Crochetière, J-C. Boulanger and C. Ouellon (eds) *Actes du XVème Congrès International des Linguistes* (pp. 367–370). Québec: Les Presses de l'Université Laval.
Long, M. (1983) Does instruction make a difference? *TESOL Quarterly* 17, 359–382.
Long, M. (1996) The role of linguistic environment in second language acquisition. In W.C. Ritchie and T.K. Bhatia (eds) *Handbook of Second Language Acquisition* (pp. 413–468). New York: Academic Press 2.
Long, M. (1997) Construct validity in SLA research: A response to Firth and Wagner. *Modern Language Journal* 81, 318–323.
Long, M. (2000) Focus on form in task-based language teaching. In R.L. Lambert and E. Shohamy (eds) *Language Policy and Pedagogy* (pp. 179–192). Amsterdam/Philadelphia: Benjamins.
Macaulay, R. (1978) Variation and consistency in Glaswegian English. In P. Trudgill (ed.) *Accent, Dialect and the School* (pp. 132–143). London: Edward Arnold.

Magnan, S. (1986) Assessing speaking proficiency in the undergraduate classroom: Data from French. *Foreign Language Annals* 19 (5), 429–438.

Major, R.C. (2004) Gender and stylistic variation in second language phonology. *Language Variation and Change* 16 (2), 169–188.

Marriot, H. (1993) Acquiring sociolinguistic competence: Australian secondary students in Japan. *Journal of Asian Pacific Communication* 4 (4), 167–192.

Marriot, H. (1995) The acquisition of politeness patterns by exchange students in Japan. In B. Freed (ed.) *Second Language Acquisition in a Study Abroad Context* (pp. 197–224). Amsterdam/Philadelphia: Benjamins.

Marriot, H. and Enomoto, S. (1995) Secondary exchanges with Japan: Exploring students' experiences and gains. *Australian Review of Applied Linguistics Series S* 12, 64–82.

Matsumara, S. (2001) Learning the rules for offering advice: A quantitative approach to second language socialisation. *Language Learning* 51, 635–679.

Matsumara, S. (2003) Modelling the relationships among interlanguage pragmatic development, L2 proficiency, and exposure to L2. *Applied Linguistics* 24 (4), 465–491.

Mauranen, A. (1994) Two discourse worlds: Study genres in Britain and Finland. *Finlance* 13, 1–40.

McLaughlin, B. (1987) *Theories of Second Language Learning*. London: Arnold.

Meara, P. (1994) The year abroad and its effects. *Language Learning Journal* 10, 32–38.

Meisel, J. (1983) Strategies of second language acquisition: More than one kind of simplification. In R. Andersen (ed.) *Pidginization and Creolization as Language Acquisition*. Rowley, MA: Newbury House.

Meisel, J. (1997) The acquisition of syntax of negation in French and German: Contrasting first and second language development. *Second Language Research* 13, 227–263.

Mendoza-Denton, N. (2004) Language and Identity. In J. Chambers, P. Trudgill and N. Schilling-Estes (eds) *The Handbook of Language Variation and Change* (pp. 475–499). Oxford: Blackwell.

Meyerhoff, M. (2006) *Introducing Sociolinguistics*. London: Routledge.

Miller, L. and Ginsberg, R. (1995) Folklinguistic theories of language learning. In B.F. Freed (ed.) *Second Language Acquisition in a Study Abroad Context* (pp. 293–316). Amsterdam: John Benjamins.

Milroy, L. (1988) Gender as a speaker variable: The interesting case of the Glottalised stops in Tyneside. *Sociolinguistics Symposium*, York Papers in Linguistics.

Milton, J. and Meara, P. (1995) How periods abroad affect vocabulary growth in a foreign language. *ITL Review of Applied Linguistics* 107 (8), 17–34.

Möhle, D. and Raupach, M. (1983) *Planen in der Fremdsprache*. Frankfurt: Peter Lang.

Möhle, D. and Raupach, M. (1993) Ausdrucksschwierigkeiten als Merkmal von Lernersprache. Sprachproduktion fortgeschrittener Lerner im Französischen. In G. Henrici und E. Zöfgen (Hrsg.). *Fehleranalyse und Fehlerkorrektur (Fremdsprachen Lehren und Lernen* 22), Tübingen, 109–128.

Morgan, R. (1970) Know your enemy: A sampling of sexist quotes. In R. Morgan (ed.) *Sisterhood is Powerful*. New York: Random House.

Mougeon, F. (1995) *Quel Français Parler? Initiation au Français Parlé au Canada et en France*. Toronto: York University, Editions du Gref.

Mougeon, R. and Rehner, K. (2001) Variation in the spoken French of Ontario French immersion students: The case of *juste* v. *seulement* v. *rien que*. *Modern Language Journal* 85, 398–414.

Mougeon, R., Nadasdi, T. and Rehner, K. (2001) A sociolinguistic analysis of phonetic variation in the spoken French of immersion students. Paper presented at the *Annual Conference of the Canadian Association for Applied Linguistics*, Québec City.

Mougeon, R., Nadasdi, T. and Rehner, K. (2002) Etat de la recherche sur l'appropriation de la variation par les apprenants avancés du FL2 ou FLE. In J-M. Dewaele and R. Mougeon (eds) *L'appropriation de la Variation par les Apprenants du Français Langue Seconde*. Special issue of *Acquisition et Interaction en Langue Etrangère* 17, 7–30.

Mougeon, R., Rehner, K. and Nadasdi, T. (2004) The learning of spoken French variation by immersion students from Toronto, Ontario. *Journal of Sociolinguistics* 8 (3), 408–432.

Muller, C. (1970) Sur les emplois personnels de l'indéfini *on*. *Revue de linguistique romane* 34, 48–55.

Myles, F. and Mitchell, R. (1999) Interrogative chunks in French L2: A basis for creative construction. *Studies in Second Language Acquisition* 21 (1), 49–80.

Nadasdi, T., Mougeon, R. and Rehner, K. (2001) A sociolinguistic analysis of phonetic variation in the spoken French of immersion students. Paper presented at the *Annual Conference of the Canadian Association of Applied Linguistics*, Laval (Québec).

Nadasdi, T., Mougeon, R., and Rehner, K. (2003) Emploi du futur dans le français parlé des élèves d'immersion française. *Journal of French Language Studies* 13, 195–220.

Nagy, N., Moisset, C. and Sankoff, G. (1996) On the acquisition of variable phonology in L2. *Penn Working Papers in Linguistics* 3, 111–126.

Nagy, N., Blondeau, H. and Auger, J. (2003) Second language acquisition and "real" French: An investigation of subject doubling in the French of Montreal Anglophones. *Language Variation and Change* 15 (1), 73–103.

Nattinger, J.R. and De Carrico, J.S. (1992) *Lexical Phrases and Language Teaching*. Oxford: Oxford University Press.

Nichols, P.C. (1983) Linguistic options and choices for black women in the rural South. In B. Thorne, C. Kramarae and N. Henley (eds) *Language, Gender and Society* (pp. 54–68). Cambridge, MA: Newbury House.

Nyrop, K.R. (1925) *Grammaire Historique de la Langue Française*. Copenhagen: Gyldendalske Boghandel Nordisk Forlag.

Olson Flanagan, B. and Inal, E. (1996) Object relative pronoun use in native and non-native English: A variable rule analysis. *Language Variation and Change* 8, 203–226.

Opper, S., Teichler, U. and Carlson, J. (1990) *Impact of Study Abroad Programmes on Students and Graduates*. London: Jessica Kingsley.

Paolillo, J. (2002) *Analysing Linguistic Variation: Statistical Models and Methods*. Stanford, CA: CSLI Publications.

Parker, G. and Rouxeville, A. (1995) *The Year Abroad: Preparation, Monitoring, Evaluation*. London: AFLS/CILT.

Pavlenko, A. (2001) How am I to become a woman in an American vein? In A. Pavlenko, A. Blackledge, I. Piller and M. Teutsch-Dwyer (eds) *Transformations of Gender Performance in Second Language Learning. Multilingualism, Second Language Learning, and Gender* (pp. 133–174). New York: Mouton de Gruyter.

Pavlenko, A. (2005) *Emotions and Multilingualism*. Cambridge: Cambridge University Press.
Pavlenko, A. and Blackledge, A. (2004) *Negotiation of Identities in Multilingual Contexts*. Clevedon: Multilingual Matters.
Pavlenko, A. and Dewaele, J-M. (2004) Multilingualism and emotions. Special Issue of *Journal of Multilingual and Multicultural Development* 25 (2–3), 93.
Pavlenko, A., Blackledge, A., Piller, I. and Teutsch-Dwyer, M. (2001) *Multilingualism, Second Language Learning and Gender*. Berlin/New York: Mouton de Gruyter.
Payne, I. (1980) A working-class girl in a grammar school. In D. Spender and S. Elizabeth (eds) *Learning to Lose* (pp. 12–19). London: Women's Press.
Pellegrino, V. (1998) Students' perspectives on language learning in a study abroad context. In B. Freed (ed.) *Language Learning in a Study Abroad Context*, Special issue of *Frontiers* 4, 91–120.
Perdue, C. (1993a) *Adult Language Acquisition: Crosslinguistic Perspectives*. Cambridge: Cambridge University Press.
Perdue, C. (1993b) Comment se rendre compte de la logique d'acquisition d'une langue étrangère par l'adulte. *Etudes de Linguistique Appliquée* 92, 8–22.
Pica, T. (1983) Adult acquisition of English as a second language under different conditions of exposure. *Language Learning* 33, 465–497.
Pica, T. (1987) Second language acquisition, social interaction, and the classroom. *Applied Linguistics* 8, 3–21.
Pica, T. (1988) Interlanguage adjustments as an outcome of NS-NNS negotiated interaction. *Language Learning* 38, 45–73.
Pica, T. (1994) Research on negotiation: What does it reveal about second language learning onditions, processes and outcomes? *Language Learning* 44, 493–527.
Pica, T. (1998) Second language learning through interaction: Multiple perspectives. In V. Regan (ed.) *Contemporary Approaches to Second Language Acquisition in Social Context* (pp. 9–31). Dublin: University College Dublin Press.
Pica, T. (2005) Second language acquisition research and applied linguistics. State of the art on second language acquisition. In E. Hinkel (ed.) *Handbook of Research on Second Language Learning and Teaching* (pp. 263–280). Mahwah, NJ: Lawrence Erlbaum Associates.
Pica, T. and Doughty, C. (1985) Input and interaction in the communicative language classroom: a comparison of teacher-fronted and group activities. In S. Gass and C. Madden (eds) *Input in Second Language Acquisition* (pp. 115–132). Rowley, MA: Newbury House.
Pica, T., Doughty, C. and Long, M. (1986) Making input comprehensible: Do interactional modifications help. *ITL Review of Applied Linguistics* 72, 1–25.
Pica, T., Holliday, L. and Morgenthaler, S. (1989) Comprehensible output as an outcome of linguistic demands on the learner. *Studies in Second Language Acquisition* 11, 63–90.
Pica, T., Holliday, L., Lewis, N., Berducci, D. and Newman, J. (1991) Language learning through interaction. What role does gender play? *Studies in Second Language Acquisition* 13 (3), 346–376.
Pintzuk, S. (1987) *Varbrul Programs for the IBM Personal Computer and for the VAX* [Computer programs]. Philadelphia: University of Pennsylvania, Department of Linguistics.
Polanyi, L. (1995) Language learning and living abroad: Stories from the field. In B. Freed (ed.) *Second Language Acquisition in a Study Abroad Context* (pp. 271–293). Amsterdam/Philadelphia: Benjamins.

Pope, M. (1934) *From Latin to Modern French*. Manchester: Manchester University Press.
Poplack, S. (1989) The care and handling of a mega-corpus: The Ottawa-Hull French Project. In R. Fasold and D Schiffrin (eds) *Language Variation and Change* (pp. 411–451). Amsterdam/Philadelphia: Benjamins.
Poplack, S. (2000) *Prescription et Pratique: Une Confrontation à Travers le Temps*. Paris: Variation, Catégorisations et Pratiques Discursives.
Poplack, S. and Tagliamonte, S. (2001) African American English in the Diaspora. *Language in Society* 30.
Poplack, S. and Turpin, D. (1999) Does the *futur* have a future in (Canadian) French? *Probus* 11, 134–164.
Poplack, S. and Walker, D. (1986) Going through [L] in Canadian French. In D. Sankoff (ed.) *Diversity and Diachrony* (pp. 173–198). Amsterdam/Philadelphia: Benjamins.
Posner, R. (1996) *The Romance Languages*. Cambridge: Cambridge University Press.
Preston, D. (1989) *Sociolinguistics and Second Language Acquisition*. Oxford: Blackwell.
Preston, D. (1996a) Variationist linguistics and second language acquisition. In W. Ritchie and T.K. Bhatia (eds) *Handbook of Second Language Acquisition* (pp. 229–265). New York: Academic Press.
Preston, D. (1996b) Variationist perspectives on second language acquisition. In R. Bayley and D. Preston (eds) *Second Language Acquisition and Linguistic Variation* (pp. 1–45). Amsterdam/Philadelphia: Benjamins.
Preston, D. and Yamagata, A. (2004) Katakana representation of English loanwords: More conservation and variable learner strategies. *Journal of Sociolinguistics* 8 (3), 359–379.
Raffaldini, T. (1987) Attrition of communicative ability among former year abroad students of French. PhD dissertation, Indiana University.
Rampton, B. (1995) *Crossing: Language and Ethnicity Among Adolescents*. Harlow: Longman.
Rand, D. and Sankoff, D. (1990) *Goldvarb Version 2: A Variable Rule Application for the Macintosh*. Montreal: Centre de Recherches Mathématiques, Université de Montréal.
Rast, R. (2006) Le premier contact avec une nouvelle langue étrangère: Comment s'acquitter d'une tâche de compréhension? *Acquisition et Interaction en Langue Etrangère* 24, 119–147.
Raupach, M. (1984) Formulae in second language speech production. In H. Dechert, D. Möhle and M. Raupach (eds) *Second Language Production* (pp. 114–137). Tübingen: Gunter Narr. 114–137.
Raupach, M. (1987) Procedural learning in advanced learners of a foreign language. In J. Coleman and R. Towell (eds) *The Advanced Language Learner* (pp. 173–153). London: AFLS/CILT.
Regan, V. (1990) Sociolinguistics and second language acquisition. *Teanga: Journal of the Irish Association for Applied Linguistics* 10, 14–25.
Regan, V. (1992) Variation and gender. *Teanga: Journal of the Irish Association for Applied Linguistics* 90–97.
Regan, V. (1995) The acquisition of sociolinguistic native speech norms: Effects of a year abroad on L2 learners of French. In B. Freed (ed.) *Second Language Acquisition in a Study Abroad Context* (pp. 245–267). Amsterdam/Philadelphia: Benjamins.

Regan, V. (1996) Variation in French interlanguage: A longitudinal study of sociolinguistic competence. In R. Bayley and D. Preston (eds) *Second Language Acquisition and Linguistic Variation* (pp. 177–201). Amsterdam/Philadelphia: Benjamins.

Regan, V. (1997) Les apprenants avancés, la lexicalisation et l'acquisition de la compétence sociolinguistique: Une approche variationniste. *Acquisition et Interaction en Langue Étrangère* 9, 193–210.

Regan, V. (1998a) *Contemporary Approaches of Second Language Acquisition in Social Context*. Dublin: University College Dublin Press.

Regan, V. (1998b) Sociolinguistics and language learning in a study abroad context. *Frontiers: The Interdisciplinary Journal of Study Abroad* 4, 61–91.

Regan, V. (2002) Le contexte d'acquisition: La variation du groupe et de l'individu. *Acquisition et Interaction en Langue Etrangère* 17, 123–141.

Regan, V. (2004) The relationship between the group and the individual and the acquisition of native speaker variation patterns: A preliminary study. *IRAL – International Review of Applied Linguistics in Language Teaching* 42 (4), 335–348.

Regan, V. (2005) From speech community back to classroom: What variation analysis can tell us about the role of context in the acquisition of French as a foreign language. In J-M. Dewaele (ed.) *Focus on French as a Foreign Language. Multidisciplinary Perspectives* (pp. 191–209). Clevedon: Multilingual Matters.

Regan, V. (2008) The immersion experience in Canada. In M.A. Ni Mhainnin and E. Tilley (eds) *Canada: Text and Territory* (pp. 39–50). Cambridge: Cambridge Scholars Press.

Regan, V. and Adamson, D. (2008) A study of variation in the native speaker speech community. In D. Adamson (ed.) *Interlanguage Variation in Theoretical and Pedagogical Perspective* (pp. 23–32). London: Routledge.

Rehner, K. and Mougeon, R. (1999) Variation in the spoken French of immersion students: To *ne* or not to *ne*, That is the sociolinguistic question. *The Canadian Modern Language Review* 56 (1), 124–151.

Rehner, K., Mougeon, R. and Nadasdi, T. (2003) The learning of sociostylistic variation by advanced French as a second language learners: The case of nous versus on in immersion French. *Studies in Second Language Acquisition* 25 (1), 127–156.

Rickard, P. (1974) *A History of the French Language*. London: Hutchinson.

Rivers, W. (1998) Is being there enough? The effects of homestay placements on language gain during study abroad. *Foreign Language Annals* 31 (4), 492–500.

Roberts, J. (1997) Hitting a moving target: Acquisition of sound change in progress by Philadelphia children. *Language Variation and Change* 9, 249–266.

Roberts, J. and Labov, W. (1995) Learning to talk Philadelphian: Acquisition of short a by preschool children. *Language Variation and Change* 7, 101–112.

Robinson, J.S., Lawrence, H. and Tagliamonte, S. (2001) Goldvarbrul 2001. *30th NWAV Conference*, Raleigh (NC).

Romaine, S. (2003a) Variation. In C. Doughty and M. Long (eds) *Handbook of Second Language Acquisition* (pp. 409–436) Oxford: Blackwell.

Romaine, S. (2003b) Variation in language and gender. In J. Holmes and M. Meyerhoff (eds) *The Handbook of Language and Gender* (pp. 98–118). Oxford: Blackwell.

Rousseau, P. and Sankoff, D. (1978) Advances in variable rule methodology. In D. Sankoff (ed.) *Linguistic Variation: Models and Methods* (pp. 57–69). New York: Academic.

Roszak, B. and Roszak, T. (1969) *Masculine/Feminine*. New York: Harper and Row.
Ryan, J. and Lafford, B. (1992) Acquisition of lexical meaning in a study abroad environment: *Ser* and *estar* and the Granada experience. *Hispania* 75, 714–722.
Sandy, S. (1997) L'emploi variable de la particule négative *ne* dans le parler des adolescent franco-ontariens. MA thesis, York University, Toronto.
Sanell, A. (2007) Parcours acquisitionnel de la négation et de quelques particules de portée en français L2. PhD thesis, Département de français, d'italien et de langues classiques. Stockholm, Stockholm University.
Sankoff, D. (1987) Variable rules. In U. Ammon, N. Dittmar and K.J. Mattheier (eds) *Sociolinguistics: An International Handbook of the Science of Language and Society* (pp. 984–997). Berlin and New York: De Gruyter.
Sankoff, D. (1988) Sociolinguistics and syntactic variation. In F. Newmeyer (ed.) *Language: The Socio-cultural Context* (Vol. IV) (pp. 140–161). Cambridge: Cambridge University Press.
Sankoff, G. and Vincent, D. [1977(1980)] The productive use of *ne* in spoken Montreal French. In G. Sankoff (ed.) *The Social Life of Language*. Pennsylvania: University of Pennsylvania Press.
Sankoff, G. and Vincent, D. (1977) L'emploi productif de 'ne' dans le français parlé de Montréal. *Le Français Moderne* 45 (3), 243–256.
Sankoff, G. and Cedergren, H. (1976) Les contraintes linguistiques et sociales de l'élision de /l/ chez les Montréalais. In M. Boudreault and F. Mohren (eds) *Actes du XIIIème Congrès International de Linguistique et Philologie Romanes* (pp. 1101–1117). Québec: Presses de l'Université Laval.
Sankoff, G., Thibault, P., Nagy, N., Blondeau, H., Fonollosa, M-O. and Gagnon, L. (1997) Variation in the use of discourse markers in a language contact situation. *Language Variation and Change* 9, 191–217.
Sanz Lecina, E. and Nespoulous, J.L. (1995) Un indice de la relation du locuteur à son discours: Les pronoms. *La Linguistique* 31 (1), 49–63.
Savignon, S. (1997) *Communicative Competence: Theory and Classroom Practice. Texts and Contexts in Second Language Learning*. Reading: Addison-Wesley.
Saville-Troike, M. (2006) *Introducing Second Language Acquisition*. Cambridge: Cambridge University Press.
Sax, K. (2000) Acquisition of stylistic variation by American learners of French: /l/ elision in the subject pronouns *il* and *ils*. Paper presented at the *Second Language Research Forum*, Indiana University.
Sax, K. (2001) Stylistically speaking: Variable use of *nous* versus *on* in American learners' French. Paper presented at *NWAV 30*, Raleigh (NC).
Sax, K. (2003) Acquisition of stylistic variation by American learners of French. Unpublished PhD, Indiana University.
Schachter, J. (1990) On the issue of completeness in second language acquisition. *Second Language Research* 6 (2), 93–124.
Scherer, K. and Wertheimer, M. (1964) *Psycholinguistic Experiment in Foreign Language Teaching*. New York: McGraw Hill.
Schmidt, R. (1996) Interaction, acculturation, and the acquisition of communicative competence: A case-study of an adult. In N. Wolfson and E. Judd (eds) *Sociolinguistics and Second Language Acquisition*. Rowley, MA: Newbury House.
Schumann, J. (1975) Second language acquisition: The pidginization hypothesis. Doctoral thesis, Harvard University.
Schumann, J. (1978) *The Pidginization Process*. Rowley, MA: Newbury House.

Segalowitz, N. and Freed, B. (2004) Context, contact, and cognition in oral fluency acquisition: Learning Spanish in at home and study abroad contexts. In J. Collentine and B. Freed (eds) *Learning Context and its Effects on Second Language Acquisition*. Special Issue of *Studies in Second Language Acquisition* 26, 173–199.

Siegal, M. (1995) Individual differences and study abroad: Women learning Japanese in Japan. In B. Freed (ed.) *Second Language Acquisition in a Study Abroad Context* (pp. 225–243). Amsterdam/Philadelphia: Benjamins.

Siegal, M. (1996) The role of learner subjectivity in second language sociolinguistic competency: Western women learning Japanese. *Applied Linguistics* 17, 356–382.

Siegal, M. and Okamoto, S. (1996) Imagined worlds: Language, gender and sociocultural "norms" in Japanese language textbooks. In N. Warner, J. Ahlers, M. Oliver, S. Wertheim and M. Chen (eds) *Gender and Belief Systems. Proceedings of the Fourth Berkeley Women and Language Conference* (pp. 667–679). Berkeley: University of California at Berkeley.

Singleton, D. (1996) Formal aspects of the L2 mental lexicon: Some evidence from university-level learners of French. In K. Sajavaara and C. Fairweather (eds) *Approaches to Second Language Acquisition* (pp. 79–85). Jyväskylä: University of Jyväskylä.

Slavoff, G. and Johnson, J. (1995) The effects of age on the rate of learning a second language. *Studies in Second Language Acquisition* 17 (1), 1–16.

Söll, L. (1983a) De la concurrence du futur simple et du futur proche en français moderne. In F-J. Hausmann (ed.) *Etudes de Grammaire Française Descriptive* (pp. 16–24). Heidelberg: Julius Groos Verlag.

Söll, L. (1983b) Situer *on/nous* en français moderne. *Studies in Descriptive Linguistics* 9, 7–15.

Spada, N. (1985) Effects of informal contact on classroom learners' L2 proficiency: A review of five studies. *TESL Canada Journal* 2 (2), 51–62.

Spada, N. (1986) The interaction between type of contact and type of instruction: Some effects on the L2 proficiency of adult learners. *Studies in Second Language Acquisition* 8 (2), 181–199.

Stewart, M. (1995) Personally speaking. or not? The strategic value of *on* in face-to-face negotiation. *Journal of French Language Studies* 5, 203–223.

St Martin (1980) English language acquisition: The effects of living with an American family. *TESOL Quarterly* 14 (3), 388–390.

Swain, M. (1985) Communicative competence: Some roles of comprehensible input and comprehensible output in its development. In S. Gass and C. Madden (eds) *Input in Second Language Acquisition* (pp. 235–253). Rowley, MA: Newbury House.

Swain, M. and Lapkin, S. (1990) Aspects of the sociolinguistic performance of early and late immersion students. In R. Scarcella, M. Anderson and S.D. Krashen (eds) *Developing Communicative Competence in a Second Language* (pp. 41–54). Rowley, MA: Newbury House.

Swain, M. and Lapkin, S. (1998) Interaction and second language learning: Two adolescent French immersion students working together. *Modern Language Journal* 82 (3), 320–337.

Sundall, L-G. (1991) *Le Temps futur en français moderne*. Studia Romanica Uppsala: Almqvist and Wiksell International.

Tagliamonte, S. (2006) *Analysing Sociolinguistic Variation*. Cambridge: Cambridge University Press.
Tarone, E. (1979) Interlanguage as chameleon. *Language Learning* 29, 181–191.
Tarone, E. (1985) Variability in interlanguage use: A study of style-shifting in morphology and syntax. *Language Learning* 35, 373–403.
Tarone, E. and Swain, M. (1995) A sociolinguistic perspective on second language use in immersion classrooms. *The Modern Language Journal* 79, 167–178.
Teichler, U. and Steube, W. (1991) The logics of study abroad programmes and their impacts. *Higher Education* 21, 325–349.
Thomas, A. (1956) *Dictionnaire des Difficultés de la Langue Française*. Paris: France, Larousse.
Thomas, A. (2002) La variation phonétique en français langue seconde au niveau universitaire avancé. In J-M. Dewaele and R. Mougeon (eds) *L'appropriation de la Variation par les Apprenants du Français Langue Seconde*. Special issue of *Acquisition et Interaction en Langue Etrangère* 17, 101–121.
Togeby, K. (1974) *Précis Historique de Grammaire Française*. Odense: Akademisk Forlag.
Towell, R. and Dewaele, J-M. (2005) The role of psycholinguistic factors in the development of fluency amongst advanced learners of French. In J-M. Dewaele (ed.) *Focus on French as a Foreign Language: Multidisciplinary Approaches*. Clevedon: Multilingual Matters.
Towell, R., Hawkins, R. and Bazergui, N. (1996) The development of fluency in advanced learners of French. *Applied Linguistics* 17 (1), 84–119.
Trévise, A. and Noyau, C. (1984) Adult Spanish speakers and the acquisition of French negation forms: Individual variation and linguistic awareness. In R.W. Anderson (ed.) *Second Languages: A Cross-linguistic Perspective*. Rowley, MA: Newbury House Publishers Inc.
Trofimovich, P. and Baker, W. (2006) Learning second-language suprasegmentals: Effect of L2 experience on prosody and fluency characteristics of L2 speech. *Studies in Second Language Acquisition* 28, 1–30.
Troth, E. (1970) How can a woman MAN the barricades? Or linguistic sexism up the wall. *Women: A Journal of Liberation* 2 (1), 5–7.
Trudgill, P. (1972) Sex, covert prestige, and linguistic change in the urban British English of Norwich. *Language and Society* 1, 179–195.
Trudgill, P. (1974a) *Sociolinguistics: An Introduction to Language and Society*. London: Penguin Books.
Trudgill, P. (1974b) *The Social Differentiation of English in Norwich*. Cambridge: Cambridge University Press.
Trudgill, P. (1984) *Applied Sociolinguistics*. London: Academic Press.
Twombly, S.B. (1995) Piropos and friendship: Gender and culture clash in study abroad. *Frontiers: The Interdisciplinary Journal of Study Abroad* I, 1–27.
VanPatten, B. (1987) *Foreign Language Learning: A Research Perspective*. Cambridge: Newbury House.
VanPatten, B. (1990) Theory and research in second language acquisition and foreign language learning: On producers and consumers. In B. Van Patten and J. Lee (eds) *Second Language Acquisition/Foreign Language Learning* (pp. 17–26). Clevedon: Multilingual Matters.
Véronique, D. and Stoffel, H. (2003) L'acquisition de la négation en français par des adultes arabophones. *Marges Linguistiques* 5, 242–259.

Vet, C. (1993) Conditions d'emploi et interprétation des temps futur du français. *Verbum* 4, 71–84.
Wales, M.L. (2002) The relative frequency of the synthetic and composite futures in the newspaper Ouest-France and some observations on distribution. *Journal of French Language Studies*, 12 (1), 73–93.
Walsh, R. (1994) The year abroad – a linguistic challenge. *Teanga* 14, 48–57.
Warga, M. (2007) Interlanguage pragmatics in L2 French. In D. Ayoun (ed.) *Handbook of French Applied Linguistics* (pp. 171–207). Amsterdam: Benjamins.
Warga, M. and Schölmberger, U. (2007) The acquisition of French apologetic behavior in a study abroad context. *Intercultural Pragmatics* 4 (2), 221–251.
Watson-Gegeo, K.A. and Nielsen, S. (2003) Language Socialization in SLA. In C. Doughty and M. Long (eds) *The Handbook of Second Language Acquisition* (pp. 155–177) Oxford: Blackwell.
Waugh, L. and Fonseca-Greber, B. (2002) Authentic materials for everyday spoken French: Corpus linguistics vs French textbooks. *Arizona Working Papers*.
Wilkinson, S. (1998a) On the nature of immersion during study abroad: Some participant perspectives. In B. Freed (ed.) *Language Learning in a Study Abroad Context*. Special issue of *Frontiers* IV, 121–138.
Wilkinson, S. (1998b) Study abroad from the participants' perspective: A challenge to common beliefs. *Foreign Language Annals* 31 (1); 23–39.
Wilkinson, S. (2002) The omnipresent classroom during study abroad: American students in conversation with their French hosts. *Modern Language Journal* 86, 157–173.
Willis, F., Doble, G., Sankarayya, U. and Smithers, A. (1977) *Residence Abroad and the Student of Modern Languages: A Preliminary Study*. Bradford: University of Bradford Modern Language Centre.
Wolfram, W. (1969) *A Sociolinguistic Description of Detroit Negro Speech*. Washington, DC: Center for Applied Linguistics.
Yager, K. (1998) Learning Spanish in Mexico: The effect of informal contact and student attitude on language gain. *Hispania* 81 (5), 898–911.
Ylönen, S. (1994) Die Bedeutung von Textsortenwissen für die interkulturelle Kommunikation – Kommunikative Unterschiede im Biologiestudium an den Partneruniversitäten Jyväskylä und Bonn. *Finlance* 13, 89–113.
Young, R. (1988) Variation and the interlanguage hypothesis. *Studies in Second Language Acquisition* 10, 281–302.
Young, R. (1991) *Variation in Interlanguage Morphology*. New York: Peter Lang.
Young, R. (1999) Ends and means: Methods for the study of interlanguage variation. In S. Gass, C. Madden, D. Preston and L. Selinker (eds) *Variation in Second Language Acquisition: Psycholinguistic Issues* (pp. 65–90). Clevedon: Multilingual Matters.
Young, R. (1996) Form-function relations in articles in English interlanguage. In R. Bayley and D. Preston (eds) *Second Language Acquisition and Linguistic Variation* (pp. 135–175). Amsterdam/Philadelphia: John Benjamins Publisher.
Young, R. (1999) Sociolinguistic approaches to SLA. *Annual Review of Applied Linguistics* 19, 105–132.
Young, R. and Bayley, R. (1996) VARBRUL analysis for second language acquisition research. In R. Bayley and D. Preston (eds) *Second Language Acquisition and Linguistic Variation* (pp. 253–306). Amsterdam/Philadelphia: John Benjamins.

Index

ab initio learners 22
accommodation 46, 47
acculturation 10, 18, 125
advanced learner(s) 4, 18, 37, 39-40, 44, 49, 54-7, 61, 65-6, 77-8, 94, 132, 135, 141
Adamson, D. ix, 5, 13, 16-18, 58, 65, 125-126, 129, 132, 137
age 40, 65-6, 85-6, 111, 122, 124-5
Anglophone learners 29, 87, 132
Armstrong, N. 72, 78, 96-97, 100-102, 104, 128-129
Ashby, W. 63-64, 69, 72-74, 79-80, 97, 100, 104, 119

Bartning, I. 18, 54-59, 61, 94
basic variety 65
Batardière, M.-T. 22, 52
Bayley, R. 3-5, 7, 16-17, 59-61, 68, 75, 78, 86, 124, 140
Blanche-Benveniste, C. 59, 64, 82-83, 97, 106
Blondeau, H. 25, 86-87, 109-110, 115, 127
Brecht, R. 23, 40-41, 44, 46-47, 125
Bucholtz, M. 3

Canadian French vi-vii, 64, 84, 87, 97, 101, 108-110, 112-113, 115, 127
chunks 55, 65-66, 73, 78, 101
classroom
– instruction 32, 37-8, 41, 46, 49
– learners vi, 18, 29, 32, 34, 36, 38, 67, 137-8
Coleman, J. 20-21, 38, 43-49, 61, 63, 142, 145, 148, 155, 161
community 2-4, 6-7, 9-13, 15-19, 24, 26, 28, 32, 36, 38, 40, 43, 45-46, 48, 55, 57-58, 66-67, 72-73, 76-77, 96, 102, 110, 119-120, 122-123, 125, 128, 132, 134-142
competence
– linguistic 2, 6-7, 93, 141
– pragmatic 6-7, 21, 23, 37, 40
– sociolinguistic v-vii, 2-4, 6, 12, 15, 17-18, 24, 26, 28, 48, 51-53, 65-66, 68-69, 76-77, 89, 92-93, 123, 126-129, 133-139, 141-142
– sociopragmatic v, 24, 27-28, 40, 138

context
– classroom 30, 48
– formal 64, 88, 111, 113, 115, 137
– informal 88, 109, 113
– instructed 126
– learning 11, 19, 30, 34, 136
– naturalistic 48, 126
– of acquisition v, 7, 9-12, 128, 135, 137-138
– phonolexical 97
– phonological 101
– sociocultural 5
Cook, V. 3, 81
constraint ordering 51, 71-3, 77, 79, 88, 98, 101, 140
Corder S. 11, 65
Coveney, A. 63-64, 81, 83-84, 91, 130
culture 1-2, 6, 9, 10-11, 44, 117, 119

DeCourcy, M. 132, 143
DeKeyser, R. 28-29, 32-33, 36
deletion
– copula 118
– informal 15
– levels of 98, 103
– native speaker 103
– rates 25, 63-4, 68, 71-2, 74-7, 97-8, 101-2, 129, 139-40
– variable 25, 63, 144
– vowel disfavours 74
– zero 76
Dewaele, J.-M. ix, 18, 25, 28-29, 35, 41, 64, 67, 88, 124, 132, 137-138

Eckert, P. 4, 120-121
Ellis, R. 59, 65, 125

factors
– affective 44-5, 47
– contextual 24
– discrete 121
– multiple 12, 60, 133
– sociolinguistic 89
– stylistic 88, 102, 144
Feagin, C. 57, 119

167

fluency v, 34-37
foreign language 6, 10, 12, 19, 24, 32, 34, 48-50, 67, 91
Freed, B. 4, 11, 19-20, 31-35, 37-43, 50, 76, 117-118, 122, 142
future temporal reference 60, 105-115, 127-129, 131, 134, 141-143

Gass, S. 5, 8, 38, 124-125
gender vii, 9, 12, 17-18, 28, 39, 41, 44-45, 56, 64-65, 67, 85-86, 89-94, 99-101, 103-104, 112-115, 117-133, 135-136, 139
grammatical competence, learner's 37
grammatical development 21, 30, 32, 53, 65
grammaticalisation 55-6, 63
Goldvarb 94, 100, 104, 114
Guy, G. 60, 140

Holmes, J. 121-122, 124
Howard, M. ix, 26, 28-29, 31-33, 38, 48, 53, 61, 98, 102, 129

identity 2-3, 6-7, 13, 16-17, 28, 118-119, 121-122, 124, 126, 132-133, 136
immersion
– classroom 16, 25, 67-68, 76, 86, 109, 126, 136, 138
– context 34, 43, 126-127, 135
– learner(s) vi, 18, 22, 25, 34, 68, 77, 86-87, 91, 94, 97-98, 109-110, 112-113, 115, 127, 130, 135, 138
– programme(s) 17, 68, 86, 110, 127, 135
individual variation vii, 74-75, 102, 139-140
input v, 8-12, 16-18, 20, 25, 33, 47, 53, 59, 62, 66, 72, 75, 84, 93, 96, 100, 105, 115, 117, 123-124, 130, 132, 134-136, 138-139
– comprehensible 8
– informal 20, 53
– native speaker 130, 136
instruction 19-20, 32, 37, 38, 41, 46, 48-49, 53-55, 66, 88
interaction 5, 7-10, 25, 28, 30, 37, 39-43, 45-47, 60, 88, 93, 102, 121-125, 135, 137, 139
interlanguage 6, 9, 13, 30-31, 52, 54-55, 57, 59-61, 67, 74, 88, 126, 141
– grammaticalisation 30, 54, 61
– variation 6, 9, 60

Kaspar, G. 125
Kihlstedt, M. 31, 33
Kinginger, C. 117, 132
Krashen, S. 85

L1 vii, 6-10, 15, 27, 44, 51, 57, 60-62, 65-67, 72-74, 76-77, 79, 82, 84-85, 87, 89, 93, 96-98, 101, 110, 115, 118, 122-127, 129-132, 134-135, 138-141
L2 v-ix, 2-4, 6, 8-24, 26-27, 28-30, 34-35, 37-42, 45, 47-49, 51-52, 54-57, 59-63, 65-77, 79, 86-94, 96-105, 109-115, 117-118, 122-124, 126-134, 136-142
Labov, W. vii, 13, 57-60, 66, 89, 94, 118, 120, 122, 129
Lafford, B. 33, 36, 38
language change 14, 134
Laudet, C. 35
/l/ deletion vii, 15, 60, 96-99, 101-103, 119, 128-129, 134, 139
learner language 5-6, 65
learners
– classroom 18, 29, 32, 34, 36, 38, 67-68, 109, 137-138
– immersion 25, 34, 68, 77, 86-87, 91, 94, 97, 109-110, 112-113, 127, 130, 132
Lemée, I. 86, 89, 92, 94, 111-112, 130-131, 137
lexical acquisition 21, 23-24, 28-29, 44, 46, 50
lexicalisation 69-70, 72
lexicalised phrases 64, 72-73, 101
Long, M. 5, 8, 18

Major, R. 17, 103, 126, 129, 132, 136
Marriot, H. 24, 26, 41, 42, 117, 132
McLaughlin, B. 61
Meisel, J. 10, 11, 66
Mendoza-Denton, N. 122
Meyerhoff, M. 4, 121-122
morphology 11, 29-31, 49, 55-56, 105
Mougeon, R. ix, 16-17, 25-26, 68, 84, 86-87, 97, 127, 130, 138
multivariate analyses 131, 134
Myles, F. 61, 73, 81, 101

Nadasdi, T. 25, 86, 109, 112-113, 127, 132
Nagy, N. 17, 25, 26, 67, 86, 87, 115, 127, 132
native speaker(s) v, vii, 8-12, 15-17, 24-28, 32, 34-36, 38-39, 41-44, 46-48, 51, 53-54, 56-58, 63-66, 68-69, 71-74, 76-77, 79, 81, 84, 86, 88-89, 91, 93, 98, 100-105, 107, 110, 112-113, 115, 124-126, 128-139, 141
– norms 24, 27-28, 46, 57, 98, 129
– patterns 16-17, 125, 133, 138-139
– speech 60, 62, 72, 74, 77, 122, 126, 131, 134, 136-138
– variation patterns 16-17, 69, 71, 77, 132
native speech community 10, 13, 18, 67, 72, 77, 110, 135, 137
naturalistic
– acquisition 19, 135

Index

- context 48, 126
- learner 17, 20, 38, 55, 137-138
- setting 9, 31, 127, 135-136

ne deletion v, 17-18, 25, 60, 62-79, 88, 93, 96, 101, 103, 105, 115, 119, 130, 132, 134, 136, 139-140

negation vi, 10, 62-63, 65, 68-69, 78, 107-108, 118, 141

norms
- gender 136
- native-speaker 27, 57
- prescriptive 15, 108

nous/on alternate use vi, 79-96, 105, 127-130, 134, 139

Pavlenko, A. 124-125
Pica, T. ix, 8, 18-19, 24, 28, 54, 63, 69, 80, 83, 108, 118, 125, 127
periphrastic 105-110, 112-115, 131
Poplack, S. ix, 57, 60, 64, 97-98, 101, 104, 107-110, 112

prestige
- form(s) 17, 120, 127, 131
- variant(s) 91, 118-120, 125, 127

Preston, D. 5, 13, 59, 137
proficiency level

Rampton, B. 3
Regan, V. ix, 3, 5, 16-18, 20, 24, 29, 38-39, 48, 52-53, 59, 61, 64-65, 67-69, 75-76, 78, 86, 101-102, 115, 123, 125-126, 128-130, 132, 136-138, 140, 143
Rehner, K. 18, 25-26, 68, 86-87, 91, 127
Roberts, J. 66, 122
Romaine, S. 124

Sankoff, D. 60,
Sankoff, G. 17, 26, 60, 64, 69, 78, 84, 97, 109
Sax, K. 87, 88, 98
Siegal, M. 24, 27, 28, 41, 42, 123, 124
Singleton, D. 53, 61
socialisation 4, 7
sociolinguistic
- competence 2-4, 6, 12, 15, 17-18, 24, 26, 28, 38, 51-53, 65-66, 68-70, 76, 89, 92-94, 123, 126-129, 133-139, 142

- markers 24, 26, 51, 87
- variables, stable 120, 132
- variation 2, 25-26, 48, 51, 59, 72, 77, 87, 102,115, 118, 128, 131-132, 142

sociopragmatic competence 24, 27-28, 40, 138

speech community 3, 10-13, 15-16, 18, 40, 62, 67, 72-73, 77, 96, 110, 128, 134-137, 139

study abroad vi-viii, 3-5, 8-9, 11-12, 19-53, 67-70, 75, 98, 102, 125, 128, 133-135, 138, 142-143

Swain, M. 6, 74, 86

Tagliamonte, S. 57, 60
target language 3-4, 6, 10, 16-17, 19, 24-26, 32, 35, 38, 40-41, 43, 48-49, 51-58, 72, 86-88, 92-93, 128, 137, 139, 142
Tarone, E. 13, 74
tense 15, 30, 57, 60, 69, 105-115, 117, 131, 134, 141
Trudgill, P. 94, 118

VARBRUL 59-60, 68-69, 71, 73-74, 76, 85, 89, 94, 98, 104, 125, 128, 131, 134, 140
variable(s) vi-vii, 10, 12-18, 20, 24-26, 35, 40, 42, 51-52, 55-56, 59-64, 66-67, 69, 71, 76, 79, 81-87, 89, 91-93, 95-98, 101-105, 107-113, 115, 117-118, 120-124, 127-139, 141-143
variable rule 59, 67
variant(s) 15-16, 18, 25, 80, 85, 89, 105, 109-110, 112-114, 118-120, 122, 127, 133-134, 136, 141
variation
- linguistic v, 1, 56, 59
- pattern(s) vii, 15-17, 48, 62, 65, 69, 71, 75, 77, 86, 89, 91, 98, 101, 104, 115, 118, 122, 125-126, 128-129, 131-141
- sociolinguistic vii, 2, 25-26, 48, 51, 59, 72, 77, 87, 102, 115, 118, 128, 131-132, 142

Waugh, L. 82

Young, R. 5-7, 9, 14, 18, 59-61, 64-65, 97, 101, 109, 117, 119, 122, 129, 139, 141

For Product Safety Concerns and Information please contact our EU Authorised Representative:

Easy Access System Europe

Mustamäe tee 50

10621 Tallinn

Estonia

gpsr.requests@easproject.com

www.ingramcontent.com/pod-product-compliance
Lightning Source LLC
Chambersburg PA
CBHW070616300426
44113CB00010B/1547